KANT ON THE FOUNDATION OF MORALITY

KANT
ON THE
FOUNDATION
OF MORALITY

A MODERN VERSION OF
THE *GRUNDLEGUNG*

TRANSLATED WITH COMMENTARY BY
Brendan E. A. Liddell

INDIANA UNIVERSITY PRESS
Bloomington and London

Published in Canada by Fitzhenry & Whiteside
Limited, Don Mills, Ontario

Library of Congress catalog card number: 75-108213
ISBN: 253-33170-6 [CL.]
253-33171-4 [PA.]

Manufactured in the United States of America

CONTENTS

FOREWORD

No ONE even vaguely familiar with Kant's *Grundlegung* will expect it to be easily understood at first reading, especially by someone not at home in the cold reaches of the Critical Philosophy. But there are commentaries in print, and good ones. Why yet another? And while translation is obviously needed, why another?

My original purpose, which has never changed, was to provide a commentary on the *Grundlegung* which (a) required of the reader no philosophical background, (b) provided a basic explanation of the theory contained in the work, but (c) did not stray into more advanced or critical areas. None of the commentaries I could find had all these characteristics: they seemed either too summary, too advanced, too extensive, or too narrowly directed toward establishing a particular interpretation. What was most lacking, it seemed to me, was a complete and fundamental exposition of the *Grundlegung* that provided the reader with a detailed analysis of Kant's whole argument—and nothing else. To supply such a commentary seemed in itself a worthwhile goal.

Progressing from one passage to another, I found that much space was being devoted to a modern English paraphrase of the archaic translation I had planned to use. The translation was accurate, yet because it followed more or less the clumsy, complex style natural to Kant, it would be relatively obscure to an English reader raised on a more pragmatic style. Why not, I thought, combine the necessary paraphrase with a new translation, so that Kant would seem to be writing in mid-twentieth century English? In creating such a version, I had to do violence to Kant's grammar, style, structure, even sentence placement. I broke single paragraphs into two, three, and even four. I replaced extended informal enumerations with more formal listings. Where a word had acquired a traditional English parallel, I used a variety of expressions when precise terminology was not important. In this way, I hoped, the text would become the communicator of Kant's thought, still requiring explanation, to be sure, but no longer demanding to be decoded. My objective was not puristic authenticity but clarity, not lofty criticism but primary exposition.

My indebtedness to Kantian scholars will be easily detected by them. I have given due acknowledgement whenever I was aware of borrowing an interpretation, but I am sure that I have borrowed more than I am aware. And I cannot deny my frequent reliance on Messrs Abbott, Beck, and Paton, whose translations I often consulted when my own knowledge proved insufficient. Since the text of the translation has been altered in style, paragraphing, and sentence structure, I have included marginal page references to the Prussian Academy edition of Kant's works, which will allow cross references to other sources. The translation itself is printed in heavier type for easier reference and so that it may be read without commentary, as suggested at the end of Chapter 2.

I was assisted in preparing the final draft by a grant from the Faculty Research Fund of Bradley University; by my colleague, Professor Thomas Satre, who judiciously edited the manuscript; and by the cheerful typing of Miss Becky McDuff. But more than to any others, I must record my gratitude to my wife, Phyllis. Without her much needed encouragement, I might never have completed this work, which I dedicate to her.

KANT ON THE FOUNDATION OF MORALITY

CHAPTER ONE

Kant's Moral Revolution

---

1. *Kant's Moral Revolution*

"It is with Kant that something really and positively new makes its appearance in post-Renaissance moral philosophy. In the process of summing up and concentrating in himself the complex heritage and the long effort of three centuries of thought, he performed a revolutionary task in the realm of ethical philosophy, as in that of speculative philosophy. Not that he wished to destroy or overthrow anything in the realm of morals —on the contrary, his effort was to restore. But in order to construct his imposing edifice he was in fact compelled *to transform completely the whole architecture of ethics.*"[1]

Kant, for most of his life a mild-natured philosophy professor at the University of Koenigsberg, Prussia, did not publish his first important work in philosophy until 1781 when he was 57 years old. Yet, from 1781 until his death in 1804, he wrote a series of philosophical works unequalled for their intellectual importance and revolutionary influence since the days of Plato and Aristotle. These include *Critique of Pure Reason* (1781), *Foundation for a Metaphysics of Morals* (1785), *Critique of Practical Reason* (1788), *Critique of Judgment* (1790), *On Religion Within the Bounds of Reason Alone* (1792), *Perpetual Peace* (1795), and

Metaphysics of Morals (1803), in addition to lesser works and revised editions of the foregoing. Just as 1776 marked the beginning of a political revolution "heard round the world" by the signing of the American Declaration of Independence, so 1781 marked the beginning of a philosophical upheaval which is still reverberating throughout the world of Western thought.

This second Copernican Revolution, as Kant liked to call his theory, was indeed revolutionary. Before Kant, philosophers had generally agreed that the foundation for the validity of our knowledge was the world of objects. The philosophers held radically divergent views as to what objects really are. Plato, for instance, had claimed that objects were imitations of absolute and immaterial realities which he called Forms; Bishop George Berkeley (1685–1753) had claimed that material objects exist only as ideas in the mind. But most philosophers had followed Aristotle, who held the more or less commonsensical view that objects themselves were the fundamental realities. Knowledge is genuine when ideas accurately reflect the nature of the objects which exist in the spatio-temporal universe. Philosophers seldom questioned our ability to know objects (even though Descartes had raised the issue), but sought to explain what seemed a patent fact, namely, that we do indeed know objects as they really exist.

After 1781, however, things were never the same, for in his *Critique of Pure Reason,* far from assuming as fact our knowledge of objects in themselves, Kant declared such knowledge to be impossible. The universe, or Nature, is actually a formal system imposed upon our sensations by the mind rather than an objective reality known by its accurate reflection in the mind. Knowledge, said Kant, could extend only to the limits of human experience itself and any attempt to philosophize about matters removed from experience—such as the existence and nature of God, the freedom of the will, and the immortality of the soul—would result in confusion and ultimate contradiction. Kant's conception overturned all the cherished dogmas of previous philosophy and, in turn, led to the Idealisms of the nineteenth and twentieth centuries, to Phenomenology, and through the latter, to Existentialism.

Nor was Kant's revolution confined to knowledge of the facts of the universe: it extended as forcefully into the area of moral philosophy. Before Kant, moral philosophers had generally agreed that the ultimate standard for moral judgment could be found in some objective value-object. Aristotle thought that Human Nature was the moral guide to action; the Scholastics of the Middle Ages looked to the Law of God as reflected in man's rational awareness of the Natural Law; Hume saw the moral standard as an inherent, natural sentiment of approbation. Although these philosophers differed as to what exactly the objective value-object or standard was, they were agreed that it was a guide by which man could decide and choose as he sought goodness, virtue, or moral character.

On the contrary, Kant proclaimed. Since it is impossible to know objects beyond experience, even one's own human nature or mind as they exist in themselves, but only as they appear to us through our experiences of them, we have no knowledge of any value-object except in so far as it *appears* to have value. But if we are to avoid a purely subjective moral standard, then we must appeal to reason as the source of moral goodness, not to any preconceived ideal of the perfection of Human Nature or to Divine Command. Morality, then, becomes a matter of inherent consistency of action, not a pursuit of some value-object.

The task of communicating this theory was formidable, for until his time philosophy was expressed in object language, a language in which nouns referred to things and events in themselves and adjectives to characteristics of things and events. Kant found it an impossible task to write in the prevailing terminology of philosophy; he needed a terminology free from the connotations of the previous eras. Anyone who proposes a truly new theory must face such a hurdle. Unfortunately, Kant assumed that readers of the *Foundation for a Metaphysics of Morals,* his first major work in moral philosophy, would be familiar with his *Critique of Pure Reason* and so would recognize his usage of certain key expressions. Experience has shown, however, that the *Foundation* is a far more accessible work than the *Critique of Pure Reason* and that it is certainly more familiar to nonprofessional students of philosophy. We must examine Kant's basic terminology before we can profitably begin to examine his moral philosophy itself. Such an introduction need not be lengthy; Kant believed that he was writing a book which would have popular appeal, so he avoided the more formal language encountered in his three Critiques.

Accordingly, the remainder of this introductory chapter will deal with four items:

a.   Kant's purpose in writing the *Foundation;*
b.   His distinction between *speculative* and *practical reason;*
c.   The meaning of *pure reason;*
d.   The meaning of *a priori.*

2. *The Ultimate Foundation of Morality*

The first question which naturally arises about any book is just what it is that the writer is writing about. Some commentators on Kant's moral philosophy believe that the *Foundation* is an attempt to discover the ultimate moral law, from which we can deduce our moral obligations; that Kant seeks a standard by which we might judge whether a particular action is right or wrong. Those who so interpret Kant's work find that Section III of the *Foundation,* which deals with the problem of freedom of choice, is not relevant to the central theme as they see it and conclude that it is a kind of appendix to the main thesis, dealing with an issue that is indeed important for morality in general but not to any particular moral system.

Another group of commentators believe that the *Foundation* is a treatise on the metaphysical subject of Freedom, and that Kant uses the field of ethics as the paradigm case for justifying the freedom of the will. Such an interpretation does make Section III an integral part of the whole work, but it overlooks Kant's emphatic denial that we can prove man's will to be free. It would seem rather odd for Kant to write an entire book to prove or justify something he believed was impossible to prove. Yet, as we shall see, Kant is trying to give a *kind* of proof for freedom of the will, though it is surely an indirect one. To ignore this would make parts of Section III pointless.

These interpretations are not groundless. Kant is certainly searching for the ultimate standard for moral actions and trying to justify belief in the freedom of the will. Since he firmly insists that freedom is a necessary part of the foundation of morality, he must include a justification for the belief in man's freedom to make moral choices. Likewise, if a fundamental principle can be established, it will serve as a standard for particular moral laws, even though we may not be able to deduce our particular moral duties from this principle alone.

But neither of these interpretations points to Kant's primary objective. In the Preface of the *Foundation* he states quite plainly: "The *Foundation,* then, has one purpose only: *to discover, and justify, the supreme principle of morality.*" He seeks the ultimate foundation of morality, that foundation on which the whole structure of moral law must rest if it is to be valid as genuine law of duty.

3. *Speculative and Practical Reason*

Any discussion of Kant's moral theory must begin with a clear understanding of the distinction Kant draws between speculative reason and practical reason. This is an ancient distinction. In his *Nicomachean Ethics,* Aristotle distinguishes between speculative wisdom and practical wisdom. Both are activities of man's rational soul, Aristotle explains, but they concern different objects of thought. Speculative wisdom (*sophia*) is knowledge of eternal, necessary truths, such as mathematics, while practical wisdom (*phronesis*) is knowledge of the right principles for living the good life.

An analogy may help to illustrate this difference. An automotive engineer may know all there is to know about the mechanical and physical laws involved in the design of a vehicle and yet still not know how to drive. He has theoretical (speculative) knowledge. His wife on the other hand may be an expert driver, yet understand very little of what goes on when she shifts gears. She has practical knowledge, but not theoretical knowledge. A rough distinction would be that theoretical knowledge is *knowing that* something is so, while practical knowledge is *knowing how* to perform some action.

In his *Critique of Pure Reason,* Kant distinguished between the two as follows: "It may be sufficient in this place to define theoretical knowledge or cognition as knowledge of that which *is,* and practical knowledge as *knowledge of that which ought to be.*"[2] Kant fails to abide by a precise distinction between speculative and practical knowledge, between reason as the source of knowledge of facts in the universe, and reason as the source of knowledge of what we ought to do. At times he states that both are types of knowledge. In the Preface to the *Foundation* he says, "Ulimately, reason is one; only its functions are different." Yet in Section II of the same work he asserts that will is nothing else than practical reason. In the *Critique of Pure Reason* he says that practical reason is "reason in so far as it is itself the cause producing actions." Generally, however, Kant refers to speculative reason as the rational faculty whereby we know facts, and to practical reason as the rational faculty whereby we know what we ought to do. Knowing what we ought to do is a kind of knowing, surely. But it differs essentially from speculative reason in this: while speculative reason has to do with what was, is, or will be a matter of fact, practical reason has to do with what may not be a matter of fact unless we choose to make it fact by acting. For example, by speculative reason I know that a full moon will rise on a certain evening next month; by practical reason I know that I ought to repay Smith the five dollars that I owe him, or that I ought to drive slowly on icy pavement.

4. *Pure Reason*

We sometimes hear of a conclusion being deduced or known by "pure reason." We generally understand this to mean that the process of reasoning was deductive rather than inductive, by syllogism or formal argument rather than by accumulation of factual evidence. Kant's meaning of "pure reason" is quite different, and the concept is basic to his system.

According to Kant, we have two ways of knowing—that means we have two ways of knowing facts and two ways of knowing what we ought to do. The one way, our everyday way, is knowing through experience, by our senses. Every fact we know about the universe is derived from experience, and every skill we learn is learned through practice. Of course we use our reasoning powers in acquiring such information or such skills, but this use of reason is not what Kant calls *pure* reason.

Pure reason is reasoning which is "pure of everything derived from experience." This definition raises an immediate question. If everything we know about the universe, including facts about ourselves, is derived from some kind of experience, what knowledge other than this can be the concern of "pure" reason? The answer to this question constitutes Kant's unique contribution to the history of thought: pure reason is concerned with the activity of reason itself. What we know of the universe is known through our experiences; but the framework of this knowledge, the systematic construction of knowledge itself, we cannot know through such experiences. To know anything about the universe requires that experiences be meaningful to us, yet the meaningfulness of any experience must be determined by some standard other than the experience itself. This standard, or framework, is a condition[3] for all our empirical knowledge, and thus it cannot itself be known by experience, since experience already presupposes this framework. If the framework can be known at all, it must be known quite independently of all experience, that is, by some activity of reason which does not rely on experience of any kind: *pure* reason.

An example will help. Imagine being seated in a football stadium just before the game. Suddenly half the crowd jumps to its feet, cheering wildly, "Here comes the team!" Heavily padded men pour from the dressing room onto the field and begin limbering up. The spectator counts forty such men, but his mind's eye "sees" them as forming a unit, a team. In his mind he unites the individual men into a totality, each man being a part of the whole. We need not linger on this particular example, since it is intended only to show that reason often takes over where perception leaves off; reason does something more, in this case forming into a conceptual unit what the eye sees as separate individuals.

Although this is an activity of reason, it is not yet pure reason, since the material the mind puts together into the conceptual unit, "team", is derived directly from the experiences of the individuals on the playing field. However, let us turn to that mental activity of putting separate sensations into meaningful wholes or conceptual units. If we do this abstractly, without considering any particular occasion of such activity, we are investigating a function of reason independently of experience. This second-order activity of reason, our investigation of reason's ability to combine individual experiences into conceptual units, does not concern itself with any particular experience at all, but with the activity of the mind itself. This second-order activity of reason Kant calls pure reason.

There are many similarities between the investigation into pure reason and what psychologists refer to as philosophical psychology. Both investigate the workings of reason itself, rather than the objects of reason, as does scientific knowledge. But Kant restricts his investigations of pure reason to the fundamental activities of reason as it forms separate experiences into meaningful conceptual wholes. This too has been a fruitful field of study for the psychologist. But where the psychologist takes this activity of reason as a datum, as a given fact leading to further inquiry, Kant asks whether this unifying activity of reason can justify itself. Does reason unify experiences arbitrarily, or is there some inherent—one might almost say innate—tendency of reason to act within a natural limitation, according to fixed rules which more or less direct such activity? Is knowledge an accumulation of haphazard, but fortuitous, formations of multiple sensations, or is reason itself so structured in its activity that it must unify sensations according to some pre-established system of "laws of knowledge"? By asking such a question, Kant takes nothing in knowledge for granted but subjects reason itself to its most basic criticism—in his own words, to a *critique of reason.*

Now let us return to the distinction between speculative and practical reason, to see how the concept of pure reason fits into each area. When we investigate the activity of reason as it takes sensations derived from the separate senses and unites them to form experiences of the universe, then we are in the realm of *pure speculative reason.* This was Kant's principal task in his first great work, the *Critique of Pure Reason.* On the other hand, when we investigate the activity of reason as it constructs rules of activity, we are in the realm of *pure practical reason.* Such is Kant's task in the *Foundation* and again in his later *Critique of Practical Reason.* When Kant speaks of a "Critique of Pure Practical Reason" he means an investigation into the fundamental and purely rational prerequisites for all moral knowledge. In the *Foundation* he seeks that ultimate principle, framework, condition, or prerequisite which will justify all other moral laws by establishing their objective validity. We can see the importance of this search. If, according to Kant, the mind "molds" raw sense experiences into coherent, meaningful units according to some rational laws of knowledge, it is most important for a theory of knowledge to discover this system of laws, and prove it to be a valid foundation for knowledge of the universe. If a similar activity of mind is necessary for moral knowledge, then it is of tremendous importance for the moral philosopher to discover this system of laws of choice and action and prove it to be a valid foundation for moral principles, for on such a justification the whole validity of morality stands or falls. If there is such a fundamental principle of morality and if we can prove that it is a legitimate basis for moral law, then we have found a single ultimate standard for all moral judgments. If not, morality is a relative matter, little more than a codification of individual preferences or social customs. It requires no great insight to see why this is the most crucial question of moral philosophy.

5. *All Moral Judgments are* A Priori

In traditional logic, the expressions *a priori* and *a posteriori* refer respectively to deductive and inductive methods of reasoning. Generally speaking, an *a priori* argument is one which derives a conclusion from given premises according to a formal rule (e.g., the syllogism). An *a posteriori* argument, on the other hand, begins with empirical data about particular objects or events and from this data arrives at a generalization. The latter is the basic inductive method.

Kant uses the terms *a priori* and *a posteriori* in different senses. He speaks of *a priori* and *a posteriori concepts,* and again, of *a priori* and *a posteriori propositions.* Generally, by *a priori* Kant means "derived from reason"; by *a posteriori* he means "derived from experience."

All our concepts of objects, events, and characteristics in the universe are ultimately derived from experience and thus are characterized as *a posteriori* (e.g., redness, tree, bicycle, Sally, star). An example of an *a priori* concept is that of change. We experience the succession of one state of an object from a former state, such as the successive notes played on a violin. But we do not actually see the change itself, or in this case, hear it. The combining of the two successive experiences into two parts of the same event, called a change, is a mental process. We perceive with the ear two successive notes, but we experience it mentally as a change. When we think about change itself, we are thinking about an *a priori* concept.

However, change is not a *pure a priori* concept, since we do experience change, in a manner of speaking, just as we experienced the team. The concept of change, when considered abstractly, is seen to be due to an operation of reason and not derived from experience alone; but this idea is still tied to the experiences of the successive states, and thus is not free from all experience. After all, we do use the expression, "Watch this water change color," and surely we do see the water changing color, even though we actually see the successive colors and not some additional characteristic identifiable as the change. Perhaps it would be better to say we see the successive colors as changing, as an event we would classify as a change.

A few concepts, however, are entirely independent of experience, since they serve as the underlying foundations for experience. An example of a *pure a priori* concept is "substance." When we slide a plate across a table, we experience the prior and the subsequent locations of the plate and also combine these different experiences into a single event, which we characterize as a change of location of the plate. But the justification for our doing this cannot be based on the experiences themselves, since the experiences are separable, as are the various locations of the plate enroute. We combine the various experiences of the plate's location into a unity called "change of place" by positing something which serves as a foundation for this unifying activity. Otherwise we might just as well say that the plate in the beginning is an entirely different plate from the plate at the end. We do not do so, however, because we underwrite the change of location with the presupposition that a mere change of location of a plate does not cause it to change into an entirely new plate.

In more philosophical terms, underlying every change there is something which endures through the change, and this substratum is given the abstract name *substance*. That the concept of substance in our example is completely independent of experience can be understood when we consider that an experience of a plate at one location turning into an entirely different plate at another location would be exactly the same as an experience of a mere change of location of a single plate. We judge that there is only a change of location because we mentally underwrite the event as unified by substance. Substance, then is a *pure a priori* concept, completely independent of experience.

But it is a *pure a priori* concept of speculative reason, since it applies to objects and events in the universe of fact. A concept which is equally independent of experience, but applies to the world of moral activity, will be a *pure a priori* concept of practical reason, an example of which is the concept of freedom of the will. Whether or not this is a valid concept is one of the key problems in Kant's moral theory.

When he turns to propositions, Kant says that an *a priori* proposition is justified by an appeal to reason, one which is derived from self-evident propositions. The propositions of mathematics are *a priori* propositions. For example, we know by reason alone, without recourse to experience, that $35 + 36 = 71$. An *a posteriori* proposition, on the other hand, is justified by an appeal to some experience. Any factual statement such as, "The earth is round," or "Rose Ann has blue eyes," is an *a posteriori* proposition. As a general rule of thumb, we can take *a priori* to mean derived from, or justified by, reason, and *a posteriori* to mean derived from, or justified by, experience.

Should anyone wonder whether a particular concept or proposition is *a priori* or *a posteriori,* whether it is derived from reason or from experience, he may test the concept or proposition by asking whether it can be characterized by *necessity.* Philosophers have long agreed generally that necessity is an essential characteristic of *a priori* propositions. For example, it is necessarily true that all bachelors are unmarried and that every effect has a cause. The necessity here is not derived from a poll of bachelors or through a scientific examination of effects but from the meanings of the terms involved. When we understand the meanings of the terms, we see by reason alone that the statements are true, and that to deny them would involve a self-contradiction.

On the other hand, a proposition which is not necessarily true, even though it may be universally true, would not be *a priori.* We have very good reasons for accepting the universal truth of the proposition, "All men will die," but we know this to be true only because human experience confirms it. An immortal man, one who never grows older and who remembers events from centuries past, would be a remarkable person indeed, but no self-contradiction is involved in such an idea.

When we approach the matter of moral propositions, we discover that a moral law, such as "Always keep your promises," seems to involve a kind of necessity. A moral law is not a universal truth based on experience, as though "Always keep your promises," had the same prudential quality as "When driving, always keep your eye on the road." The latter rule is good advice, because experience shows that failure to abide by it has unpleasant consequences. The possibility of these unpleasant consequences gives the rule its authority, so to speak. It can be called an *a posteriori* rule—or, in Kant's terms, an *a posteriori* proposition of practical reason.

The situation is not the same with the rule, "Always keep your promises." To be sure, such a rule could be taken in the same advisory sense as the driving rule. We might give such advice to an aspiring politician, and the validity of our advice would be based upon the probable consequences at the next election. But in such a context we would be giving political advice, not moral instruction. Moral rules differ from advisory rules in a most important respect: unlike advisory rules, moral rules involve necessity. A political candidate may break a political rule (at his risk) without ceasing to be a political candidate, whereas a person cannot break a moral rule without becoming immoral. Or to put it in another way, advisory rules tell us what it would be *wise* to do while moral rules tell us what we *must* do. There may be occasions when a driver must remove his eyes from the road or a politician must break a campaign promise. But in some yet to be explained way, a moral rule must *always* be obeyed. This does not mean that there are never occasions in which a person should break a promise.[4] But, when the situation is a moral one, such exceptions arise only in view of some other pre-empting moral rule, such as, "Do not kill another human being." If I have promised to visit a sick friend, I must keep my promise if I am to be moral; but this necessity must give way to the higher necessity to avoid killing someone. I could not, for instance, speed through a crowded school zone just to get to the hospital before visiting hours were over.

Moral rules, since they are necessary, are *a priori* rules—in Kant's terms, *a priori* propositions of practical reason. This raises a critical question. If moral rules are *a priori*, then they derive their authority, or moral validity, from reason, not from experience. How does reason arrive at necessary truth in moral propositions? What is the mental procedure whereby practical reason finds necessity? If these practical propositions (rules) are genuinely *a priori*, how are such *a priori* propositions of practical reason possible? To answer these questions, one must plunge into the very heart of the whole realm of morality itself. This is just what Kant will do.

The Purpose of the Foundation

---

1. *The Division of Philosophy*

The ancient Greeks divided philosophy into three sciences: *physics, ethics,* and *logic.* This division is quite 387 fitting for our purposes, and we can perfect it simply by determining the basis for such a division, so that we may be sure we have included everything, and at the same time have the necessary subdivisions correctly defined.

Kant uses a division of philosophy employed by the Stoics. He calls these divisions "sciences," meaning by "science" a systematic body of knowledge. This threefold division is based upon a principle of distinction which applies to all knowledge.

All rational knowledge is either *material,* about some object, or *formal,* about the forms of understanding and reason themselves, and about the universal canons of thinking, without reference to particular objects of thinking. Formal philosophy is called *logic.*

Material knowledge includes not only scientific knowledge, as we commonly understand it, but also aesthetics, psychology, and metaphysics. Even ethical principles are listed as material knowledge. Anything which may be classified as "what we think about" is to be labeled material knowledge. Formal knowledge, on the other hand, we might describe as the way we think about the objects of material knowledge. Formal knowledge is not knowledge of the thoughts or emotions which at any given time comprise our intellectual states, but rather it is knowledge of the procedural patterns which the mind follows when it thinks about anything at all.

Kant mentions two kinds of logic: (1) a logic concerned with the "forms of understanding and reason themselves," and (2) a logic concerned with the "universal canons of thinking." Kant does not emphasize this distinction in the first part of the *Foundation,* but in Section III this distinction becomes important, and we must take a brief note of it here. We have already seen Kant's concern with the structure or framework of understanding.[1] In the *Critique of Pure Reason,* Kant gave the title "Transcendental Logic" to his investigation of the elements of this *a priori* structure. Transcendental logic is the examination of the pure *a priori* concepts with which the mind molds raw sensations into meaningful experiences.

The other logic, normally called *formal* logic and concerned with the universal rules of thinking, Kant calls "general logic." General logic is a study of the formal structure of argument, that is, with whether an argument is in valid or invalid form. What both these logics have in common is that neither is concerned with any particular item of knowledge. In other words, logic is a *formal* kind of knowledge. Kant plays on two meanings of "formal": the formal aspects of argument, and the formal structure underlying experience.

Material philosophy, on the other hand, directed at particular objects as well as at the laws which rule these objects, is subdivided into two parts. These parts correspond to the different kinds of laws. Material philosophy dealing with the laws of nature we call *physics,* while that concerned with the laws of

freedom we call *ethics.* Some refer to the former as natural
philosophy, and to the latter as moral philosophy.

We all are familiar with laws of nature, but what could Kant
mean by "laws of freedom"? At first glance this seems self-
contradictory, since whatever happens according to law will be
determined, while a free choice or action should be free from
any determination by law. The solution to this puzzle will become clear when Kant discusses the nature of moral law. Here
we need note only that Kant makes a precise, though undefined,
distinction between laws of nature and laws of freedom (i.e.,
morals). True enough, everything subject to a law of nature is
inflexibly determined. But a law of freedom is *not* a law of
nature. It does not *describe* what always happens, as do laws
of nature; rather it *prescribes* what an agent must do in order to
fulfill his moral duty. Laws of freedom are no more determining
than are the laws enacted by a legislature but they are truly
laws for all that.

Logic cannot derive its universal and necessary (i.e., *a priori*)
laws of thinking from experience. If it did, it simply would not
be logic at all, since logic is the ultimate guideline for under-
standing and reason; its principles must be valid for every ac-
tivity of thought, and thus provable by reason alone. Natural
and moral philosophy, on the other hand, do indeed rely on
experience. Natural philosophy seeks knowledge of laws of na-
ture based on experience of what actually takes place in nature.
Moral philosophy seeks to know the laws of human choice,
even when such choice is influenced by nature. Thus
while moral philosophy tries to learn the laws of what   388
ought to happen, it must at the same time consider those
situations in which what ought to happen often fails to happen.

Kant, like others before and after him, holds the laws of logic
to be *a priori,* grounded in reason. Experience cannot provide the
necessity characteristic of these laws. But both physics and ethics
are to some extent based on experience (literally, they each

"have an empirical part"). The empirical part of physics includes what we usually call the natural sciences. The empirical part of ethics would include anthropology, psychology, sociology, or the social sciences in general. As empirical studies, both physics and ethics investigate how antecedent factors of heredity, ancestry, environment, and society affect human choice and activity. As such, these sciences formulate descriptive laws, general and universal statements of the ways events have been observed to take place. These laws do not state commands given to nature. If an unsupported stone did not fall, we would not say that it had in any sense disobeyed the law of gravity. Rather, we would hunt for a purely natural explanation of what had taken place; or we even might want to restate the law of gravity to account for this new datum in experience.

Moral laws, however, do command; they prescribe; and they are frequently disobeyed. What is more, we are able to account for this disobedience without having to restate the law; the explanation would be found in the laws of human inclination. One of Kant's insights is that everything that happens happens in accordance with some law, either a law of nature or a law of freedom.

Any philosophy which relies on experience is *empirical* philosophy; but if a philosophy proposes a theory derived solely from *a priori* principles, we call it *pure* philosophy. Logic, having no particular object derived from experience, is *pure formal* philosophy. Pure material philosophy, while it does have an object of investigation, does not find this object in experience. The name for such a pure material philosophy is *metaphysics*.

Both physics and ethics have an empirical side: physics (properly called) and psychology, respectively. But they each have an *a priori* side. So two kinds of metaphysics are possible: a *metaphysics of nature* and a *metaphysics of morals*.

So far Kant has distinguished between what we generally call science and philosophy. Science (the *a posteriori* or empirical "philosophy") is derived from perceptual evidence. "Pure" philosophy (*a priori* or rational) is a purely intellectual investigation. When this pure philosophy is merely formal, it is logic. Pure philosophy about the *content* of knowledge Kant calls metaphysics. And since pure material philosophy deals with two different kinds of objects, physical and moral, we have two kinds of metaphysics: a *metaphysics of nature,* which is *a priori* knowledge of the *a priori* laws of nature; and a *metaphysics of morals, a priori* knowledge of *a priori* moral laws.

Throughout the history of philosophy, the term "metaphysics" has referred principally to the metaphysics of nature. Metaphysics traditionally embodied the philosophical examination of the ideas of substance, qualities, causality, and personal identity; it sought to prove the existence of God, freedom of the will, and immortality of the soul; it theorized about universals, relationships, and the nature of reality. Kant argued that some of these ideas are *pure a priori* concepts: they are forms of knowledge. Substance and causality belong to this group. Other ideas, such as God, freedom, and immortality, do not fit into categories of experience at all. Since these ideas refer beyond the range of human experience, Kant denies that we can know whether such ideas refer to anything real at all. (See Chapter I, Section 1.) In brief, Kant claims that a metaphysics of nature is impossible: without experience we cannot have any knowledge of natural or supernatural objects or events. If there are any *a priori* laws of nature, they must be purely formal, contained in a transcendental logic, not in a metaphysics of nature. If traditional metaphysics is not to be an empty discipline, it will have to be either a transcendental logic or a metaphysics of morals.

At this point, by certain principles of division, Kant has arrived at a definition of a "metaphysics of morals." He has not yet tried to prove that such a metaphysics is possible. So the question still remains, can we have *a priori* knowledge of *a priori* moral laws? This question, of course, is only another way of asking whether we can discover an ultimate principle of morality. But even so, we can now see how such a metaphysics of morals would be related to the rest of philosophy. A graphic summary may be helpful.

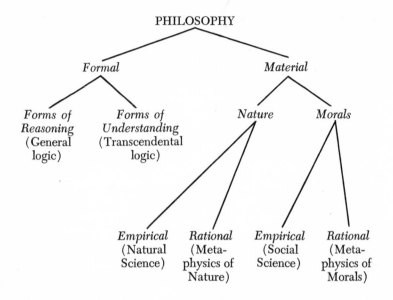

We are now able to define a metaphysics of morals as *an a priori investigation of the knowledge of moral laws governing human conduct*. Consequently, a "Foundation for a Metaphysics of Morals" will be an investigation into the ultimate basis for all *a priori* knowledge of moral law; that is, a search for the ultimate foundation for rational morality.

2. *Is a Metaphysics of Morals Needed?*

All trades, arts, and crafts benefit from a division of labor. Instead of performing all tasks, each person specializes in one particular area which differs from all the others in the special skills it requires. By doing so, he achieves a higher level of performance and greater facility. On the other hand, where everyone is a jack-of-all-trades, doing all kinds of work indiscriminately, performance will remain at the crude level of the beginner.

Thus we might give some thought to whether the distinct areas of pure philosophy would likewise benefit from specialization. Would it not be better for the whole house of intellect to censure those who pander to the public taste with a thoughtless mixture of experience and rational principle? These so-called savants have no idea of proper procedure, yet they consider themselves scholars, and deride as "idealists" those who devote themselves to purely rational pursuits. In trying to do two things at once, things which require both a distinct technique and a special talent, they bungle the whole job.

I merely want to ask whether the nature of science does not demand that we carefully separate the empirical from the rational part. Should not a metaphysics of nature be prologue to natural science, and a metaphysics of morals serve as a ground for social science? If so, we must make sure to keep the metaphysical foundations of the sciences pure of anything derived from experience, so that we can determine in 389 each case just how far reason can proceed by itself and where it finds its *a priori* principles. Also, we might discover whether this search should be pursued by all moralists (whose name is legion), or only by those who have the knack for it.

This passage is a brief plea for the same critical approach with which Kant began the *Critique of Pure Reason*. Kant objects not so much to psychological and moral investigation by one individual—he himself does both—but to the simultaneous, "mixed," empirical-rational treatment of morality. He insists, as a fundamental principle of his critical approach, that it is intellectually dangerous to attempt an investigation of rational knowledge unless we first have outlined clearly just how far reason can

legitimately proceed. The limits of rational inquiry must be carefully determined before we can develop an adequate theory of
knowledge. For obviously, if the limits are surpassed, the resulting so-called "principles of knowledge" will be illegitimate and
will produce contradictory beliefs. The first step, then, is to see
"how far reason can proceed by itself and where it finds its *a
priori* principles."

Since my immediate concern here is with moral philosophy, I
narrow the question: Are we not constrained by the gravest
necessity to erect a pure moral philosophy which is wholly free
from the merely empirical descriptions of social science? The
common ideas of duty and moral law make obvious the possibility of such a philosophy.

Since we do have an idea of duty and recognize some moral
laws to bind us, the awareness of these duties and laws must be
based upon *a priori* principles. The obligation or moral necessity
commanded by these laws cannot be found in experience (i.e.,
in any anthropological, psychological, or sociological investigation), but must be based upon principles of pure practical
reason. When Kant says that such a philosophy is possible, he
does not mean that someone has already developed it or that
the possibility is obvious to everyone who understands the common ideas of duty and moral law. He means that it is indeed
possible to develop a valid, pure moral philosophy and that our
common ideas of duty and moral law are sufficient grounds upon
which to begin the investigation.

Everyone must agree that a moral law must bind with unqualified necessity if it is to be the basis for obligation. The
command, "Thou shalt not lie," does not apply solely to men,
as though other rational beings did not have to obey it. The
same holds for all precepts which are truly moral commands.
Thus we cannot expect to find the basis for obligation in the
nature of a human being, nor in any set of human circumstances;

rather, we must seek this basis *a priori* in the concepts of pure reason itself. Those commands which are based on principles derived from experience, no matter how slight the influence of this experience—even if it affects nothing more than the motive —are not moral laws. They may even be universally applicable and thus serve as practical rules; but lacking the unqualified necessity which rests upon a purely *a priori* foundation, they cannot be moral *commands.*

If a moral law is to bind under moral obligation, then it must bind absolutely. Kant insists that this absolute moral necessity must be grounded in reason, *not in the nature of man.* In the first place, we can know man's human nature only through experience. Even though this experience be introspective, it is still *a posteriori* knowledge and cannot give us necessary truth.

Which of us can say that man is the only being who reasons? As a fanciful example, suppose we discover that dolphins have intellects comparable to ours and we learn to communicate with them. Dolphins are surely not human beings, even if they should think like we do. (For one thing, men and dolphins cannot interbreed.) Now suppose one day a dolphin lied to us. Couldn't we blame the dolphin, accuse it of immoral conduct, and say that it had done wrong? Where a cat cannot lie and so cannot do moral wrong, this dolphin intentionally said something it knew was false. So we could judge the statement as a lie and accuse the dolphin of wrongdoing, not because its conduct was "undolphinly"—dolphins may be natural-born liars—but because lying is contrary to principles of rationality and this dolphin is a rational dolphin. Obligation, or moral necessity, must be based upon rationality, not upon human nature.

General rules of prudence, such as "Honesty is the best policy," are not moral laws, since they appeal to some psychological motive, such as desire for profit and good standing in the community. Kant calls such rules "practical," but since they lack the element of moral necessity, they cannot be moral *laws.* Should a man not wish to follow the best business policy, he still has a *moral* obligation to be honest.

Thus moral laws and their principles are essentially different from all principles of action which we derive from empirical knowledge. Moral philosophy must have an entirely pure foundation. Without using any anthropological knowledge of human nature, moral philosophy imposes *a priori* laws on man because he is a rational being. Yet experience helps us to sharpen our powers of judgment: we must know the situation in order to determine which law is applicable to it, and we must know ourselves in order to assist the laws in exerting their force upon our will and our actions. For even though we are able to conceive of pure practical reason, we are influenced by so many natural inclinations that we find it difficult to put these laws into everyday practice.

Kant makes here a distinction which is often overlooked by his critics. "Moral philosophy," he says, "must have an entirely pure *foundation*." Note that he does not say that all of moral philosophy is *pure a priori* philosophy. As he already emphasized, the necessity inherent in moral obligation must find its ultimate basis in pure practical reason, but this does not mean that from a knowledge of this ultimate principle alone we can deduce our *particular* obligations. Yet this is how some philosophers interpret Kant and then accuse him of being too rigid, too formalistic. We must have the ultimate principle and the *a priori* laws of morality, but we need experience just as well, for we must know a particular empirical situation in order to know what must be done and which law applies to that situation. The moral law forbidding adultery does not apply to taking a final examination. A student found cheating on his examination could hardly absolve himself by proclaiming his innocence of adultery.

A metaphysics of morals then is truly necessary if we wish to find in reason the basis for the *a priori* principles of activity. But more importantly, so long as we lack a   390 supreme norm for the correct application of these principles, morality itself is in danger of all forms of corruption. In order for an action to be morally good, it is not enough that it conform to the moral law: it must be done *because the law commands it*. If we act from some other motive, the conformity is merely accidental. Our nonmoral motive may, in this case, produce activity which happens to conform to law, but in other cases it might just as well lead to unlawful activity.

The history of ethics gives us clear examples of what can happen when morality is based on a natural inclination. Epicurus' basic principle is that pleasure is the ultimate goal of all human endeavor. To a moral philosopher, this principle may serve as a foundation for a respectable moral system. Epicurus warns: "Since pleasure is the first good and natural to us, for this very reason we do not choose every pleasure, but sometimes pass over many pleasures, when greater discomfort accrues to us as the result of them." And he continues: "When we maintain that pleasure is the end, we do not mean the pleasures of profligates and those that consist in sensuality . . . but freedom from pain in the body and trouble in the mind."[2] Whatever leads to these modified pleasures is good, while what causes pain is bad.[3] As it is presented to us, this is an admirable moral system and whoever follows carefully the dictates of the Master will live a moral life indeed. But our own word *epicurean* suggests only too well the decadence which can result from the search for a life of pleasure.

Since the distinction between acting in conformity with the law and acting for the sake of the law, "because the law commands it," is the essential issue of Section I (Chapters 3–4), discussion of this point may be postponed until then.

Only in pure philosophy can we find the pure, genuine moral law (and in matters of practice, this is the basic issue). Unless we first build a metaphysics of morals, we will have no moral philosophy whatsoever. Since philosophy distinguishes rational

from empirical knowledge, while everyday scientific knowledge confuses the one with the other, no theory which tangles *a priori* principles with principles of experience deserves the name of philosophy. Even less does such a mishmash deserve the name of moral philosophy, for it spoils the purity of morality itself and even confounds its own purposes.

Although Kant insists that we must have a separate study of pure moral philosophy, i.e., a metaphysics of morals, he does not intend to disparage everyday rational knowledge. On the contrary, he considers commonsense rational knowledge of moral duties to be an excellent starting point leading to a philosophical knowledge of moral laws. He emphasizes here that everyday rational knowledge is not itself the foundation. It is a confused knowledge, mixing the empirical with the rational. We may well begin with such knowledge since we must begin somewhere, but our first job will be to untangle the empirical from the rational elements. It is the *a priori* basis for this mixed knowledge of moral laws that we are looking for, not any particular system erected upon this commonsense knowledge.

Do not jump to the conclusion that the celebrated Wolff, in his *Universal Practical Philosophy*, has already done what we are talking about. No, this is an entirely new field. Wolff's work was a universal practical philosophy, and so investigated willing in general along with all those activities and circumstances which relate to willing in general. But he did not examine specifically that will which is determined solely by *a priori* principles, without empirical motives. His work differs from a true metaphysics of morals in the same way that general logic differs from transcendental logic: general logic deals with the acts and rules of thinking in general, while transcendental logic investigates the acts and rules of *pure* thinking, that is, thinking which knows things purely *a priori*. A true metaphysics of morals will search for the idea and principles of a possibly *pure* will, and not the activities and circumstances of specifically human willing (which is derived mostly from psychology).

Kant's early philosophical training had been in the Wolffian tradition. Christian Wolff (1686–1754) had written a large and popular compendium of moral principles, entitled the *Universal Practical Philosophy*. Kant rejected Wolff's theories because, as Kant says, Wolff's ethical theories were based upon observations of how moral agents acted rather than upon pure practical philosophy independent of any reference to "specifically human willing." In other words, Wolff made the very error Kant warns against: he mixed a rational analysis with an empirical inquiry, with no clear distinction between the two.

The fact that laws and duty are discussed in ordinary practical philosophy, even though incorrectly, carries no 391 **weight against my argument. Even here the authors make the same error of thinking: they fail to distinguish the motives derived *a priori* from reason itself (the only truly moral motive) from those motives which the understanding has established as universal ideals on the basis of compared experiences. They lump them all together, without noticing any difference in origin, and distinguish them merely on the basis of relative applicability. In this context they define obligation, yet this definition will be anything but adequate for morality. What can you expect from a philosophy which ignores whether the source of all the possible ideas of moral activity is *a priori* or only *a posteriori*?**

Kant continues his criticism of Wolff's approach. Only one motive will give our actions true moral value, he says, and this he calls the moral motive. Wolff, on the other hand, examined the motives from which men do in fact act; finding some to be universal, or almost so, he maintained that such motives are the basis of human, and hence moral, action. John Stuart Mill (1806–1873), the noted British Utilitarian, argued from a similar position. All men do act from the pleasure motive, Mill said, and concluded that morality must then be based upon the proper pursuit of pleasure.

Vigorously opposing such procedures, Kant insists that the moral motive can be determined only by a pure philosophy of practical reason, that is, a metaphysics of morals. He thus agreed with Hume, who half a century earlier had asserted that from an investigation of what *is* so we cannot directly conclude what *ought to be* so. Moral principles must ultimately be derived from some source other than a study of facts.

3. *The Purpose of the* Foundation

Although Kant has argued the need for a metaphysics of morals, that is, for a complete examination of the *a priori* principles of morality and how they are derived from reason alone, he does not intend to pursue such a lengthy investigation in the *Foundation.*

As early as 1767, fourteen years before the first *Critique*, Kant had contemplated writing a "Metaphysics of Morals." Such a work, however, demanded an *a priori* foundation valid for speculative as well as practical reason. So Kant spent the years 1767–1781 working out his critical examination of pure speculative reason. Having published his results as the *Critique of Pure Reason*, he hoped then to begin work on the long delayed "Metaphysics of Morals." But more and more he came to recognize that there had to be a correspondingly thorough critical examination of pure practical reason, even though he had included a sketch of such an examination in the first *Critique*. And so it went. Kant did finally publish his *Metaphysics of Morals* in 1797, thirty years after he first conceived it. Ironically, the "preliminaries" constitute his tremendous contribution to philosophical thought, whereas the *Metaphysics of Morals* receives relatively scant attention.[4]

Someday I will publish a metaphysics of morals, for which this *Foundation* is the first step. The only sure foundation for such a metaphysics of morals is a critical investigation of pure practical reason, just as the only sure foundation for a meta-

physics of nature is the (already published) critical investigation of pure speculative reason.

However, on the one hand, a critical investigation of pure practical reason is not so urgently important as that of pure speculative reason, because human reason, even in minds of ordinary ability, can be directed to a high level of accuracy and completeness in moral thinking, whereas in pure theoretical thinking human reason invariably goes astray.

Still another reason for postponing the critique of practical reason in favor of the *Foundation* is that such a foundation is immediately necessary for our moral system, since we are always involved in moral situations. We may sit on the sidelines watching the play of speculative philosophers without being much affected by the outcome. But we cannot tolerate such noninvolvement in moral matters. We must have the rules *now,* and we demand that they be the right rules. Even though the *Foundation* presupposes a comprehensive critique of practical reason, such a critique need not be complete in order for the *Foundation* to have immediate practical value.

On the other hand, if a critical investigation of pure practical reason is to be complete, we must be able to prove that it is united to pure speculative reason by some common principle. Ultimately, reason is one; only its functions are different. Yet in order to prove this unity, I would have to include considerations outside the present context and these would confuse the reader. So I call this book *Foundation for a Metaphysics of Morals* rather than *Critique of Pure Practical Reason.*

Again, a metaphysics of morals, despite its distasteful name, might become quite popular and be revised for ordinary readers. Thus it is better to set the groundwork apart   392 (along with its inescapable subtleties), allowing the later book to be simpler.

Speculating that his "Metaphysics of Morals" might become something of a best seller, Kant wished to prepare the way for such a popular work by treating the "subtleties" in the separate *Foundation*. For instance, in the *Metaphsics of Morals*, Kant distinguishes between Duties of Right and Duties of Virtue. But such a discussion must rest upon an analysis and justification of the objective status of duty in general, which Kant provides in the *Foundation*.

The *Foundation*, then, has one purpose only: *to discover and justify the supreme principle of morality*. Such a study is complete all by itself and ought to be carried out all by itself.

Undoubtedly my findings in this basic study (which has as yet received scant attention) would appear much clearer if the supreme principle were to be applied to all of morality; and the success of this application would be further proof of their correctness. However, I must forego this advantage for such a course would have little real value, even though it would satisfy me personally. The fact that a principle is easy to apply and seems to cover all situations is no guarantee that it is correct. On the contrary, we might become biased in favor of such a principle and so be prevented from pursuing our search and critique objectively, without considering consequences.

To be precise, Kant's purpose is twofold: to *discover* the supreme principle and to *justify* its objective validity for the whole of morality. Sections I and II are devoted to the discovery; Section III is his attempt to justify the principle as objectively valid.

4. *Outline of the* Foundation

I have adopted a method which seems to me most appropriate for our purpose. First, we will analyze ordinary moral knowledge in order to determine its supreme principle; then, knowing the principle and its source, we will reapply it to ordinary moral knowledge. I have divided the work as follows:

Section I: Transition from ordinary rational knowledge of morality to philosophical knowledge.

Section II: Transition from popular moral philosophy to a metaphysics of morals.

Section III: Final step from a metaphysics of morals to a critique of pure practical reason.

There is a discrepancy between Kant's explanation of his procedure and his three-part outline of the contents. He says that he will first analyze ordinary moral thinking in order to find the principle underlying such thought; then, having found this principle, he will consider whether ordinary moral thinking is consistent with this principle. Yet the three sections of the *Foundation* do not correspond with this plan. Sections I and II are both analytical but Section III is a critical examination of freedom, not applied ethics. Kant never returns to ordinary moral thinking (except in his four examples in Section II, which hardly comprise a major section of the book). At the close of Section II, at that point where he had proposed to reverse his procedure, he apparently changed his mind. He says: "If we are to prove that morality is no mere fantasy . . . we must show that a synthetical use of pure practical reason is possible. However, we cannot do this *without first undertaking a critical investigation of this faculty of reason.*" Consequently, in Section III he outlines the path to a full critique of practical reason. The synthetical return had to wait for the *Metaphysics of Morals*.

A possible explanation for this discrepancy is that Kant wrote the Preface before he completed the *Foundation,* adding the outline as an afterthought. Perhaps his first draft did include both the analytical and synthetical approach he mentions. Then, realizing that he could not complete his original project without first examining the limits of practical reason more thoroughly, he postponed the synthetical application to common moral thinking. In its place he examined freedom of the will as the "foundation" for a critical examination of pure practical reason.

Having changed his outline, he naturally would have revised the title of Section III in the preface. The three titles given above do correctly summarize the contents of the three sections. We can imagine Kant revising the section titles in the preface, but through some oversight failing to change his prose description of his procedure.

The titles for the three sections sound somewhat technical, yet they are precise. Section I begins with ordinary rational knowledge of morality. This knowledge is not "ordinary" in a man-in-the-street sense. In Kant's day the prevailing moral philosophy was an adaptation of Ciceronean stoicism,[5] and the moral propositions Kant uses are representative of this moral philosophy. Kant obviously believes them true, but he does not argue for them. He is interested in finding the underlying principle that presumably would justify any other consistent set of moral propositions.

Section II begins with an analysis of the concepts of law and the moral imperative. Through these concepts—taken from "popular moral philosophy"—he again advances to the supreme principle. Then he outlines some ways in which this principle may be applied to particular moral situations, providing us with a vest pocket "metaphysics of morals."

In Section III Kant attempts to justify the objective validity of the supreme principle. He offers a critical examination in capsule form of the limits of moral knowledge and of the autonomy of the will. This section contains some of the most compact writing Kant ever produced and it will require careful attention. Yet, paradoxically, its very compactness forced Kant to a clarity of expression which we might wish were characteristic of his other writings.

5. A Note to the Reader

The reader would do well at this point to pause and reread the text of the *Foundation* without the commentary. A philo-

sophical commentary of this kind has the disadvantage of break-
ing the text up into bits and pieces in order to analyze and
discuss issues in detail. But the text itself should afterwards be
read straight through in order to obtain a full view of the
argument as the author presented it. Such a rereading is strongly
recommended at the end of each chapter.

SECTION I

TRANSITION FROM ORDINARY RATIONAL KNOWLEDGE OF MORALITY TO PHILOSOPHICAL KNOWLEDGE

CHAPTER THREE

PART 1—The Propositions of Moral Value

Morality is necessarily related to goodness, but not to every kind of goodness. There are good steaks, good paintings, good engines, good deeds, and many other events and objects we judge good for this reason or that.[1] Morality is directly concerned with good *actions* and good *agents:* it has at most an indirect connection with other goods. The production of a good dinner may, in certain circumstances, have a moral value. A talented chef employed at a high salary may be said to have a moral obligation to produce a good dinner. But morality is principally concerned with *moral goodness:* that is, with actions and motives which describe the just man of good character.

Three elements of every action situation are morally significant: (1) the *source* of the action, or that which initiates the activity, commonly called the *will;* (2) the *result* intended as the consequence of the action, such as saving a man's life; and (3) the subjective reason for acting, called the *motive,* such as saving a man's life in hope of a reward. Each of these factors can be judged good or bad. Even in the same situation our moral judgments may differ regarding the different factors. We may judge that saving a man's life is a good result, while at the same time we may judge the motive bad, because it springs from greed.

But by what standard do we judge the will? In order to find

the answer to this question, we must understand what a good will is. Since the concept of a good will is central to Kant's moral philosophy, it will help to state Kant's meaning briefly at the outset. A good will is one which chooses to act simply because it recognizes that an action is the right thing to do. That is, when an agent with a good will understands an action to be the right thing to do, this understanding alone serves as a sufficient motive for him to will that action.

We now have in very sketchy form the basis for Kant's three propositions of moral value. He proposes a moral principle corresponding to each of the three factors in an action: the *will*, the *result*, and the *motive*. In Kant's view, the good will is the primary (or ultimate) objective of morality, because the good will is the best guarantee for good agents and moral deeds. In addition, an agent will most likely perform a good deed if he acts from the best motive. But regarding the results, Kant asserts that they have no bearing on the goodness of the agent or the moral value of his action. Kant's moral education was in the Stoic tradition, a tradition which emphasized the inherent goodness of an intended action without regard for its actual results and our basic obligation to perform such actions irrespective of our personal feelings in the matter. Kant relates the three factors to morality without arguing his case. For one thing, he apparently believed that his analysis was the obvious one. But even more importantly, these propositions themselves do not serve as the basis of his moral philosophy. He employs them as a starting point, as much as to say, "Let us begin with an examination of some basic ethical concepts." He is searching for that principle which is the foundation for these propositions.

In prospect, *the three propositions of moral value* are these:
1. *The First Proposition:* the essence of moral goodness is in the good will.
   a. Reason is the foundation for the good will.
   b. Acting from duty is the essential characteristic of the good will.

2. *The Second Proposition:* to act solely from duty constitutes the moral motive of the good will.

3. *The Third Proposition:* to act from the moral motive, from duty, is to act out of respect for moral law.

1. *The First Proposition of Moral Value*

Nothing in the universe—in fact, nothing whatsoever —can we possibly conceive as *absolutely* good except a *good will*.   393

Morality must ultimately rest on something which we judge to have unqualified goodness or else morality has no foundation but expediency. For surely if we judge people, actions, and motives to be good, we appeal to some standard or other, and eventually our appeal must rest on a goodness which is itself the standard and which is not judged by anything else. This goodness must be the ultimate "good-in-itself." But such a good need not be an absolute good. There are many things good in themselves, such as beauty, proportion, life, happiness—things we desire in and for themselves alone. But an unqualified, absolute good is something more: it is that which is *sufficient by itself* to make its possessor morally good, and is *necessary* for moral goodness. With it a person will be, and without it he will not be, a morally good person.

In order, then, for a moral system to be justified, it must be based on an unqualified good. In Kant's view this unqualified good is the good will. One might think that the production of good deeds alone is sufficient justification for a moral system. However, an absolute dictator might force his subjects always to do from fear what they ought to do and we would hesitate to call their deeds morally good. Nor would we call his laws moral laws. No, the distinctive characteristic of a moral system is that, *by an instructive process*, it seeks to produce good deeds *by an appeal to good character*. A good character is the best guarantee of good deeds. If agents perform good deeds through fear alone, the good deeds may be omitted when the fear is removed. But if they do good deeds because they are good men, they will consistently do good deeds, no matter what the circumstances.[2] The emphasis must be on goodness of character. And what is it that constitutes good character in a person? Kant's answer is, the good will. By a good will Kant does not mean good fellowship, such as in the expression "good will ambassador." Nor does he mean an outpouring of love as did the angels at Bethlehem who sang, "Good will toward men." For Kant, and in the moral sense, a good will is that will which actively and consistently chooses to do the right thing, to perform the good deed; and it does so from the right motive.

To this extent it is surely true that the essential function of morality is the discovery and formation of the good will. But what of the claim that this good will is the *only* unqualified good? Could not love, or knowledge, be equally good without qualification? Would not a person who enjoyed doing good be more apt to do good deeds than would a person who did not enjoy it but acted merely from a sense of duty? Kant is well aware of the strength of his assertion and immediately gives reasons for his stand.

No doubt many things are good and desirable in certain respects. For example:
- (a) **Mental abilities** (or whatever you wish to call them): intelligence, wit, wisdom;
- (b) **Emotional characteristics**: courage, determination, perseverance;
- (c) **Blessings of fortune**: power, wealth, honor;
- (d) **Essentials of happiness**: health, the good life, contentment with one's lot.

But without that expression of character, every one of these natural goods may also produce the worst evils. Unless the good will guides their influence in deliberating on and choosing the moral good, they will lead to pride and conceit. The unbiased spectator will find little pleasure in the presence of a person who has unfailing good luck but lacks a pure, good will. We might say that the good will is the necessary condition for one to be even *worthy* of happiness.

While the properties in the above list are certainly good, they are only good under certain conditions. As often happens, they may contribute to evil. An intelligent thief is worse than a stupid one; a cruel wit worse than a cruel boor; a courageous assassin more to be feared than a timid one, and even more dangerous is a resolute persevering, courageous, intelligent assassin. Such examples only confirm Kant's belief that these characteristics are judged good only in conjunction with something else, namely, the good will. In its presence, they even assist the good will in producing good results. But combined with a bad will they produce actions which we judge to be worse precisely because of the presence of that particular characteristic.

Not even those characteristics which help the good will do its work can be called absolutely good in themselves. Their goodness is a reflection of the good will, and so is a limited, qualified goodness. A person who deliberates calmly, controlling his emotions and passions, seems to have all the essential elements of good character. These qualities were highly praised by ancient philosophers, yet they fall short of being absolutely good. Indeed, without a good will they may be extremely wicked. The calm villain is much more dangerous and hateful to us than the blustering one. 394

We can readily agree that an agent must have a good will in order to be morally good. But is the good will a *sufficient* condition? Could perhaps something else in addition to the agent's good will be required for him to be a morally good person? This question emphasizes a basic distinction which is crucial in Kant's theory: that between a good *agent* and a good *action,* between the person who acts and the deed he performs. What good an agent *produces* is independent of his moral character as such. Stolen money may buy care for orphans as well as money honestly earned.[3]

To say that an action is morally good, or morally right, is to speak ambiguously; it may mean that the agent did *what he had a moral obligation to do,* such as when a person saves a drowning man; or it may mean that the agent performed the action *with the right motive,* that is, because it was the moral thing to do. In the first sense an agent may do what is right but receive no moral credit for his deed, such as when he saves a life purely in the hope of a handsome reward. In the second sense, an agent would always receive moral credit for his deed; he acted *because* it was the right thing to do.

Kant's position is that a person receives moral credit for his action *only* when he does it for the right reason. What is more important, Kant maintains, is that he receives the *same* moral credit whether or not he succeeds in performing the action.

The goodness of the good will does not consist in what it causes or produces, or in how well it achieves a given goal. Rather, its goodness consists solely in its own activity, that is, in the way that it wills. In its own right, it has an immeasurably greater value than any other inclination, more than all other inclinations combined. Even if, through bad luck or the stingy providence of a stepmotherly nature, the good will were impotent in putting into effect its intentions, even when doing everything humanly possible, still the good will, all by itself (as distinguished from a mere wish), would sparkle like a jewel of intrinsic value. It makes no difference whether or not it be useful or productive. When the good will is in fact successful, this merely adds the setting to its luster, making the good will more attractive to the novice. But experts, who know better, do not judge the good will by success.

Kant's position is simply this: the moral merit of an agent—or the goodness of his character—does not depend upon the achievement of the intended result. If the agent acts from a good will, then he acquires *just as much moral* credit for his action, whether he fails or succeeds. Kant is not immediately concerned with the production of beneficial results. He is trying to outline the essential characteristic of moral goodness in an agent. A person who acts with a good will acts because he believes that what he intends to do is the right and moral deed. So long as he tries, by "doing everything humanly possible," to do the right thing, it matters not a bit whether he succeeds *so far as his moral character is concerned.* From the vantage point of morality, the results are secondary since morality is primarily concerned with establishing that special character which will produce beneficial results, given the appropriate conditions. But morality cannot take into account all the various unknowns of chance, the varieties of human ability, and (as Kant, the confirmed bachelor, put it) "the stingy providence of a stepmotherly nature." All that morality can do—and it is quite enough!—is to guarantee that the agent, *given* the necessary ability and circumstances, will try to do his best to do good. But considering that we generally do succeed in fulfilling our intentions and that the good will is the most reliable guarantee that a person will intend the right action, we can see clearly that the good will is the most reliable guarantee that good results will in fact be produced. Consequently *the good will is both a necessary and a sufficient condition for moral goodness.*

1a. *Reason as the Foundation for the Good Will*

Without a good will, an agent cannot receive moral credit for his action; with a good will he receives moral credit regardless of the outcome of the action. But Kant must still discuss the other motives which (moral philosophers have claimed) always lead an agent to will what is good. What of love for our fellow men, as

Hume suggests? Or the desire for happiness, as Aristotle argued? These are worthy motives which would seem to earn moral credit for anyone acting from them. How are these motives to be distinguished from the good will? In order to answer this question we should have a clear definition of the good will. Is it simply a desire to do the right thing? This is too vague: a person could desire to do the right thing merely to avoid trouble with the law. We would expect this basic question to be answered at once. But Kant detours.

How strange is this notion of a will having unconditional value all by itself, disregarding any question of 395 **its success. Could it be that in a moment of fanciful delusion we have unwisely jumped to the conclusion that Nature intended for reason to rule the will? Perhaps we ought to examine this commonsense belief more closely.**

One question, Kant believes, must be discussed before we can investigate the nature of the good will. We might easily take for granted that reason is the deciding factor in many of our choices: we decide by "reasoning it out," or we might "act on principle." Whatever the process by which this happens, it does appear to us that at least on some occasions our decisions are based upon a rational analysis of the situation rather than upon our desires or impulses. That a good will does in fact rely on reason, we cannot deny; any action not purely impulsive relies on reason to some extent. But we need to prove that it is reason *alone* which is the proper foundation, or the proper guiding force, of the good will.

We may take for granted, as a principle of Nature regarding organic beings (those which have life), that every organ has an express purpose, and that no other organ can as well fulfill that purpose. If the goal of man, as a being endowed with reason and will, were his survival or his well-being, that is, his happi-

ness, then Nature bungled the job in making reason the proper organ for achieving this goal. Instinct could do much better than reason in initiating the many actions man must perform to gain happiness, as well as establishing a general rule of conduct. And instinct could provide a greater chance of success.

If such a creature of instinct had the added blessing of reason, this faculty could only be used for contemplating man's happy lot, admiring it, finding joy in it, and giving thanks to Nature for it. But reason would have no power to control desire; such a feeble and inept guide would never be allowed to meddle with Nature's purposes. In short, Nature would take great pains to keep reason from any practical function and would never allow it the conceit to exercise its dim wit towards working out a way to achieve happiness. Nature would have set up both the end and the means to happiness and in Her wisdom would have put both into the faithful hands of instinct alone.

The first thing we notice in this argument is Kant's axiomatic belief in the purposive plan of nature. He curiously abandons his critical approach in stating this axiom, for it is a proposition about the entire universe throughout time and Kant has argued[4] that we cannot have knowledge of such matters. But this is secondary, since the axiom itself is certainly questionable. It may be true, but it is not so obviously true as Kant makes it out to be.[5]

The argument actually rests on two axioms, one of which is indirectly stated in the above paragraph: (1) reason is the proper ruler of the will; and (2) every natural faculty is appropriate for its function, and no other can perform this function as well, if at all. There is no point in quibbling about the first axiom, since to deny reason's function as the appropriate guiding source of human activity (willing) is to eliminate all morality, as well as rational activity of any sort. The second axiom is generally true. The eye is the sole faculty of sight; the ear is the best organ of hearing.

If reason is the primary directing agency of those actions we must properly call human, and if every faculty is the best one for its purpose, then reason will best enable man to reach his true goal, whatever that goal may be. Reason, not instinct, *is* the primary faculty for achieving the true goal which nature has established for a "being endowed with reason and will." But is this goal happiness? No, says Kant, for reason is not the best faculty for achieving happiness: instinct could do a much better job. Man's goal must be that for which reason *is* the best guide. Consequently, happiness is not the goal of man. Furthermore, if happiness were man's goal, and instinct man's primary guide in action, instinct would never allow reason any practical function, but would relegate it to the role of an impotent observer.

We know, as a matter of fact, that the more a sophisticated reason tries to pursue the pleasures of life and happiness, the less it succeeds in attaining these goals. This fact causes many persons—those who are honest enough to admit it—to have a certain distrust of reason; they become misologists. This is especially true of those experienced in rational activity. They look at all the so-called advantages which reason offers—not only the acts of luxurious living, but even scientific knowledge (a luxury of the mind, so to speak)—and feel that all this is more trouble than it is worth, and a far cry from happiness. Eventually they come to envy, rather than despise, the common folks who act more from the influences of   396 emotion and desire than from reason.

In short, reason cannot guarantee that we will get what we want or need—reason even increases our needs. Inborn instinct could do a far better job. But while it is one thing to minimize the value of the so-called advantages for happiness and content- ment which reason offers, it is quite another to be surly and ungrateful to that Providence which guides the universe. We can indeed conceive of a purpose for which reason is most eminently suited, a supreme goal to which all merely private pursuits, even happiness, must give way.

Kant's approach seems somewhat inconsistent. If a man seeks true happiness with full rational inquiry, he is far more likely to find it than one who seeks happiness by following his instincts for pleasure. The inconsistency lies in the supposition (for the sake of his argument) that a person who uses his reason to seek happiness will become more and more disillusioned, morose, and unhappy. But that just is not so. The trouble is Kant's manner of speaking. When he speaks of "the pleasures of life and happiness," we must remember that he is thinking of the refined epicure rather than of the Aristotelian "great-souled man," who seeks happiness in rational activity.

The goal of reason, or man's ultimate goal—which for Kant mean the same thing—must be something other than happiness. Kant speaks of the good will as absolutely essential "for one to be even *worthy* of happiness." As we shall see, man's goal must be one which he is able to achieve on his own merits. Since happiness cannot be guaranteed even in a lifetime, due no doubt to the quirks of that same step-motherly nature, then man must have some other goal which he *can* be sure of attaining on his own. Kant believes man's goal is worthiness to be happy, a goal every man can achieve whatever the fortunes of his life, though of course not without some difficulty. And if worthiness of any kind depends on the worth of him who is worthy, what kind of worth constitutes the worthiness to be happy? Obviously, *moral* worth. The goal of reason, then, or the goal for a being with a rational nature, is moral worthiness. And the necessary and sufficient condition of moral worthiness is the good will. Thus *the primary goal of (practical) reason must be to produce a good will.*

Reason does have a practical function: it is meant to guide the will. So, in accordance with Nature's plan to provide each organ with the power appropriate to its purpose, reason's true function must be to produce a good will, *a will good in itself*, not merely good for something else. For such a goal, reason is absolutely necessary.

This is not to say that the good will is the only good, or the whole of goodness; but that the good will is the highest good, that which makes anything else good, even the desire for happiness. Consequently, it is quite fitting that Nature, in Her wise way, should promote reason in its quest of the absolute good, and thus make the search for happiness (at least in this life) secondary, often ignoring it completely. Reason, seeing that its supreme calling is to produce a good will, can find its real satisfaction in achieving a goal which reason has set for itself, even when this goal confounds the objectives of our other inclinations.

We must be careful not to make Kant an anti-hedonist, at least not to the extent to which he is often interpreted. In this paragraph Kant very clearly allows that happiness is *a* goal of life, but a qualified goal, one subject to the primary objective, the production of the good will. The demands of morality often countermand, "ignoring completely," the demands of our natural propensities for the happiness of contentment. Nothing can take precedence over morality. Thus to achieve moral worthiness is the unconditional goal of life. Kant recognizes that many times the morally good deed is opposed by desire. A person need not make this a choice of good over evil, though often it turns out to be that. The good will is not the only good, nor the complete good; there are many other good things, many other good actions. But these other things and actions are conditionally good. The good will is the *supreme* good, the good that gives the other goods moral value, since the others must be sought with a good will, or else they bring no moral credit to the agent. In any conflict between the good will and any other good whatsoever, the good will must prevail.

What is the importance of this argument? Kant wishes to emphasize the role of reason; he is explicitly searching for the *a priori* grounds of morality. He therefore takes the very first opportunity to anchor firmly in our minds the basic dependence of the good will upon reason. Thus when he later examines the rational foundation of morality itself he need not interrupt the argument to prove that reason is the true foundation of moral action.

1b. *The Concept of Duty: the Moral "Ought"*

Thus we must analyze the idea of a will which has an independent, intrinsic goodness. Anyone with a good mind has that idea which points to an ultimate moral standard by which everything else is judged, so we need not teach this idea so much as make it clear and precise. This idea is *duty*, which includes in it the notion of a good will, yet a will which is faced with many subjective hindrances to its function. But these obstacles do not obscure or conceal the good will; on the contrary, they emphasize its luster all the more by contrast. 397

How does the concept of duty contain that of a good will? In this and the following passages, in fact throughout the rest of the *Foundation,* Kant relies heavily on the common notion of duty as the primary example of our common rational knowledge of moral concepts. So it is most important that we have a clear understanding of what Kant means by "duty".

We saw in Chapter 1 that the understanding provides pure *a priori* concepts to which sensations must conform if they are to be meaningful. We discussed the concept of substance, whereby two successive experiences are *given* a relationship by the understanding even though the raw sensations as such do not themselves reveal this relationship. In the same way, but in the practical rather than the speculative sphere of reason, there is the *moral a priori* concept of duty. To this we must now turn.

For Kant, who takes his departure from Hume, no factual situation is ever sufficient *of itself to* produce a duty, that is, to oblige an agent to perform a certain action. Although it often happens that we jump immediately from the awareness of the factual situation to a concluding "ought,"[6] this is not by what the logician calls an immediate inference. The traditional explanation is that, in making such an inference, we are implicitly subsuming the factual situation under an obligation-rule which applies to situations of this kind. Our train of thought (though not always on a conscious level) might run something like this: "There is a man who is in great pain; (I ought to relieve pain whenever I can;) so I ought to relieve his pain." Our obligation is derived from the "ought"-rule, which is enclosed in parentheses to indicate the possibility, or probability, of subconscious inclusion. The point is that nothing in the mere fact alone of a man's being in pain obligates me to help him—*unless* I acknowledge the principle that I ought to relieve pain whenever I can. As Hume put it, what *is* the case cannot by itself imply what *ought to be* the case. Something else is needed: a ground of obligation.

But why cannot a factual situation by itself obligate someone? For Kant, the reason is that the notion of obligation contains the idea of *moral necessity*.[7] When I have an obligation to do something, or when I have a duty to do it, or when I ought to do it— all meaning the same thing in a moral context—there is a *moral necessity* about the action in relation to me as agent. By moral necessity we mean that, in those situations in which there is no overriding counter-obligation, *no excuse whatsoever* can absolve me of the obligation, no appeal can relieve me from such a duty. Moreover, no other reason for acting is so final or so powerful.

Kant, a Prussian, refers to moral obligation by the term "duty" *(Pflicht)*. We tend to view duty as a stern taskmaster, which cuts into our comfort and compels us to painful endeavor, self-privation, and inner strife. We might choose, in place of "duty," some more contemporary expression, but this would require a major overhaul of the conceptual framework of the *Foundation*, and would dress Kant in a gown too anachronistic for recognition. As a compromise, we will continue to use "duty", remembering that by "*a* duty," Kant means what we understand by "a moral obligation"; and by "duty", he means the essence of the moral "ought," what we might uneuphoniously label "ought-ness" or "obligatoriness". In this way we may possibly lessen some of the harsh overtones of subservience while retaining the essential element of moral necessity; and it is the latter which Kant emphasizes.

Duty, or moral necessity, cannot be derived from mere experience. Any concept involving necessity is *a priori,* and consequently cannot depend upon experience. Yet a particular duty must involve some experience. How would we know what we ought to do if we had no experience of the obligating situation? But it is practical reason which assigns the necessity to one particular course of action and not to another. Thus the moral necessity of an action is based on reason, not on experience, and the conceptual form of this moral necessity, which we call duty, is a *moral a priori* concept (that is, an *a priori* concept of practical reason).

In an anlysis of duty, Kant says, we discover the good will, "yet a will which is faced with many subjective hindrances to its function." Using a number of examples designed to show what it means to act from duty, Kant begins by explaining that the good will appears most clearly to be acting from duty, or for duty's sake, when it chooses to do what reason says it ought to do in opposition to what the agent might feel like doing.

We can ignore all those actions which conflict with duty, no matter how useful they may be, since it is absurd to ask whether an action opposed to duty can be done for duty's sake. Likewise, we can ignore those actions which, though in accord with duty, are done without any personal inclination towards them. We can easily tell whether such actions are done for duty's sake, or from some other personal reason. But it is very difficult to decide whether an action which we ought to do, and which at the same time we feel an inner compulsion to do, is done for duty's sake. Consider the following examples:

A merchant has the duty not to overcharge an unwary customer. Where competition is lively, he is wise to have a set price for everyone, so that a child may buy as cheaply as anyone else.

Everyone receives honest service. But this is not enough for us to decide that he is honest for duty's sake, or that he acts solely from principles of honesty. Honesty for him is the best business policy. And it would be odd to imagine that his honesty stems from a real love for each of his customers. He is honest not for duty's sake nor because of an inner compulsion but rather for personal gain.

Actions are related to duty[8] in one of three ways:
1. They may *conflict* with duty and obviously do not involve a good will.
2. They may be *in accord with duty* but are not performed for the right reason, i.e., from the moral motive:
   a. The motive may be some inner compulsion, such as love or a sense of honor; or,
   b. The motive may be a desire for the consequences.
3. They may be done *from duty*, in recognition of the moral "ought." Such an action Kant calls *aus Pflicht* (from duty, for the sake of duty). Such an action is both dutiful *(pflichtmässig)* and done from duty *(aus Pflicht)*, whereas the actions which are dutiful but done from inclination are not done *from duty*.

Kant lumps all motives other than the purely moral motive of acting solely from duty into the generic class of inclinations or desires, which is to say, motives based upon self-interest. In this class we will find such extremes as, on the one hand, benevolence, philanthropy, and parental love; and selfish greed, the desire for sensual pleasure, and fear on the other. This is unfortunate, for it oversimplifies the problem. Some of these motivating factors are good, and we surely ought to strengthen them; others are bad and should be vigorously controlled, even though we may not be able to suppress them entirely.

However, Kant's point itself is rather simple. We can perform a duty in one of two ways: either because it is our obligation *(aus Pflicht)*, or for some other reason. Whatever the other reason may be, Kant calls it an inclination, a desire, a selfish motive. He distinguishes between a direct inclination ("I *like* to give to charity") and a selfish purpose ("By giving to charity I will be popular"). But the distinction is not important to the moral motive. If a person acts from any reason other than recognition of his obligation, then for Kant he is not acting solely from duty. The storekeeper who serves all customers equally, without cheating, is an honest man; but if he is honest for purely prudential business reasons, we cannot call him a virtuous man.

Everyone has a duty to preserve his own life, over and above his positive inclination to do so. But even frequent 398 **careful precautions will have no moral value if they stem from natural inclination, since the maxim has no moral foundation. True, such a person preserves his life in accordance with his duty, but not for duty's sake. Suppose, however, hardships and sorrowful despair rob a man of every possible reason for living, and suppose he is angry at Fate rather than sinking into despondent self-pity. If he still preserves his life, not because life is desirable (he may even wish he were dead), but because such is his duty, then his maxim has a moral foundation.**

By this example of the despondent man, Kant broadens his distinction between acting *from* duty and acting *in accordance with* duty. The distinctive element in this paragraph is the introduction of the term *"maxim."* Kant defines a maxim as a *subjective principle of action.* Roughly speaking, a maxim is the personal rule or policy I follow when I act, for I never act without acting from some personal policy or other. As a principle or rule, a maxim is a general policy; it applies to some more or less extensive *class* of actions. Everything I do I can describe in some general way, even though frequently such descriptions are artificial. For instance, I am now engaged in an activity which belongs to the class "writing on paper with a pen." Suppose that every time I wished to write, I withdrew to a quiet spot in order to concentrate. My maxim would be, "When I want to write, I will first retire to some secluded spot." This principle would be one of my general rules of acting. It outlines a procedure for acting in a certain kind of situation, writing. The maxim describes the type of situation in which I act, and it may also contain my reason for acting. In Kant's example of the duty to preserve one's life, the maxim of the contented man would be something like, "As long as life is pleasant, I will do what I can to preserve it." An alternative maxim might be, "When life becomes intolerable, I will commit suicide." These are principles upon which the man acts, or will act, given the appropriate situation. They are *his own* (i.e., subjective) principles. He need not suggest that others do as he does. Such personal or subjective rules of acting, present in every human decision to act (though not necessarily on a level of conscious awareness), Kant calls maxims.

What maxim guides the man who hangs onto life even when he lacks any inclination to do so, solely because it is his duty? His maxim would be something like, "I *must* try to live as long as possible." The moral foundation of this maxim is rooted in the good will. That is, the maxim owes its existence as a subjective rule to the good will, which acts for duty's sake and not merely from inclination. Thus the man who clings to life because it is his duty is acting with a moral maxim. His maxim has moral value. The man who lives his life because it is pleasant acts from a *good* maxim, perhaps, but such a maxim lacks moral value.

We have a duty to be kind whenever the situation permits it. Many persons have so sympathetic a personality that they find real pleasure in making others happy, and without any motive of vanity or self-interest they find joy in the well-being they bring to others. Nevertheless such actions have no *moral* value, no matter how much they agree with duty, or how much good they produce. The very same actions could just as well proceed from a desire for honor. When such a motive causes a person to do those good deeds which luckily agree with duty,

he acts honorably and deserves praise and reward. *But not esteem.* The maxim behind these actions lacks a moral foundation, since it is based upon some motive other than doing one's duty.

Now suppose that this same humanitarian is dealt such distress that he loses all joy in helping others. He still has the means to help others in need, but their need seems insignificant beside his own. If, in spite of his lack of inclination, he pulls himself out of his numbing lethargy and assists others for duty's sake alone—then, for the first time, his action has true moral value.

Or take the case of a man, otherwise a decent person, who is naturally unsympathetic, being unmoved by the suffering of others. Perhaps he is blessed with exceptional endurance and strength, and believes others should accept their lot as he does. (Such a fellow would hardly be the meanest man alive.) Can he find in himself a nobler motive for devoting himself to relieving the distress of others than one derived merely from a warm heart? Certainly he can, even though Nature failed to fill him with brotherly love. Indeed, only here do we find the true mettle of a man's character. If he helps others for duty's sake, despite his inclinations to the contrary, he exhibits character of the highest *moral* value. 399

The first section of this passage deserves special emphasis. There Kant explicitly states what many have claimed that he denies, namely, that an action may be good without having moral value. Surely, Kant says, many actions are good and are done from praiseworthy motives, such as love for one's fellow man; yet such actions do not have *moral* value. They are not done from the moral motive, but from desire or some other human motive. When such actions are praiseworthy or honorable, then we surely have the right to praise or honor the agent; but we do not esteem him. Esteem is due the virtuous man, the man who acts from the moral motive, the man of moral character.

But a question can be raised here which Kant never clearly

answered, and because he did not, he is taken to imply something which he could not have intended. This concerns the case of a man who acts in accordance with duty, is aware that it is his duty, but also has another motive. For example, there is the man who gives to charity because it is his duty but who also enjoys doing so from a motive of brotherly love. (Seldom are human motives simple and clear-cut.) Does Kant mean to say that this is not a good action? Decidedly not. Does he mean that the agent is not acting morally? By no means. What Kant wants to say is that in such cases *we cannot tell* whether the man would still have performed his duty if the inclination were missing. Maybe he would, maybe he wouldn't; there is no way we can judge. But Kant is not concerned to give us a standard for judging the actions of others, or even of our own—at least that is not his primary objective. He is making a distinction between the moral motive and other motives. Yet he is often taken to mean that unless an action be done solely from duty, it has no moral worth. This point deserves some further discussion.

Morality plays a crucial role in our lives, urging us to do good rather than evil; to practice virtue instead of vice; to love, not hate. To the extent that man willingly does good, practices virtue, and loves, and does so because it gives him pleasure, the less he stands in need of a moral law. But when he ought to do something for which he has no inclination, a moral *command* is needed. It is just at such a time, when a man has no inclination to do his duty and yet does it, that Kant says moral credit is gained. But whether this is the *only* occasion in which a man can receive moral credit is another matter.

In order to understand Kant's point of view, let us consider a mother who finds delight in caring for her infant child. We can praise her for her attention to her child's welfare. But one day the child suffers serious brain damage. The mother still loves her child and spends all her efforts in caring for it with little or no hope of any return of affection. Certainly the mother does her duty towards her child, who would deny it? But she does it out of love, not for duty's sake. She gains our admiration, but not our esteem. For what would the mother do should she eventually lose her love for her child? If the child became only a tiresome burden, would she continue to do her duty or would she give over the child to someone else's care—in effect abandoning her duty? (Let's ignore the question of comparative care for the child.) We don't know what she would do, because the motive from which she acted was insufficient to guarantee performance. If we knew that she was acting from duty, we could more accurately predict what she would do. What answer then can we make to our question concerning the possibility of acquiring moral credit when the moral motive is joined with some non-moral motive? Our example shows a parent who achieves heroic stature in the face of trying adversity. But does her love-motive earn her any moral credit? Kant's answer would begin with another question: will she continue to fulfill her obligation should her love-motive fail? Is her reason for acting subjective only, or does it also include some awareness of the objective necessity of the action itself? If she continues to care for her child, then she does so with a moral motive (since all other motives have failed), and in that case she surely receives moral credit. However, if she does not continue, she obviously receives no moral credit, since she fails to do her duty. Consequently the question —does a person achieve moral credit when the moral motive is is joined with a non-moral motive?—cannot be answered. The moral motive appears only when it is the sole motive. Thus Kant is justified in denying moral value to non-moral motives, and this in turn gives strong support to his first proposition that the good will is the necessary *and* sufficient condition for moral value.[9]

In making the distinction between merit and moral merit, we must guard against the tendency to confuse the difference in kinds of merit with a difference in degrees of goodness. The loving parent of a retarded child may do much more good and gain much more credit than one who gives money to charity purely from duty. To think otherwise is to miss Kant's point. He is not comparing actions; he is comparing *motives*. An action done from duty in the face of contrary inclination gains more merit than the same action done from some other motive.

A man even has an indirect duty to seek happiness. The more he is troubled by the burdens of anxiety and need, the more he may be tempted to fail in his duty. Even apart from duty, everyone has the most fundamental urge to be happy, since the idea of happiness more or less sums up in our minds the satisfaction of all our desires, cares, and needs. But the specific paths which lead to happiness always seem to thwart some desire or other, and men have never found a meaningful definition of happiness which incorporates the satisfaction of all desires. Why then should we be surprised when one particular desire, promising a definite satisfaction at a definite time, outweighs a foggy idea? Thinking in this vein, a man with gout may decide to live as he pleases, choosing the certain pleasures of the present to the hazy, uncertain promise of a future happiness supposedly to be derived from good health. Yet here also, even if he lacked the general desire for happiness and if health were not a real factor in his deliberations, he would still have to seek his own happiness for the sake of duty. Only by obeying the law of duty will his search for happiness have true moral value.

The gloomy life is not necessarily the moral life. Kant's insight into human nature is apparent when he observes that virtue is more easily achieved by the happy man than by the Gloomy Gus. For one thing, Gloomy Gus is too wrapped up in his own misery to think of much else. The more aids we have for acting in accordance with duty the better. Kant does not say, however, that these should be aids to acting *from* duty. A man usually acts from duty when these helpful inclinations are absent. Should we then try to avoid happiness? Would it not be better to be miserable so that we could always act purely from duty? Kant would be the first to insist that this is ridiculous.

No doubt this is the way we should interpret those passages in Holy Writ commanding us to love our neighbor, even our enemy. For no one can command us to feel a love for another. The law of love is independent of feeling and may even be opposed to feeling. It commands us *to act,* not to experience an emotion. As a practical law, it is grounded in the will and not in the heart, in principles of action and not in emotional impulses. Only the activity of love can be commanded.

The command to love one's neighbor is not a command to feel something; it is a command to do, to act. When Jesus told the crowds, "Love your enemies; do good to those who hate you" (Matt. 5:44), he was not giving them two injunctions, but one stated in two ways. "Love," Jesus said, "That is, *do good.*"[10]

Before we proceed to the second and third propositions of moral value, a brief summary of the discussion will draw together the threads of the argument. The first proposition is this: The good will is the only absolute good, the necessary and sufficient condition for any morally good action. The good will is also the goal of human existence, since it is the goal of reason, human nature's guide. The function of the good will is to produce good character, and a good character actively and consistently produces good actions by acting from the moral motive, that is, from duty. A man may perform good deeds, but unless he does them from duty, he acquires no moral credit even though he earn other merit.

When we put all this together into one formula, we have a manageable statement of the first proposition of moral value. *The first proposition of moral value is: the absolute good, and the ultimate foundation of morality, is the good will, which gains moral credit from acting in accordance with duty for the sake of duty itself.*

2. *The Second Proposition of Moral Value*

The second proposition of moral value is: the moral value of an action done from duty is found in the maxim 400 *which guides the will and not in the desired results of the action.* What matters is not success or failure in achieving the result, but solely the rule which guides the will in choosing to act, regardless of what the agent may be inclined to do. We have already decided that no desired results, however beneficial, can give absolute and moral value to our action.

The *motive* for acting determines the moral worth of an action. That is, if an agent acts for duty's sake, rather than from inclination, then his action has moral value. There remains, however, the question of what constitutes the moral motive. We have already seen that the success or failure of the intended action adds nothing to the will's goodness, although it obviously makes a great difference in the quantity of material goodness actually produced.

Many moral philosophers believe that it is equally important, if not more so, for an agent to seek the right things, and that an agent cannot earn moral credit if he intends to do something which will in fact produce harm. But Kant never suggests that this is an unimportant consideration, for to do so would be to ignore the basic function of morality. What Kant proposes is that the *moral* value of an intention is independent of the *material* goodness of what is willed. It makes no moral difference what is willed, so long as the agent wills it from the moral motive. This appears difficult only when we confuse the moral value of the will with the material goodness of the action. Surely it is better to produce good rather than evil; but is it better to produce good actions from bad motives, or bad actions from good motives? The answer depends on the standard used for "better." If we want results, then good actions are better, no matter what the motive. If we want good character, then good motives are better, whatever the results. But in view of the general correspondence between motive and action, it is far better to have good motives, since they are the best guarantee of good results.

What then is the essence of the moral motive? What reason for acting gives an action moral value?

But if we cannot find moral value in the relation of the will to the desired result, where can we find it? *Only in that rule which determines the will*, without any regard for the results to be attained by acting. We can picture the will as standing at an intersection between its *a priori* formal rule and its *a posteriori* material rule: the one is rational, the other is empirical. Now the will must be guided by something; so when it chooses to act for the sake of duty, it must be guided solely by the formal rule of reason since every empirical rule of desire has been ignored.

The standard we seek is the rule[11] which determines the will, that is, the rule of duty or obligation. Kant pictures the will at a crossroads between the rational motive of acting solely for duty's sake and the empirical motive of acting from a desire for a particular result. In other words, whenever we will to act, we act either on a rational principle or from a desire of some kind. The will must will from *some* motive or other, so when it wills from the moral motive it determines itself by a rational rule, not merely by a desire for some object. This is true even in cases where the object of desire would be the same as the object of duty.

Briefly, then, the moral motive is an *a priori* determinant of the will and desire is an *a posteriori* determinant. By saying "determinant" of the will, or that the will is determined by reason, Kant does not suggest anything of a deterministic psychology.[12] When he speaks of determinants, he means motives, those grounds upon which we do in fact decide to act. If we ask someone, "What made you do that?" we do not necessarily imply that the person was compelled. Most of the time we are asking for his motive, since to suggest that he was compelled to act is to deny that he acted with any motive at all.

Before discussing the third proposition of moral value, let us summarize briefly the points made so far:

a. The good will is the necessary and sufficient condition for the moral worth of an action or agent.
b. This moral worth does not depend on success or failure in producing a result.
c. The moral worth does not depend on the goodness of the purpose for which the agent acts.

d. The moral worth consists, rather, in acting from the moral
motive, that is, according to a principle of reason.

3. *The Third Proposition of Moral Value*

Kant says that the third proposition follows from the two
preceding propositions. The first and second propositions established the good will as the necessary and sufficient condition for
the moral worth of an agent and defined the good will as that
which performs its duty from the moral motive. The third proposition does not follow in the way a conclusion follows from its
premises, i.e., as a logical conclusion. Rather, the third proposition supplies the missing explanation: we do not yet know what
it means to act from the moral motive, that is, to act from duty.

**The third proposition, which follows from the first two, I
would express as: *Duty is an action which, out of respect for
law, I acknowledge as necessary for me to perform*.**[13] **I can be
drawn to some object, and see it as the result of some proposed
action, but I cannot respect it; for it is merely an effect of the
will, not the activity of willing. I may approve of my own inclinations and love those in others which serve my own purposes,
but I cannot respect these inclinations. Only something which
is related to my will as a foundation, not as a consequence, and
which disregards or overcomes inclinations, can be an object of
respect. In short, only *law* can command the will through respect.**

The moral motive is the condition for acting with a good will.
To act for duty's sake is to act solely because one has an obligation. But the source of obligation or duty is law, for only under
law does an action acquire that characteristic of necessity which
elevates it to the status of a command of duty. Thus, to act from
duty is to act in accordance with the law because the law commands unconditionally; in short, *because it is the law*.

When a person does something in accordance with the law

(whether moral or civil law), he may do so from the fear of sanctions if he violates the law, or because he enjoys doing what the law prescribes, or because he desires the benefits of the law. For example, a man might drive within the speed limit because he fears being arrested, or because he enjoys driving slowly, or because he hopes to avoid an accident. In none of these cases does he act from respect for law. Only if he acts solely because the law so prescribes does he act from what Kant calls respect for law.

Respect[14] is not an emotional experience, but an intellectual awareness and recognition of the unqualified value of that which we respect. We respect the law when we recognize that we ought to act solely because we have a rational awareness of the unconditional moral value of what the law commands. We value most things as means, but in respect for law we value the law for itself, not as the result of decision or argument, but just because it is the law.

> **Since in order to act from duty I must disregard the influence of my inclinations, and thus any object of de-   401 sire, the sole remaining objective influence on my will is the practical law. The corresponding influence is my respect for the law, expressed by the maxim* that I ought to obey the law even when it frustrates my inclinations.**
>
> * A maxim is a subjective rule of acting. The objective rule, that is, the rule every one would accept as a subjective rule were reason to have full sway over desire, is the practical law.

Many kinds of motives can determine an agent's choice to act according to duty. A person might enjoy what he does, desire the result, or act from fear, and so on. However, when an agent acts without compulsion but lacks any of the above motives, then he acts solely because the moral law commands him to act.

In the footnote Kant defines a maxim as "the subjective rule of acting." He contrasts this to the objective rule, the law, and says that these two would always be the same were our desires always under the control of reason. Were we perfect, we would always *want* to do what we *ought* to do. As things are with us, however, it is not necessary that we *want* to do what we have an obligation to do. It suffices that we respect the law, that we recognize the law as having sufficient authority to determine our choice.

Let us further examine the difference between *maxim* and *law*. As we have seen, a maxim is the rule we follow when we act. Its form is something like this: When I am in this kind of situation, I will do such-and-such. We "know how to act" in a situation when we know what kind of situation it is and have some knowledge of the rules governing our conduct in such situations. This general rule is what Kant calls the subjective principle, the maxim, whenever it is acted upon. Sometimes the maxim contains the motive. For instance, the maxim, "When I am in a school zone I will drive slowly," may contain the motive, "so that I will not be arrested for speeding." Of course we seldom consciously express these rules; but we could, and would do so if we were trying to justify some particular action.

A law, on the other hand, makes no reference to motive, since *the law is concerned only with the action,* not with the reason for acting. The law cannot command us to act from a certain motive; it can only command us to act.[15] Whether I avoid committing murder from fear of punishment or from respect for life, I have obeyed the law. But I do not act from a moral motive unless I obey the law because it is the law, that is, from respect for the validity of the command imposing obligation on me. Only when I conform my maxim to what the law commands, and do so out of respect for the law, then only does my maxim have moral value. If the motive is moral, so is the maxim.

Which is more fundamental, to have a maxim accord with the law, or to have a moral motive? For Kant the moral motive takes precedence.

Thus the moral value of an action does not come from any desired effect, nor from any rule of action motivated by such a

desired effect. Any such effect, as for example my own well-being or even the happiness of others, could conceivably result from purely natural causes. But the supreme and absolute good requires a rational will. Consequently, the preeminent moral good must be found, not in some desired effect, but solely in a will which is determined by the idea of law. Whoever acts from the idea of law achieves this preeminent moral goodness by his very willing; he need not wait upon results.*

---

* Some may accuse me of hiding a vague feeling, which I call respect, instead of offering a clear definition of the word. Respect is a feeling, I admit, but not one aroused by some outside influence. Respect is essentially different from any feeling based on desire or fear, for it is self-induced from a rational concept. Whatever I recognize directly as a law binding me—that is, whenever I am aware of being subject to a law independently of external influences—I recognize with respect. Respect involves two elements: the immediate determination of the will and awareness of this determination. In this way respect can be called the effect of the law on the will, not the cause of the law. We might define respect as the awareness of a value which cancels out love of self.

Respect is something *like* desire or fear, but wholly independent of either. Only the law can be the object of respect, since law is the only thing we impose upon ourselves and yet recognize as commanding under necessity. Since it is law, we are subject to it no matter what we might desire, which shows how respect resembles fear. However, we do impose this law on ourselves; and in this way respect is like desire.

Any so-called respect for a person is, strictly speaking, only respect for what the person exemplifies (such as honesty). We see self-improvement as a duty, and so we tend to see a person who has improved himself as the basis of a law that we imitate him. This law is what we respect, not the person himself. All so-called moral interest is nothing else but respect for law.

We are looking for the ultimate basis of morality. However, we cannot expect to find it in results, since good results frequently proceed from obviously immoral motives and actions, even from nonhuman causes. And since the moral value of an action depends on the motive, we must look to the motive as the "preeminent" moral good. This motive is respect for law. It can be found only in a rational being, since nonrational beings have no conception of law and obviously cannot act from respect for it. Furthermore, any person who wills to act out of respect for law is a person with a moral motive. He thereby earns moral credit, whether or not he succeeds in his purpose and even when he is mistaken about what the law commands.

The expression, "feeling of respect," is not misleading, since respect is like other feelings in certain aspects. Because it is grounded in the will, it is like desire; as respect for law it is like fear. However, respect is a product of reason, while desire may spring from emotion. We might agree that there is a kind of moral feeling, but it is essentially a different kind of feeling from that which we call self-righteousness. Surely there is a certain influence on the will when we recognize a moral law. Nothing else can affect us in just that way; no other feeling is just like that feeling.

We can see Kant struggling with a thorny psychological distinction here and finding the going rough. In his explanation he inadvertently includes matters which are premature, for example, self-legislation and respect for persons. Perhaps this footnote was added later to clarify a concept essential to his analysis of the force of moral law.

4. Resume

Lest one should think that Kant has already found the ultimate basis of morality in the moral motive, he should keep in mind that all these propositions of morality are derived from common rational knowledge. Kant has not yet analyzed the concept of law, which is all-important to an understanding of the moral motive. Nor has he yet discussed how the will is determined solely by the moral motive. But from his examination of common rational morality he has derived the following underlying principles:

1. *The sole unconditional moral good is the good will, the will which acts for duty's sake rather than from desire.*
2. *The moral value of an action lies solely in its motive, to act from duty.*

3. *One acts for duty's sake when he acts out of respect for law.* Kant began with a common notion of moral goodness and found the source of this goodness in the moral motive. The remainder of Section I will give an analysis of this moral motive and its relation to law.

CHAPTER FOUR

PART 2—The Form of Law: Universality

1. *The Concept of Law as Law*

The act of highest moral value is one done solely from respect for law. But when we ask what constitutes respect for law, we immediately raise the question of what is the nature of law, and which laws are we to respect. There are volumes and volumes of laws in any law library. Since no one knows all of them, respect for law must mean respect for something common to all laws. This is the question to which Kant now turns: what in a law commands our obedience?

But what kind of law by itself alone can determine a will and make it absolutely good, not by considering   402 any beneficial consequences but only by the awareness of the law itself? Since any motive based on the results of obeying the law has been excluded, the only rule remaining for the will is that all its actions should conform to the law *as law.* That is to say, *I must never do anything from a maxim which I could not propose to be a universal law.* Thus without having to consider any particular laws or kinds of actions, we find that *merely conforming to law as law* is our rule of the will. Only with this rule can we prevent duty from being a pompous

flight of fancy. And, as a matter of fact, commonsense moral judgments are generally based on this rule.

By respect for law as law, Kant cannot mean any particular set of laws, but the idea of law as imposing obligation. Whatever the law, it must be obeyed *because it is a law.* In the realm of moral law, he means conforming to a moral rule because it is what one ought to do. No matter what the particular moral rules governing the situation, we ought to abide by it, *because* it tells us what we ought to do.

An illustration may help clarify this key concept. Suppose a parole officer told his parolee, "Obey the law and you will stay out of trouble." A week later the parolee is apprehended in possession of a concealed weapon. The parole officer asks, "Didn't I tell you to obey the law?" But the parolee replies, "Oh, I kept *one* law, but you didn't say anything about the others." Such an excuse simply could not be taken seriously. "Obey the law" clearly meant that the parolee was to obey *all* laws. The command was a *formal rule,* a standard. It said in effect, "Whatever you do, make sure you do not break any laws." The officer did not have to specify any particular laws; he gave the parolee a standard for deciding what to do in *any* situation, a rule to cover *all* situations. A purely formal moral rule, one which covers every moral situation, would be no more explicit than Jesus' "Be ye perfect." Such a law includes everything, but nothing in particular.

In what way does such a formal rule give us a standard for deciding the moral alternative in any particular situation? For an answer, we must look to that aspect of the particular moral rule which is common to all moral rules. Now, each particular situation differs in some respect from every other; but there is one feature they all have in common: one alternative in each situation is the moral alternative, commanded by a rule or law. That is, the common factor must be found in the nature of the rule or law itself, not in the particular command of the particular rule or law. The only factor common to all law, Kant proclaims, is *universality*. Every law is impersonal, impartial, or—which comes to the same thing—universally applicable to everyone in the same situation. The law of driving on the right-hand side of the road applies only to drivers, true, but it applies to all drivers equally and without exception.

If universality be the common element of all law, then the law of morality must incorporate universality. As Kant puts it, conformity to law as law is conformity to the universality in law. The question now becomes: how do we conform to the universality of law? Kant's answer is his statement of the rule of morality: *Never do anything from a maxim which you could not propose to be a universal law.* That is, we must not do anything which we could not propose as the moral law for everyone. Whenever we want others to act differently than we do, whenever we make our own situation an exception to the rule ("But mine is a special case!"), we violate the canon of universality. We act in conformity to law when we can consistently will that everyone should act as we act in such a situation, and even more, that it should be everyone's duty to act so. "How would you like it if everybody did that?" we often ask, thus confirming Kant when he says that "commonsense moral judgments are generally based on this rule."

With this principle, that we must never do anything from a maxim which we could not propose as a universal law, Kant concludes his argument based on commonsense rational morality. Having analyzed the three propositions of moral value, he finds in the concept of *conformity to law as such* the central theme relating them to one another. The good will is one which conforms its maxim to law as law, thus acting from the moral motive (respect for law as law) in performing its duty (that action which conforms to law). This principle or ultimate rule provides two things: a way of deciding when our actions are in accordance with moral goodness, and a yardstick for determining whether our motives are moral or not. When we act in accordance with the principle of conformity to law as law, then we perform a morally good action; and if conformity to law as law is the reason why we act, then we act with the moral motive. This principle, moreover, will apply to any action whatsoever, for it is a purely *formal* rule, without reference to any circumstances or persons.

2. *The Case of the Prudent Lie*

The next step is to describe what it means to propose one's maxim as a universal law. Kant uses an example familiar to everyone, the case of a man who makes a false promise in order to gain some advantage.

As an example, consider this question: When things are going badly for me, may I make a promise without any intention of keeping it? The question has two clearly different meanings: on the one hand, will such a promise be to my advantage? and on the other, will it be right to make such a promise? Without question such promises are often advantageous, at least in the short run, although on this basis I should anticipate the possibility that long-run disadvantages might follow from the lie. And no matter how clever I might be, I cannot foresee all possible consequences. The long-term result of giving one's word falsely could outweigh any short-term advantages I would gain, which might make it more prudent to follow the universal rule never to make a false promise under any circumstances. But clearly this maxim is based on nothing more than fear of consequences.

In an essay entitled "On a Supposed Right to Tell Lies from Benevolent Motives," Kant expands on this example. A friend, pursued by a murderer, runs to my house and I hide him. The murderer arrives and asks if my friend is hiding inside. May I lie to save my friend? Kant's answer is that I may not, since it is always wrong to lie. He argues that we do not find in *antici-pated* results the *absolute* moral criterion we need. Suppose we universalize the maxim: whenever I hide a friend from a mur-derer, I will lie to protect him. Surely, it would seem, we could willingly allow anyone to lie in such a situation. Isn't it better to save a life than to tell the truth here? Generally speaking, yes, but in such a case we cannot be sure that our purpose in lying will actually result; moral decisions require some absolute cri-terion, not one offering merely high probability. Even if I do lie, I cannot be certain that I will be believed; and if I am believed, I cannot be certain that my lie will ultimately prevent the mur-derer from carrying out his plot. Suppose, for instance, that my friend, hearing me stall the murderer at the door, escapes through a rear window. The murderer believes me, searches elsewhere, finds my friend outside, and kills him. By my lie, I helped cause the very result I had intended to prevent. The *anticipated* conse-quences upon which I based my decision to lie *did not occur*. And so, Kant concludes, from an examination of what we expect to happen we can never derive that assurance of moral goodness. But this is only an elaboration of what we already know, that neither the moral import of the maxim, nor the moral worth of the action, can depend upon the results desired, no matter how beneficial such results may be.[1]

Kant insists, first, that an action must be based upon a *rational* principle, not an empirical one; this principle is respect for moral law as such. Secondly, this rational principle extols the universalizability of maxims, without primary consideration of consequences. The expected consequences alone cannot serve as a basis for the universalization of a maxim; the purpose alone cannot determine the moral goodness of an action. An action in-tended to produce good results may be laudable, but it will not on that account have moral value, unless it is also done from respect for law. Surely it is praiseworthy to save one's friend out of friendship, but friendship can in some cases lead us to do immoral deeds. Respect for moral law, on the contrary, can never lead us to immoral actions, even though, in ignorance, we produce bad results.

To tell the truth for duty's sake is one thing: but it is something else altogether to tell the truth because we fear the results a lie might cause. In the first case, the very idea of my having a duty to tell the truth involves a law which commands me, whereas in the second case, I must first try to determine what will result from my action. Actions which violate a law of duty are always morally bad, but actions which violate a maxim of prudence may occasionally work out to my benefit (even though this is not generally so).   403

The quickest and surest way to answer the question, "Can a false promise be in accordance with duty?" is to determine whether I could propose my maxim—"When in trouble, get out of it by making a false promise."—to hold as a universal law, binding myself and everyone else. Would I want everyone to be allowed to make a false promise when that is the only way he could escape trouble? Certainly I can choose to lie, but I cannot propose that there be a universal law for lying. Were there such a law, I could never make a promise at all, since it would be impossible to find anyone who would take my word regarding what I promised to do; or if someone unthinkingly did take my word, he would try the same thing on me. As soon as I try to universalize my maxim, it negates itself.

It is always and certainly immoral to act against duty. It is, obversely, always and certainly moral to act for duty's sake. But it is neither always nor certainly moral to act from expediency, since expediency may lead us to do what is morally wicked from an expectation of future benefits. We cannot allow our desires for certain consequences to determine what is our duty. Duty must be determined on some other grounds than consequences.

I cannot consistently will that everyone should be permitted to tell a prudent lie, still less that it should be everyone's duty to tell such a lie. The reason is simple. If, through some quirk of moral fate, my maxim did become universal law, no one could ever tell a prudent lie. Since everyone might freely lie whenever he believed it to be advantageous, no one would believe anyone in anything, and thus no one could promise anything at all. We must not, however, base the immorality of a prudent lie on these consequences, any more than we base morality on consequences. The point of the principle of universalization is that, when we wish to do something which cannot be universalized, our intention is to do something which other people are *not* allowed to do. We insist that others not be allowed to tell prudent lies, in order that our promise will be taken as truthful. We want an exception made in our case. But law admits of no exceptions. That is what Kant means by saying, "I can choose to lie, but I cannot choose a universal law for lying." The outlaw thrives on other people's respect for law; he could not wish for the entire population to become outlaws.

This rule of universalizing our maxim is *not* a rule which makes an action morally good. The rule gives us a process for deciding, a formula for judging whether our action is consistent with duty or not. We may determine, by this rule, that the action is compatible with duty, and still not perform it for duty's sake. We act from duty under two necessary conditions: knowing *what* is our duty, and doing it *because* it is our duty. Kant's rule of universalization is primarily a matter of the way we come to know our duty. As Paton succinctly puts it: "Consistency is the test, but not the essence, of moral action."[2]

Consequently I need not be a genius in order to know how to act with a good will. Though I may be a babe in the woods as far as understanding all the varieties of worldly circumstances is concerned, I need merely ask: Can I propose my maxim as a universal law? If I cannot, then I must reject the maxim, not because it may lead to any harm to myself or others, but because it cannot be used as a rule for universal law, a law which commands the immediate respect of reason. Although I may not understand the whole question—which is a question for a philosopher—at least I understand this much: respect is an estimate of a value superior to any based on desire; respect for moral (practical) law, by making my action necessary for me to perform, makes it my duty; and every other motive must bow to duty, for duty is the condition for an absolutely good will, a will whose value is supreme. By this reasoning we reach that principle which is the foundation of commonsense rational morality.

Kant believes that this question, "Can I (consistently) propose that my maxim be a universal law?" is the basic question in a moral decision. If I cannot consistently propose it, then my duty is to avoid any action based on it. On the other hand, the ability to propose my maxim as a universal law does not mean that I must act on the maxim. I need not make any promises at all, for instance, unless failing to make a promise involves some other maxim.

Respect for morality and for law is a recognition of the unqualified value inherent in moral actions, actions which are the mark of a good will. Since respect for the moral law is the basis for the good will, which is the only unqualified good, such respect has supreme moral value. For obviously, in Kant's mind, the necessary condition for an absolute good must likewise be absolutely good. As we saw in the previous chapter, this does not mean that we have two absolute goods. One cannot say that respect for law and the good will are distinct things: the goodness of the good will *is* its respect for law.

3. *Philosophical Knowledge of Morality*

The purpose of this first section has been to analyze the commonsense propositions of rational morality in order to find the principle upon which they rest. The main steps of the argument are these:

1. *The only absolutely good thing is the good will, that will which acts not merely in accordance with duty but also for duty's sake.* When we perform a good action, one which we ought to do, we achieve moral credit only when we do what we ought to do *because* it is what we *ought* to do. If we act only to obtain the possible consequences, we gain no moral credit, no matter how beneficial the action.

2. *The moral goodness of an action is determined by the maxim, not by the purpose to be achieved.* The motive determines the moral goodness, not the goodness of the desired consequences. Though we may judge an action by its results, we judge the agent by his motive.

3. *The moral motive is acting from respect for law.* A person who knows his duty and does it because it is what he ought to do, is acting with a special kind of attitude, namely, an awareness that the law imposes obligation upon him. Acting from duty is the best reason for acting, since the goodness of the will cannot depend upon other motives. To act for the sake of duty is to act from a recognition of the ultimate value of moral goodness.

4. The law, which stands as the condition of a good will, which determines our duty, and which we must respect, is not a particular law, but *the concept of law as such,* that is, the concept of moral command and obligation. In moral matters we can determine the lawfulness of our actions by proposing that our maxim be universalized. If we can honestly and consistently do this without making our own case an exception, then our action accords with moral law and conforms to duty.

5. The philosophical principle which underlies the three commonsense propositions may be expressed in the following way: *The fundamental and necessary condition for any moral value in a will or action is the moral motive, arising from a recognition of duty, expressed in moral law.* A person may act lawfully with an evil intention or motive, while another may act unlawfully while trying to be moral. If a person acts because he

sincerely believes what he is doing to be the moral thing to do, then he gains moral credit, no matter what benefit or harm he actually produces.

Throughout the argument summarized above, Kant keeps reminding us that moral goodness depends upon reason, not upon experience. The moral motive is grounded in reason, on *a priori* principles. The fundamental principle is a principle of reason, and we have found it not by an investigation from experience but by rational analysis. However, it is one thing to conclude a principle from a given set of premisses or postulates: it is quite another to prove the principle valid as the true ultimate principle of morality. Kant could have tried to prove the truth of the principle by deriving it from premisses he could justify on other grounds. But then the principle would depend upon the other premisses and would not be the ultimate principle.

Kant's task, then, is to prove that the principle is self-justifiable, so to speak, and then show that the derived principles are true because the ultimate principle is true. In the above argument he asked: *given* the truth of the three propositions of moral value, what must be the fundamental truth? His answer did not prove the fundamental principle true; only that its truth is a necessary condition for the truth of the other propositions. To prove the fundamental principle itself requires a different approach.

4. *The Necessity for Proof*

David Hume had argued that we have a native sentiment of benevolence, a moral awareness akin to feeling, which guides us in our moral judgments.[3] Kant agrees, to an extent.

Of course, commonsense moral reasoning does not use the abstract, universal form of this principle, but it al- 404 ways uses something comparable as its criterion for moral judgment. We could easily illustrate how commonsense uses something like this principle to judge what is good or bad, what is dutiful and what opposes duty. Like Socrates, we would

not have to teach anything new but only to clarify the principle in order to show commonsensically that one can be honest, good, even wise and virtuous, without any knowledge of science or philosophy. In fact, we could have assumed from the beginning that a knowledge of duty must be within the reach of even the most ordinary men.

Most people, having attained a certain level of maturity, generally make sound moral judgments. For the most part, we know right from wrong and have a fair idea what the difference is. And the vast majority of our judgments are made without any theoretical knowledge of abstract principles. The question is not whether we make sound moral judgments—the world would be in far worse shape if we did not—but whether the principles which these judgments tacitly presuppose are capable of justification independently of the general soundness of our judgments. Since experience and maturity evidently provide a day-to-day basis for practical wisdom, one might raise the question whether such an independent justification is even necessary.

We must admit that practical judgment has a good advantage over theoretical judgment in everyday human reasoning. In theoretical matters, whenever ordinary reasoning exceeds the boundary of experience and sensation, it winds up in meaningless and self-contradictory tangles, or at least in a welter of unclear, wavering uncertainties. But in practical matters, moral reasoning begins to show its power as soon as it eliminates all sensuous influences from its laws. Its decisions become clearer, it hones its own conscience, it searches other claims of morality— all in order to judge for itself the value of different actions.

And in this, ordinary men have as good a chance of finding the right answer as philosophers have, perhaps a better chance. While the philosopher has no practical abilities which the ordinary man lacks, the ordinary man is free of the mass of irrelevant and trivial ideas which so often lead the philosopher astray. The wiser way, then, might be to rest content with the judgments of ordinary practical reason, using philosophy merely for insuring completeness, clarity, and workability of our rules— and of course in moral arguments. Why should we drag common- sense reasoning from its cozy simplicity in moral judgments and push it with philosophy onto a new road of inquiry and instruc- tion?

In the *Critique of Pure Reason,* Kant argued that theoretical reason, when it attempts to decide questions outside the realm of experience (such as the questions of the infinity of space, or of the origin of the universe), will come to contradictory con- clusions. These conflicts he called the Antinomies of Pure Reason. It seems, says Kant, that practical reason has the advantage over pure (or speculative) reason, for it is just in such matters re- moved from experience that practical reason finds its surest em- ployment. We can determine our duty only by an *a priori* judg- ment, not by experience; duty involves a kind of necessity which experience cannot justify.

Yet in the moral judgments which persons of commonsense usually have little difficulty in making, sophistication often seems to be a disadvantage. Who hesitates, if not the man who sees "objectively" both sides of an issue? The intellectual is inclined to ponder: "Wait a minute. Is what I *think* my duty *really* my duty?" A fanatic, on the other hand, is never afflicted with such doubts. Would it not be better, then, to follow our commonsense moral judgments and use philosophy as an *ancilla fidei,* a servant for belief? Why should we disturb ourselves with a variety of "doubts, distinctions, disputes, and devilish devices of dis- quietude"? What good is philosophy, anyway, in living the moral life?

How wonderful it is to be innocent, yet how easily the innocent are seduced. Those wise in practice need theory, not so much as a guide, but to guard their prin- ciples and make them stronger. Everyone recognizes that his needs and desires—which promise happiness when satisfied—

405

raise powerful obstacles to those commands of duty which reason proposes as worthy of respect. But reason commands the will under necessity, promising nothing to desire. Reason, we might say, ignores and scorns the demands of inclination, which in turn will not let themselves be cowed by reason's commands. Here is the source of that dialectic of human nature, from which we tend to belittle the validity of laws of duty, or at least to doubt their purity and strictness, so that we may adapt them wherever possible to our own feelings and desires. This, of course, rots the very roots of morality and degrades it, which result not even commonsense reason can accept.

To the question, what good is philosophy in moral life, Kant gives a two-part answer. In this paragraph he shows that prudential wisdom by itself is subject to subversion; in the following paragraph he explains why practical reason is necessary to prevent the distortion.

Common wisdom is not infallible. David had his Bathsheba, Antony his Cleopatra, and W. C. Fields his Mae West. When a man clearly knows his duty but is strongly tempted by his own desires and deepest needs, will he still follow reason without being seduced by the undulations of Lady Happiness? How frequently we begin to "think this thing through," take a second look at the situation, and finally put reason in the back seat. "Would God want me to do this, *really?* Doesn't He want us all to find *happiness?* He is Good. He couldn't want us to be in *pain* and *misery*, could He? . . . Of course not!"[4]

This self-deception is quite human and happens to us all at one time or another. The moral issue, however, is more serious than it might appear at first. The "dialectic" between reason and inclination is liable to cast doubt upon reason's judgment, so that we are even more likely to violate the moral law. Furthermore, if reason's judgment is disputed, then any decision to act will be based on factors other than reason and the moral motive. Human as we are, when we find ourselves in a conflict between reason and some other inclination, the decision often goes against reason. Even when we act according to duty, our decision is frequently based on inclination, not on respect for moral law. Unless moral judgments can safely and finally be grounded on a firm *a priori* foundation, we are always in danger of subverting reason by inclination. And unless we can rationally justify our moral judgments, we can never have any assurance that our judgments are valid.

This is why ordinary human reason must seek the help of moral philosophy. Human reason by itself is sufficent, so long as it avoids theoretical speculation. But in moral matters it must be aided by moral philosophy in order to gain information and clear instruction about the source of its principle, and how this principle may be used in the face of counterclaims from our needs and desires. In this way human reason may avoid the confusion of opposing moral claims and escape the danger of losing its principles in a swirl of ambiguous theory. In short, whenever ordinary moral reason tries to improve itself, it tends to move unawares into a dialectic, and it needs philosophy to determine the answers. The same thing happens in the theoretical function of reason. In both cases, reason can find the answer only by a critical examination of human reason itself.

Our quest must be for a stable foundation for morality, for a principle which cannot be subverted by maxims based on needs and desires. To find such a principle, we must leave the world of commonsense morality and enter the realm of *a priori* practical reason, that realm of purely formal concepts and principles which constitute moral philosophy. Having found the principle of the good will to lie in respect for law, we must determine *a priori* what this law of all morality is and what is its relation to the moral understanding. The first task then will be to investigate the concepts of morality themselves, by *a priori* analysis. By doing so, we should arrive at the first structure of a valid metaphysics of morals.

SECTION II

TRANSITION FROM POPULAR MORAL PHILOSOPHY TO A METAPHYSICS OF MORALS

CHAPTER FIVE

PART 1—Prologue to Section II

---

1. *The Structure of Section II*

This section, the longest of the three, comprises about half of the *Foundation*. It is the best known and most quoted section, containing those ideas which many consider the core of Kant's ethical thought. Here we find an explicit description of the categorical imperative, the idea of man as a being of inherent value and dignity, the concept of a kingdom of ends, the autonomy of the will, and the raising of the critical question of the validity of the categorical imperative as a genuine law governing human conduct. It is a well-packed section, including a famous quartet of examples, three or more formulations of the categorical imperative, and criticisms of opposing theories.

Because of its length, Section II will be presented in four chapters. Chapter 5 will examine the first few pages, in which Kant recapitulates his discussion of Section I, indicates what is to come, and gives reasons why we must follow this procedure. In Chapter 6, Kant begins the main argument, investigating what it means to act from principle or from the idea of law itself. He will argue that men act from either of two kinds of principle: one based on self-interest, the other based on reason.

Chapter 7 is an interlude in the main argument that has led

some to interpret Kant's *Foundation* as primarily an ethical treatise,[1] rather than as a search for the foundations of morality itself. The interlude *is* primarily ethical, suggesting certain rules of conduct, specifying examples of moral action, and posing ideals for man's moral understanding.

In the fourth part of Section II, Chapter 8, Kant returns to the main argument, showing that the basic principle of morality —the categorical imperative—is only valid as a genuine law of human conduct if the will is self-legislating. All other moral foundations prove invalid. He thus arrives at the basic question of the critique of practical reason (the main issue of Section III): how is it possible for the will to give law to itself?

Some readers may be puzzled by the title of this section. Section I consisted of a transition from ordinary rational knowledge. Section II, however, does not begin with this philosophical knowledge, but proposes a transition from *popular moral philosophy* to a metaphysics of morals. What is the popular moral philosophy to which Kant alludes? As we shall see, he thinks very little of some varieties of popular philosophy, calling them a "disgusting mishmash of examples strung together by crackpot principles," lovingly produced by boneheads. Kant never explicitly describes the popular moral philosophy which he employs, nor does he explain why he takes this approach.

We can, however, discover his reasons for ourselves from his other writings. Likewise we will have to examine the rationale of his method. We should notice here, however, that there is a great difference between a popular moral philosophy and a philosophy derived from ordinary rational knowledge. The latter has an *a priori* structure, whereas the former may be based on any number of grounds, such as emotion, love, fear of God, benevolence, and so on. In each case, however, Kant's method is the same: he takes what is already at hand and draws from it the *a priori* ground upon which such principles must be based if they are to have any validity for moral decision.

2. *Experience and the Idea of Duty*

Kant begins this section with a review of the *a priori* method used in Section I: namely, that any examination of moral value must be divorced from empirical conditions.

Even though we discovered the idea of duty by ana-lyzing how commonsense moral reasoning functions, we must not think that we derived this newfound idea from experience. On the contrary, when we examine our experiences of the way men do act, we find no instances which provide us with unquestionable examples of actions done purely for the sake of duty. Indeed, of the many actions which accord with duty, some persons suggest that since the motive is always in question, so the moral value of the action is doubtful. 406

For this reason, every age has its philosophers who absolutely deny that duty is a real motive in human choice. Without first finding out whether their own ideas of morality are correct, they turn all human motives into sophisticated varieties of self-interest. They express a profound regret that human nature, which nobly holds up to itself the respected ideal of duty, is yet too weak and corrupt to live by it. Reason, they say, ought to rule human activity, yet it merely serves the satisfaction of some single desire or (in better men) the harmonious satisfaction of all desires.

We have all met the amateur psychologist who will question our apparent motives for any action. If my father happens to make me angry, the cause is not so much what he does as it is my subconscious rivalry for my mother's love. Or if I dislike a certain teenage vocalist, it is not his voice or bearing which dis-pleases me, but a hidden homosexual attraction that causes my overt reaction of displeasure. Etc., etc. Behind such callow analyses lies the truth that no motive is unmixed. There may be hidden elements involved in every human choice; we can never say with certainty that any particular action was done solely and purely from duty or for the sake of moral righteousness. We cannot derive the pure concept of duty from any examination of man's actual performance, nor will such evidence explain what it means to act from duty.

David Hume believed that no idea by itself could ever cause us to act. Actions he said are passional, initiated by internal stimulus or desire. We must "feel for" something before we "act for" it. Reason's role is merely to determine the best way to satisfy our desires or achieve our goals (which for Hume were the same things). Hume recognized that men have feelings in common; life is not psychological chaos. He explained man's general preference for goodness and the peaceful life by postulating a "universal sentiment of approbation,"[2] a kind of emotional conscience common to all men. All we must do to learn about this sentiment is to study the moral judgments of men.

To some extent, of course, Hume is correct. Kant's basic disagreement with Hume on this point is that the *a priori* concept of an action done purely for the sake of duty could not originate from any examination of what men do, since there may never have been such a case.

As a matter of fact, it is absolutely impossible for experience to prove beyond question even one case in 407 **which the agent's maxim for performing a duty was moral, that is, a case in which he acted purely from the idea of doing his duty. Certainly there are times when the most careful self-examination reveals nothing to us but the moral motive of duty as powerful enough to persuade us to do the good deed in question, something demanding great sacrifice. Yet it is still possible that what seems to be the idea of duty is in fact a hidden impulse of self-interest moving the will. We like to puff up our egos with the notion that we act from noble motives but, as it turns out, not even the most careful examination can discover the bottom of the well of our subconscious impulses. Our diffi-**

culty is that in moral matters we are dealing not with visible actions but with the unseen inner principles of action.

If we are to base our examination on experience, then how can we determine what goes on deep within the psyche, far removed from any possible introspective view? Hidden motives are just that—hidden. We can never, from an empirical examination, conclude absolutely that no hidden motive is involved in a particular case. We all like to believe that our motives are pure, especially in moral situations, but we can never be sure. Since the moral worth of an action is determined by the motive, then no experience of what an agent *does* will give us any sure knowledge of the moral value of the action. But, if we have no sure knowledge of actions done from duty, perhaps there are none.

Consider a further consequence of claiming that we derive the idea of duty from experience only. By this we would assure victory for those who belittle all morality as being only a figment of a vain, human imagination, stretching beyond its limits. (They already believe that all other ideas are drawn from experience.) Because I think well of my fellow man, I readily believe that most human actions conform to the norms of duty. However, if we carefully watch our intentions and goals, we generally find the ever-present and dearly beloved Self at their heart, not the stern command of frequently painful duty.

We cannot call someone an enemy of virtue simply because he doubts whether there has ever been an act of genuine virtue. He may be an objective observer who, as he grows older, is led by his added experience and sharper moral insight to see the difference between an ideal and reality. Since there may never have been such an act, the only way for us to insure our understanding of duty and secure a basic respect for law is a firm belief that reason itself, without depending on experience in any way, can tell us what we ought to do—   408 even if no one has ever acted purely from reason.

We are concerned with those deeds which the world may never have seen, with deeds which the behaviorists believe to be impossible, namely, deeds which reason inexorably commands. For instance, we insist that a friend be completely sincere, and we continue to insist on it even though no such friend ever lived. The duty of perfectly sincere friendship comes under the idea of duty in general, so is independent of experience, and arises from reason guiding the will on *a priori* grounds.

The older and wiser we become, the more evident it is that, as Buttercup observes, "Things are seldom what they seem." If we are to retain our conviction that an action done for duty's sake is at least possible, we must appeal to reason alone, not to experience. Experience will tell us only what was, what is, or what may be—what may please, displease, cause pain or joy. Reason alone informs us of what we ought to choose. But reason cannot command the will under necessity if it derives its rule from experience.

Take friendship. We know what a perfect friend ought to be. But has anyone ever known such a friend? No, for a man would have to be more than human to be a perfect friend. We know that our friends, however loyal and true, are imperfect and might possibly fail us. Yet we still expect them to be perfect. We still insist that a friend *ought* to be perfect. But if we never saw or knew a perfect friend, how do we know what one should be like? Only by reason, says Kant. Our reason, understanding the nature of true friendship, determines what a true friend ought to be. This idea, arrived at independently of empirical evidence, is *a priori*.

Obviously experience cannot provide instances from which we could derive absolute laws. But even more, unless we want to reject the truth of morality and its applicability to anything at all, we must allow that moral law is so all-embracing that it rules not men only, but any being which is rational. The moral law must be absolute, not subject to conditions, provisions, or exceptions. How could we respect something less than absolute, something subject to the changing conditions of human existence? How could a law which applies to human beings also be a law which applies to all rational beings—including humans— unless that law were derived, not from experience, but *a priori* from pure practical reason?

Morality must be applicable to all rational beings, and not merely to human beings.[3] We know human beings only through experience, but rational beings we can know by reason. If the principles of morality are independent of experience, then any rational being would be capable of discovering them and would be equally bound by them. We do not know, of course, whether there are rational beings other than ourselves. But if there be such beings (e.g., rational angels), they are morally responsible agents. They must obey the moral law as much as any of us humans.

This directly opposes those who claim that we can distinguish moral right from moral wrong by a study of man's nature (psychology), his primitive cultures (anthropology), his present culture (sociology), his needs and projects (pragmatism), his spiritual needs (theology), or his physical needs (physiology). Morality, Kant insists, is based on man's *rationality* and it is as a rational creature that man become a moral one.

No advice can be worse than to suggest that morality be derived from examples. Any example of morality must first be judged by some moral standard to find out whether it can serve as a good example to imitate. How then can an example itself serve as the ideal of morality? Even the Holy One of the Gospel, before we can call Him good, must be judged by an ideal of moral goodness. He says of Himself: "Why do you call me (whom you see) good? God alone (the ideal of goodness, whom you cannot see) is good." But where else do we get the idea of

God's supreme goodness except from the *a priori* idea
of moral perfection and its logical relation to the idea 409
of free will?

Imitation is out of place in moral decision. Examples allow
nothing more than encouragement, by proving that what the law
commands can be done and by providing specific instances of
what the law commands in general. But in seeking a moral ideal,
we can never substitute examples for the true original in reason.

Once again, but from a different approach, Kant denies that
morality can be based on what men actually do. Examples serve
only to illustrate what has already been judged by some general
principle. Nor can moral principles be derived from what most
or all men do. We may discover in men's actions a certain common principle and to that extent an examination may be useful.
But it is one thing to learn that men follow a certain principle
and quite another to justify that principle as one they ought to
follow, i.e., as a valid moral principle. We can never justify our
actions by arguing that "everybody is doing it." That is lazy
man's morality and is more often than not an excuse of the
crudest sort.

The remark about the "Holy One of the Gospel" raises an
age-old question: is God called good because we recognize His
goodness or is He called good simply because He is God? For
Kant, the answer is simple. If we call God good, it is because God
conforms to our *a priori* standard of what goodness is. If there were
no rational beings, God would not be called good, since He would
fulfill no conditions in any rational understanding. And yet God
would be no less perfect than He is. We have certain conceptions
of goodness, and we call good those beings which conform to
them. Such requirements for goodness are rational, not empirical.
For we call God, whom we cannot see, good. How could we
call God good if our idea of goodness were based on what we
saw only?

Morality cannot be based upon any foundation other than

reason. Moral rules must be justifiable by *a priori* concepts, such as the ideas of duty and law. The deeds of humankind may show us that men do live by such moral rules, but their deeds cannot justify themselves. We may learn of the law through experience, but we recognize it—see it as *law*—by reason alone. Law contains within itself the necessity of compliance, and experience grants no such necessity.

3. *The Need for an* A Priori *Investigation*

Kant is well aware of the lack of popular demand for an *a priori* investigation. Were all men philosophically inclined, the desirability of such an examination would be obvious to everyone. Yet even in that case, few would be eager to undertake such a difficult search.

Suppose there were no genuine supreme principle of morality, no principle derived from pure reason and independent of any experience. Were this so, I could see no point to a search for *a priori* concepts and the principles associated with them. (We could not even distinguish ordinary knowledge from philosophical knowledge.) But the search for an *a priori* principle is especially relevant to our era. In a contest of preference between a pure rational knowledge that lacks any empirical ground (i.e., a metaphysics of morals) and a popular moral philosophy —well, we can easily guess which side would win.

No thoughtful person will deny the necessity of theoretical research, particularly in the scientific field. But though the need for research is less obvious in moral philosophy, it is just as great. Furthermore, investigation into the abstract principles of moral conduct must precede any popularization of the principles. Yet the opposite procedure is generally followed: moral standards in effect are taken as the source of a moral theory, rather than moral theory being used to judge the standards we follow. Kant waxes sarcastic about such a reversal of procedure.

We must grant the value of a popular version of moral philosophy, but only after we have gained a firm grasp of the principles of pure reason. Thus our first task must be to prove the metaphysical basis of morality, and only then to seek popular approval. But how thoughtless it would be to reverse this order, to seek popularity first, leaving the discovery of true principles to follow. To begin with, such a procedure would prevent any claim to genuine *philosophical* popularity, since no skill at all is needed to explain a simple-minded theory.

What is more, this so-called popular theory would consist of a disgusting mishmash of examples strung together by crackpot principles, the kind of nonsense so often heard in conversations with boneheads. But persons with any sense at all will be confused and discouraged without knowing why. Even philosophers, who easily see through the confusion, find few followers when they seek to persuade men that worthwhile popu-   410
larity must wait upon a firm grasp of true principles.

Those who do feel some need for *a priori* principles, who are aware that these principles must be based on man's primary claim to moral responsibility, his reason—even they do not undertake the search without at the same time trying to popularize it. Yet it should be a separate enquiry. Kant mentions below a few of these mixed theories, previewing his refutation (at the close of Section II) of the spurious theories of morality. But Kant follows his own rule: only after he has completed his *a priori* investigation of the genuine foundation of morality does he reject these other principles.

Just glance at the work of moral philosophers who try to be popular. We find principles based on man's unique human nature (or sometimes his rational nature), the ideal of perfection or happiness, a moral sense, the fear of God—a pinch of this, a dash of that, making a delicious hash. But none of these writers ever wonders whether he ought or ought not

seek principles in a knowledge of human nature, which he
knows only by experience. Even if he raises this question—that
is, even if his principles be purely *a priori*, based solely on ideas
of reason and on nothing else at all in experience—he never
wonders whether he should pursue moral philosophy as a distinct branch of pure philosophy, namely as a metaphysics* of
morals (to use a term of low popularity). Thus these writers fail
to complete their investigations. They speak out too soon, rather
than requesting their readers, who clamor for a popular version,
to wait until the work is properly finished.

> * We can distinguish pure moral philosophy (metaphysics) from
> applied moral philosophy (applied to the human situation). We
> make the same kind of distinction between theoretical and applied
> mathematics and between abstract and applied logic. This distinc-
> tion emphasizes that moral principles must be *a priori* and self-
> validating, rather than dependent upon the particularities of human
> existence. But, on the other hand, it also emphasizes that from the
> *a priori* principles we must be able to derive practical moral rules
> which do apply to our human circumstances.

To have a positive knowledge of our duties, we must first
possess a metaphysics of morals which completely lacks any
dependence on anthropology, theology, physics, and, especially,
cultish doctrines such as theosophy. In fact, if we do possess
such an *a priori* foundation for our moral principles, our compliance with the command of duty is much more likely. For when
the pure idea of duty and the moral law join forces, without
help from any sensuous inclinations, their combined effect on
the human heart exceeds any other motive or desire
known to us.* Aware of its own worth and coming to   411
realize that it can act as its own master in human affairs,
reason loathes the lesser motives and gradually enslaves them.
But when reason tries to decide on the basis of a moral theory
which mixes feelings and desires with *a priori* ideas, reason
wavers between this motive and that, none of which can be
derived from a valid moral principle. Such motives may acci-
dentally lead to good results, but they may just as well produce
the opposite.

* The eminent Herr Sulzer wrote me to ask why moral theories are so ineffective, even though much in them is quite reasonable. I have put off answering him until I could offer a complete explanation. The fault lies with teachers who fail to make their ideas clear. They look elsewhere for motives which will induce their charges to be moral, but by trying to find a compelling theory, they ruin the whole affair. For even the man on the street can see that an act of honesty, performed with a firm determination, without any hope of reward here or hereafter, and in the face of the strongest obstacles of human necessity or sensual temptation—that such an act exceeds in value and outshines any act performed for some non-moral reason. To imagine such actions inspires us to imitate them. Even fairly young children feel this, and we should never try to explain duty to them in any other way.

No motive appears to the will so powerful as that of pure obligation. Men will occasionally do what they feel they ought to do in the face of misfortune and death. We honor the true heroes of history who braved danger to do what they believed to be right. But when we see the motive of someone's honorable action to be the allurement of gain, the applause of the crowd, or the thirst of desire, our picture of moral honor fades and the agent appears no more the true hero but merely mortal, like us. Leander performed a mighty deed in swimming the Hellespont each night. But his purpose was to spend the evening with his ladylove, Hero. When he drowned, he drowned in the pursuit of his desires, not in the performance of his duty. He is an inspiring example to separated lovers but not an example of moral righteousness. Kant saw many practical difficulties for those who try to follow a "mixed" theory of morality. We see such difficulties today in the quandry of many young people regarding sexual desires. On the one hand they live in a society which emphasizes sexuality in almost every area. Songs are filled with obvious references to physical intimacy: the atmosphere churns with ideas of individual standards and the testing of the older morality. On the other hand, they are told that pre-marital intimacy is sinful, that it leads to a lessening of genuine love, that early marriage is unwise. What is right, what wrong? Their minds "waver between this motive and that, none of which can be derived from a valid moral principle." If their ardent urges are dangerous, why so much emphasis on satisfying them? If they follow where passion leads, why are they condemned for doing what was so alluringly suggested? The mixed theories provide no solution, and the average young man and woman are woefully confused.

Kant's footnote offers valuable practical insight. One should never represent moral goodness to children in any guise but its own. If we can assume a parent's basic knowledge of right and wrong, then we must see that it is an error for him to "motivate" a child into morality. Suppose a parent trains his child to follow the moral law because in that way he will achieve his own best interests. When the child grows to adulthood, he will then decide questions of morality on the basis of the same motive of self-interest. However, if the child is trained to do what is right because it is the moral thing to do whatever the apparent consequences to his own interests, then when the child is grown he will decide, not from self-interest, but from moral character. Suppose we see two men, both doing what we know to be morally wrong. One of the men is acting from self-interest, while the other is acting from an erroneous belief about what he ought to do. Who is more likely to be changed by an appeal to principle? Obviously the man in error. His fault is one of honest mistake, but the other is pursuing what he desires, whether it be moral or not. When we consider that most men do have a commonsense idea of what is right and wrong, we can see the immediate and long-range benefit of training a child always to do what he knows to be right *because it is right.*

Someone may ask: "Isn't it better to teach a child to do the right thing *for some reason,* rather than merely because it is right?" Such a question indicates a lack of understanding of the nature of moral goodness. Moral rules are not set up as means to some other end: they are established so that people may know or judge what is the right thing to do. That an action is the right thing to do is the *best* reason for doing it. Any other reason is a non-moral reason, annulling any possible moral credit for the action. If a person obeys a moral rule because he wishes to reach heaven, his motive is not a moral one but a desire for spiritual reward. He acts, not because the action is itself right, but because it is a means to something he wants. There is a subtle paradox about this. If a person does what is right because he believes it to be the right thing to do, he will always reach heaven. However, if he does what he believes will gain him heaven because he wants to gain heaven, he could conceivably fail to reach that celestial estate. It is a matter of motive. For Kant, the moral motive, acting for the sake of moral rightness *(aus Pflicht)*, is the best of all possible motives and the only one which can guarantee salvation, if salvation is in any way a matter of human fortune.

Having argued his case for an *a priori* investigation, Kant briefly summarizes his argument.

1. Moral concepts are derived from reason.
   a. They cannot be derived from experience.
   b. The more empirical the principle, the less it will be a valid moral law.

What conclusions can we draw at this point? First, every moral idea is *a priori*, having its foundation and source in reason alone. The purity of this source makes such ideas the basis of worthwhile and ultimate moral rules. Whether the ideas arise in ordinary moral thinking or on the highest theoretical plane, they clearly cannot be taken from experience since empirical knowledge lacks necessity. Whenever moral ideas become mixed with experience, they lose their validity and the actions they cause lack unconditional value.

2. Moral ideas are based on reason alone.
   a. Since we know human nature by experience, this knowledge cannot be the source of morality.
   b. Only from reason can moral principles acquire their universal validity.

Secondly, the ideas and laws of morality, both in theory and in practice, must be derived from pure reason alone and presented in a pure, unmixed setting. Furthermore, we must discover the entire scope of pure practical *a priori* knowledge—that is, the limits of pure practical reason. However, we must not seek moral principles in the particular nature of human reason—even though speculative philosophy must follow this very course. Moral laws apply to any being that can reason, and so we must derive moral rules from the abstract idea of a rational being as such. 412

3. Without an *a priori* moral philosophy:
   a. We cannot define duty in general.
   b. We cannot determine our duties in particular.

Any moral philosophy which applies to human beings must incorporate some empirical study of mankind (e.g., anthropology). But we must first develop moral philosophy as a pure metaphysics of morals, without involving experiences of mankind. (The philosophical method simplifies this procedure.) Clearly, if we lack an *a priori* metaphysics of morals, we would be foolish to look for the common moral element in all dutiful actions in order to have a standard for theoretical conclusions. Nor would we have valid principles of morality for everyday moral decisions or for moral instruction. Yet only by such valid principles can genuine moral habits be instilled in the human soul, prompting it to seek the highest possible good.

Paraphrased, Kant's summary might read: "If we do not justify morality by basing it on man's reason, we will not understand what it means to say that there are duties which we ought to perform. Furthermore, it will be impossible to point to a single action as an unquestionable instance of duty. It will be impossible to teach children moral principles except on grounds of expediency. And finally, we will have lost the surest and best possible appeal for good, the appeal to moral character."

To anyone who reads contemporary ethical literature, especially works by those who deny an *a priori* foundation for morality, Kant's appeal seems all too timely and his argument weighty. Almost without exception such writers are forced to a position of moral relativism or, even further, to a denial that morality is anything but emotional persuasion. Kant's position is quite clear: If we have duties which are indeed duties, then their claim upon us must be based on reason. If we cannot discover the source of their claim, our belief that there *are* duties may be a delusion. So, in order to have an unshakable foundation for our moral beliefs, we surely must search for such a source. And we must search for it *in* reason alone, *by* reason alone.

4. *Preface*

So far in our undertaking we have examined ordinary moral judgments (which are certainly worthy of our respect) to find their philosophical foundation. Now we will investigate popular moral philosophy, which is derived principally from examples, as a first step towards a metaphysics of morals. Since metaphysics encloses the entire sphere of rational knowledge (including abstract ideas), experience and examples are little help. So in order to progress from popular morality to the metaphysics of morals, we must examine how reason derives the idea of duty from universally applicable laws.

Section I dealt with the concepts of the *good will, duty,* and *law.* By an analysis of these concepts as they are found in the principles of ordinary moral thinking, Kant determined that *universality* is the fundamental characteristic of the ultimate principle of morality.

However, we can do only so much with an analysis of concepts. To discover a *principle* of morality, we must examine principles, particularly principles found in moral theories, in order to learn what it means to act on principle or from the idea of law.

Though universality is the *a priori* characteristic of morality, there remains the problem of *relating universality to human action*. By an *a priori* analysis of what it means to act on principle, Kant will deduce the supreme principle of morality as a general moral law, which he calls a *categorical imperative*. From this he will proceed to the idea of *autonomy* as the ultimate foundation of morality. Autonomy will finally be seen as an Idea of pure practical reason, of which experience offers no examples.

CHAPTER SIX

Part 2—Practical Reason and Its Imperatives

---

1. *The Role of Practical Reason*

Knowledge that a particular action will produce some good result need not be derived from practical reason.[1] I might know that by easing trade restrictions international economy would be improved. But if I have no opportunity to make such changes, my knowledge remains no more than a theoretical estimate. Practical reason comes into play when the agent's own action is what is in question. But not all actions spring from judgments of practical reason. A man may act on blind impulse: he may go beserk and kill anyone he happens to meet. We would call a man in this condition irrational. Another may act from instinct, as when he jerks his hand off a hot surface. Such action would be nonrational, involving no reasoning at all.

Under what conditions would we call an action *rational?* For Kant, the answer is simple: an action is rational, done with practical reason, *when the agent acts from some guiding principle.* It is not enough that the agent knows what he wants and how to get it done. The madman may know he wants to kill and how to do it, but he would not be acting by any rule. Roughly speaking, a person acts rationally when his action arises from and is consistent with some personal *policy.* If I walk to the corner to cross the street rather than cross in mid-block, I act from the policy, "I will cross streets at corners." Such a policy, or *general rule of acting*, Kant calls a *principle*. There are, of course, many possible reasons for crossing at the corner. I might happen to be there at the time and simply cross. But if I walk down to the corner to cross, because it is my policy to do so, then I am *acting on principle.* In Kant's words, I am acting not only according to the policy, but *because of* it, or, "from the idea of it."

Everything in nature works according to law. Only a being who reasons can act from the *idea* of law, that is, act on principle. We call this ability the will. And since the ability to determine one's actions on principle requires reason, we can see the will and practical reason as one and the same ability.

Every event, human or nonhuman, occurs according to some law. Walking down the block accords with the law of gravity, as much as does the flow of water over a waterfall. Rational beings act not only according to laws of nature but use them to advantage. Applied science is nothing more than using laws of nature to our advantage (and in some cases to our disadvantage). In contrast to laws of nature, to which we always conform, there are other laws which we ourselves create: civil and moral laws. The basic difference between the laws of nature and laws of man, is that the former are purely *descriptive.* They are universal statements of the unvarying ways natural events occur. Being descriptions only, they do not command; so we do not speak of disobeying them. Laws of man, on the other hand, are *prescriptive;* they do command and are indeed often violated. But mere knowledge of a law of man does not by itself result in compliance. The link between knowledge of the law (principle, rule, or policy) and the complying action is the *will,* which Kant identifies with practical reason, our capacity for translating policy into action. Given favorable circumstances, when we will to act, we act.

And if we act because of some policy, we act rationally. This process—knowing, willing, acting—is the exercise of practical reason.

Many times we do *not* act in accordance with our policies. The philanderer who has the policy, "Take advantage whenever you can," may on occasion resist his impulses. The saint may occasionally slip. When we act against principle are we therefore acting irrationally? Not necessarily. We may act contrary to one principle, true, but that does not mean that we act without any principle whatever. Sometimes we reject one policy in order to act from another policy. To do so, of course, implies an inconsistency somewhere in our values. When we act rationally we act on some policy or other—but not always on a good policy.

Should there be anyone whose reason infallibly determined his will, he would necessarily choose to perform those actions which reason recognized to be objectively necessary. His will would necessarily concur in the decisions which reason, free from the influence of desire, commanded as necessary for him to perform, that is, as good. But for someone else, reason may not be strong enough to coerce the will, because of the influences of subjective inclinations and desires which oppose reason's decision. Whenever a will lacks complete harmony with reason—as in our human condition—then   413
those actions which reason recognizes to be objectively necessary may not be chosen by the will. When such a decision is subjectively contingent, then reason's influence on will through objective laws is called *constraint*. Constraint is defined as the relationship between objective law and a will which is less than completely good; it denotes the influence which reason, in recognition of law, exerts on the will of a rational being, a will which need not necessarily obey.

Consider the case of an individual who *always and by his very nature* acts in complete accord with his reason. His reason will have as its basic policy: "Do that which is good in itself, rather than what you want to do." If a particular action is good in itself, then it is good on its own merits, that is, *objectively good*. And if objectively good, then reason will dictate that it be chosen *without reservation*. In Kant's language, such an action is *objectively necessary*. The person whose reason completely rules his life will always choose to perform these objectively necessary actions. They become *subjectively necessary* by becoming the objects of his personal policy; and they become such on *a priori* grounds, not from inclination. We might express this in more contemporary language by saying that such a person *naturally* chooses to do what reason tells him he ought to do.

But for one in "the human condition," beset with the pull of desires, inclinations, and incentives contrary to what reason commands, actions do not always conform to reason's direction. We may know that something ought to be done, yet choose to do quite the opposite. There is nothing very mystifying about it. We simply choose to do other than we ought to do. When reason's influence is weak, i.e., when we lack will *power*, we follow the sweep of inclination.

But even when we shun doing what we ought to do, we still feel a certain tug toward our duty. This "feeling," which we have already discussed, Kant calls *constraint*, the relation of a will to its obligation. The relation in question is that between a will not entirely determined by a recognition of its obligation and reason which recognizes that obligation. Such is the case of a will *not completely* good, yet which still feels "that spark of celestial fire called conscience."

2. *Imperatives*

Since man, as a rational being, is capable of acting from principle, we must examine the principles from which he acts, so that we may understand the relation of reason to will and of morality to acting.

The rational awareness of an objective principle which constrains will is a *command of reason;* and the expression of this command is called an *imperative*.

This little paragraph is disarmingly simple, but two important points are raised. First the command of reason is *a priori,* arising in the moral understanding. It is the recognition of a law which constrains a will not completely good. For a completely good will there would be no constraint, since the will would naturally follow the objective principles. But in our imperfect state we tend to take an objective principle as a maybe-I-will-maybe-I-won't kind of thing. Our reason says, "Do!" while our will says, "Not necessarily." For us, such principles are constraining, morally impelling, but *not subjectively necessary.* We are aware that nothing compels us to act on them; and distaste, aversion, or laziness sometimes lead us to do something else. Nevertheless, the rational recognition of the principle is a part of the situation: for the awareness itself *that* a principle is objectively binding constitutes a rational command for us.

The second point is important for an understanding of Kant's terminology. Commands of reason, he says, are expressed (formulated) as *imperatives.* If someone were to rewrite the *Foundation,* he might substitute the expression "Moral rule" or "ought-statement" for "imperative." Imperatives are frequently associated with orders or other verbal commands. Kant does not use "imperative" in a grammatical sense but in a logical sense of "prescription," which includes both grammatically imperative sentences and ought-statements. Any ought-statement pertaining to human action will be classified as an imperative.

All imperatives are expressed by "ought," a word which indicates the connection between reason's objective law and a will which, because of its own nature, is not bound to obey this law. The connection itself is called constraint. Imperatives assert that something would be good to do or that something else would be good not to do; but they assert such judgments to a will which may not choose to act simply because something is suggested to it as a good thing to do. However, a practical good does determine the will by means of ideas of reason: in this case will is determined not on subjective grounds but on objective grounds, those which are valid for every rational being as such. Subjective grounds, such as the pleasant, affect the will through personal experiences; they provide no universally valid principles of reason since they relate only to the sensations of this person or that.*

Although Kant asserts that "all" imperatives are expressed by an "ought," his own formulations of the categorical imperative never use the term "ought" but are in the imperative mood. This is only a minor point. "Ought" does express the relation between an objective principle and a will subject to the pull of inclination. "Ought" expresses constraint.

"Imperatives assert that this would be good to do, or that would be good not to do." This fundamental axiom interrelates a good action, its recognition by reason, and the human will. Kant assumes the ancient principle that the will is determined by the recognition of goodness and seeks only what appears to it as good. When we choose to act, we act for some goal which appears to us, in one form or another, as good.[2] But there are many kinds of good things which we might catalog in the following way:

a. *Subjective goods:* things good *for me,* as *I* see them; things which I judge good in their relation to me. For example, my health, security, job, money, etc. A thing may seem good to me yet bad to someone else, as in the case of my marrying a person desired by another.

b. *Objective goods:* things good in themselves, for everyone, in every situation, not dependent upon particular persons or upon particular situations. For example, happiness, virtue, love, knowledge, salvation, etc.

We must not make the distinction as narrow as Kant does, as being between desire for pleasure and reason. Some subjective goods may be unpleasant; the pleasure may not be the main consideration. One need not consider pleasure at all when he judges something good for himself. Must a political candidate look upon the presidency as a pleasant goal? (He may, but I daresay he should know better.) Kant's point does not depend upon a hedonistic distinction. Objective and subjective goods are distinguished in one basic way: whether or not what is judged good is judged on the basis of reason or on the basis of personal inclination or interest. If reason represents something as good for *every* rational being (and virtue is the example *par excellence*), then it is an objective good; but if reason represents it as good only for me or only for a particular personal situation, then it is a subjective good.[3]

Both kinds of good, objective and subjective, are recognized by judgments of reason. Rational activity may be directed toward a subjective or objective good or toward both at once. It would be a mistake to say that an object of one class can be chosen only by reason and that an object of the other can be chosen only by desire. Objective goods are indeed chosen by reason, or better, recognized by reason, but so are subjective goods. The difference is in the *basis* for choice or recognition. Objective goods are good in themselves, valid goals for everyone; subjective goods are good for me but not necessarily for everyone nor in every situation. Furthermore, as we shall see, both varieties of good can be related to the will by an "ought," but not on the same grounds.

In a footnote to the last paragraph, Kant presents an interesting corollary.

---

* When desire depends upon an experience of some need, we call it *inclination*. On the other hand, when a will which is not necessarily subservient to objective laws of reason follows the rules of reason, we call it *interest*. (Thus the divine will cannot be said to have an interest.) But the human will can have an interest in something without choosing to act from it. *To have an interest* means to be interested in the action: the action itself interests me, since my will is guided only by the laws of reason. But *to act from interest* means to be interested in the result of the action: my will follows the counsel of reason solely to achieve the anticipated pleasant results of the action. In Section I we said that when we perform an action from duty we must disregard any interest in the results and confine our interest to the action itself and its basis in reason (i.e., law).

Although not a new point, this footnote presents a partial answer to the question, "When we act from duty, don't we *want* to act that way? Don't we have an inclination to do our duty?" The answer is both yes and no: an inclination for the performance of duty, yes, but not necessarily for what a specific duty entails. We can choose to do something without any desire for the results which the action will produce. To some extent we *do* want to do our duty, over and above the awareness that we ought to. And it *is* a different kind of "feeling" than in those cases where we find some pleasure in acting. But exactly *what* the difference is has not been made clear.

We have been talking mostly about a human will. What of a Holy Will, or God's Will? If we can consider God, and perhaps the angels, as rational, do objective principles bind them too? "Ought" God do anything?

Although a perfectly good will would in every case be bound by objective laws (laws of goodness), we cannot **414** **think of it on this account as *obligated* to obey these laws since by its very nature it is moved to act only by the idea of goodness. Thus no imperative binds the Will of God nor, more generally, a Holy Will. "Ought" does not apply to such a will, since its choice necessarily accords with law. Consequently, imperatives express only the relation between objective laws and the subjective, imperfect will of this or that rational being (e.g., a human will).**

No, we can never say that God, or a Holy Will, "ought" to do anything; the word "ought" loses its moral meaning in such a use. For "ought" (in a moral sense) expresses the relation between something which reason presents as good without condition (a good-in-itself, an objective good to be sought by all rational beings), and a will which is so constituted that it does not have to choose that good. But if there be a will which by its very nature is completely guided by reason, then such a will cannot know obligation. In plain terms, such a Holy Will always and necessarily *wants* to do what it *ought* to do. Its inclinations are always and necessarily subject to an objective, rational appraisal of the good. Moral obligation is meaningless for such a being, as much as for non-rational beings. The latter have no conception of ought; the former does not require it. "Ought" applies only when an alternative choice is possible, but for a Holy Will there is no such possibility. "Ought," then, and the whole of morality, is a human concern. God has to become man in order to drink the cup of duty.[4]

3. *The Two Kinds of Imperatives*

Kant's analysis to this point can be summarized as follows:
a. Rational beings not only act in accordance with laws of nature but may also act *because of* reason's recognition of certain laws.
b. When reason and will are completely harmonious (as in a Holy Will), the dictates of reason are always followed. Human wills lack such a harmonious relation with reason: what reason dictates may not always be obeyed.
c. Constraint, that unique tension between reason and will, occurs when reason presents a particular action as objectively necessary (good for everyone) but the will is inclined to an opposite course of action.
d. We express this particular stress between reason and recalcitrant will by an "ought." "Ought" specifies the necessity of performing some action which is not necessarily desired by the will. Such "ought" statements, called imperatives, apply only to wills not completely good.

All imperatives command either *hypothetically* or *categorically*. A *hypothetical imperative* commands the will to perform a particular action as a necessary means to some end which the will desires (or might desire). A *categorical imperative* commands the will under objective necessity, without reference to any ends.

Now every practical law points to some possible action as being good and thus necessary for any will which is guided by reason. All imperatives then are expressions which determine an action to be necessary in virtue of some principle found in a will which is good to some degree. If the action appears good merely as a means to something else, the imperative is hypothetical. But if the action is shown to be good in itself and hence necessary as a matter of principle for a will that follows reason, then the imperative is categorical.

The distinction between hypothetical and categorical imperatives is related to the distinction between hypothetical and categorical assertions. A hypothetical (conditional) assertion is one which shows the relation between an event and its condition or supposition: "If it rains, the vote will be small." A categorical assertion is an unqualified statement: "Some Vietnamese are short." Similarly, a hypothetical imperative expresses a command to the will but does so *under some condition:* "If you want to be polite, you ought to study a book of etiquette." The "ought" is conditional upon the desire to be polite. Not so with the categorical imperative; it depends upon no conditions whatever. "Keep your promise" expresses a command which is unconditionally necessary.

These paragraphs make explicit some premisses which explain how imperatives interrelate the will and reason. The imperatives commanding the action as necessary are implicit judgments that the action commanded is good. These are not two separate judgments: rather, the judgment that an action is good is *also* a command that it be performed. Furthermore, if practical reason judges an action as good, it judges it to be *necessary.* An action which is good *ought* to be done. A hypothetical imperative expresses the necessity of pursuing the means to some desired end: "If you want a strong bookcase, you ought to use screws." The use of screws is presented as a necessary step in building the bookcase wanted. A categorical imperative, on the other hand, expresses an objective necessity, an action which is not good as a means to something else but good in itself and thus necessary for its own sake. Only an action good in itself can be presented as an action necessary without any conditions attached to it.

The moral problem is a double one: *how does reason know* what is good; and, when the good is known, *how does reason move the will* to choose it? Imperatives, then, serve a dual function, corresponding to the two sides of the moral problem.

An imperative, then, tells me which of those actions I am able to perform are good; it does this by stating the rule commanding such an action and relating this rule to a will which may not perform the action merely because it is a good action. For in some instances a person may not know that a particular action is good; and even if he knew that it was good, he might still have a maxim which conflicts with the objective principles of practical reason.

In order to see how an imperative can *inform* us of the good, we have to remember that goodness is a determination of value and that valuating is a function of reason, not of will. Let us suppose I am in a situation which confronts me with a number of alternative courses of action. I do not know initially which of these will be good to do and which not. If, however, I can determine which of the courses of action is commanded by reason (whether hypothetically or categorically), I can conclude that that action at least is a good one. For reason could not consistently command an action as necessary if reason did not at the same time judge that action to be good. But I cannot reverse the procedure: the judgment that an action is a good one does not permit me to conclude that it is commanded by reason. There might still be an alternative action in that situation which is *also* good and which *is* commanded by reason, and that action must take precedence over the first good action. For instance, suppose I am weary but have promised to visit my sick friend. Now surely taking a nap would be a good thing to do, but since I have promised, reason commands me to keep my promise. Practical reason, then, forces me to conclude that not only is keeping my promise a *good* thing to do, but it is *better* (in this situation) than taking a nap.

The more serious problem arises in determining how reason, simply by judging that visiting my sick friend is better than taking a nap because it is my duty, can move my will to choose my duty rather than to take a nap. Where does reason get its power? To answer this question we must look more closely at hypothetical imperatives, which are directives based upon subjective interests. By understanding how they function as commands, we will be better able to comprehend how an objective command of reason can move a will without relying on desire.

4. *Hypothetical Imperatives: Conditional Commands of Reason*

The hypothetical imperative merely says that the action is a good means to some possible or actual goal. 415 If it relates the action to a possible goal, we call the imperative *problematic;* if the goal is actually sought, the imperative is called *assertoric.* But the categorical imperative, which declares an action to be objectively necessary in itself without any reference to any goal whatsoever, we call an *apodictic* imperative.

The terminology used in this section is not currently in vogue. Kant borrowed his terms from the names of the logical forms of judgment, as he did the terms "hypothetical" and "categorical." The term "problematic" means, roughly, "contingent." A problematic judgment is based upon some condition which may not obtain, such as: "*If* he reaches the 30-yard line, it will be a first down." An assertoric judgment (one which "asserts") is likewise a conditional statement, but one in which the condition has already been fulfilled. Thus, "If he reaches the 30-yard line— and he has!—it's a first down." Or, "*Since* he reached the 30-yard line, it's a first down." The term "apodictic" means roughly the same as "objectively necessary." It is a statement of necessity, such as: "A team must progress ten yards in order to make a first down." Apodictic judgments are unconditional.

The first kind of hypothetical imperative to be discussed is the *problematic imperative* (later called an imperative of skill).

Whatever a rational being can do, that we may take as a possible objective for some will. Consequently, there are an unlimited number of possible principles of action, referring to the means necessary to achieve these objectives. Every practical science proposes certain goals to be attained and uses imperatives to describe the means for attaining the goals. These we can call *imperatives of skill*. In such imperatives the relevant question is not whether the goals are reasonable or valuable, but only what must be done to attain them. The means used by a physician to cure his patient and the means employed by a murderer to poison his victim have equal value to the extent that each accomplishes the respective purpose.

A young child cannot know all the goals which he will seek during his lifetime and so his parents teach him skills in choosing the correct means to a great variety of arbitrary goals. Since parents cannot be certain which goals *will* be chosen, they teach skills regarding goals which *might* be chosen. But in their zeal to teach the skill of choosing the correct means, they frequently neglect to train the child's judgment about the *value* of those things he may later choose as his goals.

The imperative of skill commands nothing more than the means required to achieve a certain end. We learn the means–end relationship from many sources, and we are well aware that there may be many ways to achieve a particular end. Take the situation of a man who wants to burn a pile of leaves. He might use a match, a magnifying glass, a cigarette lighter, a napalm bomb, a flame thrower, or a fire-by-friction kit. A variety of things will start the fire. But in a particular situation (with the available means at hand) we would not say, "If you want to burn leaves, you ought to use napalm," but would say something like, "If you want to burn the leaves, you ought to use a match."

Where is the necessity in this situation? There is surely no obligation to use a match. There is only the *practical* necessity of using the appropriate means to achieve the desired end. We are concerned only with the *means* necessary to achieve some end, whatever its value as an end. Cyanide is much better than aspirin for poisoning someone. Kant is aware of the dangers of such abstraction. We may become so engrossed in the means to some end that we fail to evaluate the end itself. Scientists during World War II were more intent on detonating a nuclear device than in evaluating the results they hoped to achieve thereby. But whatever the value of the end, the imperative of skill expresses the necessary means for achieving it.

But we must remember that the skill imperative is conditional. *The necessity of performing the action rests on the desire for the end.* If a person does not want to burn the pile of leaves, reason has no basis for its command to use a match. Furthermore, since it derives its practical authority from the person's desires, it is a *subjective* imperative. The necessity relates to one person only and involves only one particular goal for that person. Some other desired object or purpose will demand other means, involving a different imperative. This individuality of ends will help to distinguish the problematic imperative from the assertoric imperative.

One goal, however, we can assume that all rational beings actually pursue (at least those rational beings who can be subject to imperatives in the first place, i.e., dependent beings)

and, furthermore, that everyone pursues this goal through some natural necessity. This goal is *happiness*. Those imperatives which show certain actions as necessary for achieving happiness are called *assertoric imperatives*. The action is proposed not as a practical necessity for some merely possible goal, but as necessary for a goal we know for sure that everyone pursues, since it springs from his very nature. When someone has   416 skill in choosing the means to his own well-being (i.e., his happiness), we call him *prudent*, in the narrowest sense of the word.* Imperatives which refer to the means of achieving happiness, while they are rules of prudence, still are merely hypothetical: the action is commanded as necessary, not in itself but as a means to an end.

* "Prudence" has two meanings: (a) the interpersonal sense, denoting a man's skill in influencing others in order to use them for his own purposes; and (b) the personal sense, referring to his own ultimate benefit. Thus any advantage of interpersonal prudence must finally be grounded in personal prudence. One who is prudent in the interpersonal sense, but not in the personal sense, should be called clever or shrewd, but not prudent, properly speaking.

The second type of hypothetical imperative involves a different kind of good. First, we know that men *do* seek the goal, happiness. Secondly, it is an end which encompasses *all* our activities to such an extent that some philosophers (e.g., Aristotle) believed happiness to be the proper foundation of morality.[5] Thus, the imperative of prudence is *assertoric:* "If you want to achieve happiness—and you surely do!—then you ought to. . . ." The more we know of the proper means to happiness and act on the knowledge, the more prudent we are. The belief that some action is a proper means to happiness finds expression in an imperative of prudence. The necessity of acting still depends upon our desire for happiness but, since everyone desires happiness "through some natural necessity," the authority for the imperative is a broader one than that for an imperative of skill. It is not derived from a desire for some particular objective but from our human nature itself. Yet the necessity is not thereby objective, since it is not based upon rationality, but upon our specifically human nature. We know man to have this goal through our experience, not through reason.

Our natural goal *is* happiness, true, but reason is not capable of leading us to it, even if we had holy wills. Too much depends on circumstances beyond our own control, such as health, sufficient necessities of life, harmonious relations with our fellow men, etc. There are no guaranteed means to happiness. Must we despair of achieving our goal in life? Not at all. Although it is highly unlikely (due to stepmotherly Nature) that we will fully achieve our *natural* goal, we can surely achieve our *moral* or *rational* purpose, which is to be *worthy of happiness*. Thus the rational goal is in accord with man's natural goal, and not in opposition to it. The seeming opposition arises when an action which reason represents as necessary for being worthy of happiness is not the same as that action which desire or inclination suggests as a means for achieving happiness itself. This situation is the model case of moral struggle and exemplifies the fundamental difference between the hypothetical and categorical imperatives.

5. *The Categorical Imperative: the Unconditional Command of Reason*

Finally, there is that imperative which straightforwardly commands us to do something without basing the command on some goal to be achieved by the action. This is a *categorical imperative*. The categorical imperative disregards the particular circumstances of the situation as well as the proposed results of the action; instead, it commands in virtue of the form of the action and from the law governing such situations in general. The essential moral goodness of such actions depends on the motive, no matter what the results might be. Such is the *imperative of morality*.

When a particular action appears necessary as a means to happiness, its necessity is still conditional, depending upon the agent's desire for that end. When reason represents an action as necessary in order to be worthy of happiness, however, it does so regardless of whether happiness will actually be achieved. The action, in fact, is not presented as a means at all; reason does not present an objectively necessary action to the will in this way. No, the will is presented with an action which ought to be done solely because the action is necessary on its own account. The imperative which presents the action to the will does not rest upon some condition, nor does it depend upon some desire of the agent. Rather, it presents the action as *categorically* and *unconditionally* necessary, necessary in spite of any possible conflicting desires or inclinations. The goodness of such an action is not found in the result to be achieved but in the action itself or, more accurately, in the willing of the action, in our motive for doing it. No matter what the result may be, the action must be performed because it is the moral thing to do. Thus, says Kant, only the categorical imperative is the imperative of morality, for only a categorical imperative commands what is unconditionally and morally necessary.

The difference between these three kinds of imperative can be stated in the different ways each constrains the will. To make the distinctions clear, let us call them respectively *rules of skill*,[6] *counsels of prudence,* and *commands* (*laws*) *of morality.* We might also call the first a *technical* imperative (concerned with art), the second a *pragmatic* imperative (concerned with one's own benefit),* and the third a *moral* imperative (concerned with free conduct as such, namely, with moral action).

Now only law contains the idea of unconditional, objective, and universally valid necessity; thus laws must be obeyed, no matter what our desires may be in the matter. Counsels, on the other hand, while they do involve a kind of necessity, do so under a contingent and subjective condition, that a man believes the action counseled to be a means to his happiness. But the categorical imperative is not subject to any conditions and is a command in the strict sense of absolute, practical necessity.

> * This seems to me the proper meaning of "pragmatic." Pragmatic sanctions, for instance, are derived from statutes enacted for public welfare, not from any natural law pertaining to states. Pragmatic history is that which is written to teach prudence, by showing how we might do better for ourselves than other peoples have done in the past.

These, then, are the three types of imperative:

a. *Technical Rules of Skill.* These indicate the necessity of employing a particular means to a particular end. The necessity of acting is subject to a desire for that end. If one desires to achieve that result, then he must (ought to) use these means.

b. *Pragmatic Counsels of Prudence.* These depict the necessary actions one must perform in order to achieve happiness. The necessity depends upon the agent's belief that the action will indeed produce happiness. A person desires happiness by his very nature as a human being and believes the indicated action to be a means to happiness; then he must (ought to) perform the action.

c. *Unconditional Laws of Morality.* These command certain actions as necessary without regard for the desires of the agent, nor for the goodness of the results of the action. The action must be willed because it is objectively necessary, an action which is good in itself.

We might also catalog these imperatives according to the breadth of the conditions from which they derive their authority. A rule of skill is dependent upon one particular desired goal of one agent. A counsel of prudence, extending to all the actions of an agent, is still dependent upon his own desire for happiness and belief that the particular action in question will help achieve it. A law of morality is universal, unconditional, and independent of any agent's desire. Moral law prescribes that *anyone* in a given situation must obey that law if he is to be moral. Morality is a matter of unconditional necessity and does not depend upon wanting to be moral. A duty is a duty, whether or not the agent wants to do it.

These then are the three ways by which reason commands the will to perform an action. The question which we have postponed—*how* does reason influence the will?—may now be raised.

6. *How Are Imperatives Possible?*

But this raises the question: *how are all these impera-*
tives possible? The question does not ask how we come   417
to perform the action which the imperative commands,
but simply how an imperative constrains the will by imposing obligation on it.

The question of the possibility of imperatives is *not* the psychological question which deals with the processes of human decision and resultant action. Kant is asking how the imperatives impose necessity on the will. How does an imperative constrain the will? The question deals with the relationship between reason and will, not with actual human behavior.

We do not require a lengthy explanation to show how the imperative of skill is possible. Anyone who chooses a particular goal must choose the necessary means to that goal—at least if he chooses with reason, and if the means are within his power. So this imperative is an *analytic* command for the will. When I choose to act in order to produce some effect, I must at the same time think of myself as the causal agent who uses the means to that end. The imperative, consequently, simply commands me to perform those actions necessary to obtain the goal I have chosen. Of course, synthetic propositions must be used for deciding what means will produce the desired result, but they refer only to the actions which will realize the goal; they do not refer to the basis in the will for choosing to perform the actions. For instance, if I want to bisect a line according to an exact method, I must draw from each end two intersecting arcs. I know this by means of synthetic propositions of mathematics. But when I recognize that this is the only way to produce what I want, then it follows analytically that in choosing to bisect a line I also choose to perform the operation necessary to do it. To think of something as an effect which I cause by a particular action, and to think of myself as acting in that particular way, are one and the same thing.

Suppose I want to make ice cream. I have learned through experience that ice cream can be made only by using some type of milk base. The proposition, "Ice cream is made with a milk base," is not analytic for in the future chemicals may serve as well as milk base for making ice cream. But as things now stand, if I chose to make ice cream, I must also choose to use a milk base in making it. That is, if I desire a certain end, then to be consistent I must also will the means.

In a consistent way of willing things, if we will a particular end, we must likewise will the means to that end. Or as Kant puts it, in the idea of willing the result, we necessarily include willing the means to that result. And this is what Kant means by calling the imperatives of skill analytic. If I fully choose to obtain the end (and do not merely wish I had it), I must by necessity choose to perform the means to the end. Even though the cause–effect relationship is learned through experience, it is the means–end relationship[7] which practical reason recognizes as necessary. Whether or not I actually perform the necessary means is another matter and does not involve the means–end relationship itself. No one outside the trade has an obligation to make ice cream, but a man who wants to make ice cream, who knows that a milk base must be used, and who yet persists in trying to make ice cream with cement and turpentine, is simply irrational.

If we could precisely define happiness, then the imperatives of prudence would be the same as the imperatives of skill and thus would be analytic. Here, as well as   418
in the former case, choosing the end would, if the agent chooses rationally, impose a rational necessity of choosing the means (within the agent's power) which would produce that end. Unfortunately, the idea of happiness is so vague that no one can definitely and consistently say what he wants and chooses, even though he wants and chooses happiness. The reason is that all the components which he includes in his idea of happiness are empirical, i.e., derived from experience; but his idea of happiness is itself absolutely complete, including total well-being, both in the present and in any future circumstances.

But not even the most farsighted and capable finite being can get from such an idea any definite conception of what he really wants. If he believes happiness to consist in wealth, how much trouble, envy, and plots will he thereby bring upon himself? If he thinks it consists in knowledge and foresight, how many inescapable evils (now concealed from him) will he discover? How many more desires will be aroused—as though he did not already have enough—by his discovery of new needs? If he thinks happiness to be long life, can he be sure that it will not be merely one long misery? Or suppose he simply takes happiness to be health; how many times has he been held back by physical illness from those excesses which perfect health would have made alluring? We could go on and on. In brief, we are not all-knowing; and so we simply cannot determine from principle and with certainty what to do to become happy. Since we cannot find any definite rule for achieivng happiness, the only rules we can act on are empirical counsels, such as rules of diet, frugality, courtesy, restraint, and so on, which we know from experience will best promote a happier life generally.

We can conclude, then, that imperatives of prudence cannot command, strictly speaking: they cannot present actions as being practically necessary on objective grounds. These imperatives are better called *counsels* (*consilia*) rather than *laws* of reason (*praecepta*), since it is impossible to find a sure and universal answer to the question, "What action will make a rational being happy?" Happiness is an Ideal of the imagination, not of reason, and is derived from experience—so it cannot be the foundation for a command of reason. We can never expect experience to show us, beyond doubt, the action which would produce the entire series of consequences—a series which   419 is in fact endless.

Even if we could determine with certainty the means to happiness, the imperative of prudence would then be an analytic proposition; it would differ from the imperative of skill only in having its goal actually desired, whereas the imperative of skill states its goal merely as possibly desired. But since both command an action as a means to some desired end, both imperatives are analytic, for they command that one who wills the end must in each case will the means. And so we see no problem as to how the imperative of prudence is possible.

Briefly put, the imperative of prudence, or counsel of prudence, *would* be analytic *if* we knew the precise means–end relationship for acquiring happiness as well as we know those relationships in the technical rules of skill. In making ice cream, we can have a precise idea of what we are hoping to achieve and what must be done to achieve it. And reason perceives that, as matters stand, if we choose to make ice cream, then by practical necessity we must choose the actions which produce ice cream, whatever they may be. In willing happiness, on the other hand, reason still perceives the necessity of acting to produce happiness. The important difference, however—so important that a counsel of prudence is not a command at all for finite beings— is that we have neither a clear idea of what happiness is nor definite ideas of how to achieve it. We have certain notions about happiness, true, but they are vague, confused, obscure, and uncertain. Happiness is so all-encompassing that it would require a superhuman mind to conceive it fully. Consequently, the counsels of prudence are commands only in an advisory sense.[8]

7. How is the Categorical Imperative Possible?

The only real problem we must investigate is how the imperative of morality is possible. Since it is not hypothetical, we cannot base its objective necessity on a presupposition as we did with hypothetical imperatives. Nor can we show by examples from experience that there is in fact an imperative of morality. It might possibly be that every imperative which appears to command categorically may be subconsciously a hypothetical imperative. Consider the precept, "Do not make a false promise." Now, we take this as something more than advice for avoiding some evil, as though it said, "Do not make a false promise for you may lose your credit if you get caught at it." On the contrary, we judge a false promise to be bad in itself and that the imperative forbids it categorically.

But no example can prove beyond question that a will which obeyed a command, apparently influenced by the law alone, was not in fact determined by other influences. It is always possible that some hidden fear of disgrace or a secret dread of other dangers may unconsciously influence the will. How could we prove that no such hidden cause exists when we have no experience of it? But if such a hidden cause does exist, then the so-called moral imperative, which seems to command categorically and unconditionally, turns out to be no more than a pragmatic rule, one which shows us how best to act in our own interests.

The initial problem is that the categorical imperative is not analytic. There is no means–end relationship, since the categorical imperative depends upon no conditional factor as does the hypothetical imperative. It commands universally and unconditionally, with a moral necessity. We cannot justify the imperative of morality by any appeal to experience. We have already seen that no historical instances can be given as unquestionable illustrations of purely moral behavior, simply because we can never be sure there were no hidden motives. In fact, it is possible that there have never been instances of purely moral behavior; it is therefore impossible to use actual examples as proof.

Consequently our investigation of how a categorical imperative is possible must be *a priori*. If we could prove 420 by experience that there really is such an imperative all we would need to do would be to validate it. But we do know this much: only a categorical imperative can be a practical *law*. Other imperatives may be called rules of choice, but not laws, since anything which must be chosen merely as a means to some arbitrarily selected goal may itself be considered contingent. As soon as we lose our desire for the goal, the imperative loses its force. But an unconditional command allows the will no option to choose otherwise; it alone commands with that necessity which we expect from law.

The principal reason that examples will not work is that the categorical imperative is *a priori:* it binds the will under necessity. Necessity can be justified only by an appeal to rationality, not to experience; and since the categorical imperative does command without any conditional presupposition, it is *a priori*. In the case of making ice cream, we find that using a milk base is part of the process, so in willing to make ice cream, reason demands that we use the milk base. But reason does not demand that we make ice cream. On the other hand, we must keep our promises, no matter what the situation. We have no allowable alternatives.

We have seen how the hypothetical imperative is analytic: the concept of willing the end contains the concept of willing the appropriate means to the end. But in the categorical command of reason, there is no such means–end relationship. Nor will logic alone reveal any particular action to be one's duty. Any relationship between reason and will with respect to a dutiful action is nonanalytic: Kant calls such a relationship *synthetic*. The categorical imperative expresses a *synthetic a priori* relationship between reason and will.

In the second place, there are weighty reasons for our difficulty in determining how the categorical imperative (the law of morality) is possible. This imperative is a *synthetic a priori practical proposition*,* and, because so much trouble arose in validating synthetic *a priori* propositions in theoretical knowledge, one could easily conclude that equal problems would arise in practical knowledge.

> * I relate the action to my will by an *a priori* (necessary) connection, without assuming as a condition any desire on my part to perform the action. The relationship is completely objective, based on an idea of reason which has full power over subjective motives. This practical proposition, therefore, cannot assume an analytic relationship between willing an action and having some inclination to perform it. (We do not have such a perfect will.) Rather, this synthetic proposition connects the action directly to the idea of a rational will, yet the action is not analytically contained in that idea.

The discovery of the *synthetic a priori proposition* has often been cited as Kant's major contribution to philosophy. While this is not exactly true—others before Kant had been aware of such a class of propositions—Kant was the first to analyze explicitly their role in human knowledge. Kant agreed with Hume that propositions are divided logically into two groups: analytic propositions and synthetic propositions. *Analytic* propositions are those which are true by the very concepts involved. We need only understand what the subject of the proposition means in order to know that the predicate is true of that subject. Thus, "All bachelors are unmarried," "All fathers are male," and "All circles are round," are analytic propositions. *Synthetic* propositions are simply propositions which are not analytic. If the predicate adds something to our understanding of the subject, then in forming the proposition we have "synthesized" two non-related concepts into one proposition. Thus, "Washington was the first President," "All men are mortal," and "Rose Ann has blue eyes," are synthetic propositions.

Besides the logical distinction of analytic versus synthetic, there is the epistemological distinction of propositions into *a priori* and *a posteriori*. *A priori* propositions, characterized by necessity and universality, are grounded in reason, while *a posteriori* propositions are derived from experience and thus lack the characteristics of necessity and universality.[9] "All men are mortal," while true of every man in the past, is not true by rational necessity, since there is nothing inconsistent in the idea of an immortal man. We know that all men die because experience has so taught us; thus the proposition is *a posteriori*. On the other hand, "All bachelors are unmarried," is necessarily true, anywhere, anywhen, past, present, and future. It is true because it is a truth of reason and not merely of fact. The concepts are understood by reason to be logically related. The proposition, accordingly, is *a priori*.

Hume had proclaimed that there is only one way of pairing these propositions: all analytic propositions are *a priori*, and vice versa; all synthetic propositions are *a posteriori*, and vice versa. Kant, however, disagreed strongly. It is true, he said, that a proposition which is analytic is *a priori*, since analytic propositions are constructed by reason; and it is also true that *a posteriori* propositions are synthetic, since experience does not provide us with material for statements true by the very meaning of their terms. Nevertheless there are propositions which are universally and necessarily true, Kant noted, which are *not* true because of the conceptual equivalence of their subjects and predicates. They are *synthetic a priori* propositions. Examples of such propositions are, "Every event is caused," "The shortest distance between two points is a straight line," "For every action there is an equal and opposite reaction," and "Something endures through every change." These propositions are necessarily true, and true of any time or place in the universe. What is more, their truth is not derived from experience; in fact, they are used to judge experience. For instance, I know that the straight distance between two given points is ten feet, but a line drawn from one point to the other is measured to be ten feet and 1/16 inch. I may then conclude that no matter how straight the drawn line may look, it is not straight.

Practical propositions—i.e., imperatives expressing what a person ought to do—are likewise distinguished as analytic and synthetic, *a priori* and *a posteriori*. We have already seen that hypothetical imperatives are *analytic:* they command under necessity and are thus *a priori*. The force of the command to choose the means follows from the practical meaning of the will's choice of the end. But moral commands, since they do not command an action in order to achieve some end, command an action as necessary (a duty) for its own sake. Such practical propositions are *a priori* but are not analytic: they are *synthetic a priori* practical propositions. Reason relates an action to the idea of a good will and duty, but the meaning of good will and duty do not include any reference to a particular action. How then can reason command a particular action as unconditionally necessary? Or, in Kant's words, how is a synthetic *a priori* practical proposition possible? How does reason give moral law? The difficulties of the *Critique of Pure Reason*, in which Kant sought the basis of synthetic *a priori* theoretical propositions, seem equally great for moral propositions.

8. *The "One" Categorical Imperative*

In order to give a rational foundation for obligation, to justify the possibility of the categorical imperative, we must first determine whether we ever make such judgments of practical reason. It is certainly easier to validate a known proposition than some abstract idea which is never expressed. We have a fairly clear understanding of what the categorical imperative must be:

    a. It must express an unconditional command of reason.

    b. It must be independent of desire or inclination.

    c. It must be applicable to every moral situation, not limited to this person or that lifetime.

Kant proposes to combine these characteristics in a single formulation, which will then be the supreme principle of morality.

To solve this problem, let us first ask whether from the very idea of a categorical imperative we may derive a formulation which contains all that a categorical imperative must be. Even if we find this formulation, there still remains the special and arduous task of finding how such an absolute law can be possible. We will postpone the latter difficulty until the last section.

The bare idea of a hypothetical imperative tells me nothing until I know under what conditions the imperative comes into being. But when I think of the categorical imperative, I know immediately what it contains. Besides the spe-   421 cific law applying to the situation, the categorical imperative commands only the necessity that my maxim* conform to that law. But since the law is not subject to any conditions, *the categorical imperative can command only that my maxim conform to the universality of law as such.* The conformity itself is what the imperative commands as necessary.

---

  * A *maxim* is a subjective rule of acting and must be distinguished from the objective rule, the practical *law*. The former is a personal policy of acting which reason determines in view of subjective conditions, such as desires or even ignorance. The maxim is the rule according to which the agent does in fact choose to act. The law, on the other hand, is an objective rule—an imperative—valid for every rational being; it is the rule by which the agent *ought* to act.

Consider the idea of a hypothetical imperative once again. What is the command of reason here? We do not know until we know what end has been chosen. Reason cannot command me to use milk base until I choose to make ice cream. That is why hypothetical imperatives are not commands at all in the strict sense but are what we might call rules of practical consistency. Surely I do not *disobey* any command if I try to make ice cream with cement and turpentine, unless it be the law of practical consistency. The most that could be said is that I act foolishly, unreasonably, or such like. Although my action cannot be justified as productive of ice cream, it is not an immoral action.

But examine the categorical imperative. In it we see a command in the strict sense. When I disobey it I am immoral, for my maxim—that policy or rule which is my actual and personal basis of choice—does not accord with moral law. The law says, "Do this," while my maxim says, "In this kind of situation I will do something else." The moral law is the objective principle, which is not restricted to me personally but applies unconditionally to any rational being in a comparable situation. What happens when I act morally? Simply, my maxim, my subjective rule, coincides with the objective command. When we remember that every action is done according to the agent's own personal maxim and that he acts morally when his personal maxim coincides with the objective principle, then the general law of morality must be: *make your maxim coincide with the objective principle.* Or, always make sure that the action derived from your maxim is the same action which the law commands. Or more simply, choose to do what you ought to do.

This is all well and good: I must see that my maxim coincides with the objective principle. But what is the objective principle? Particular moral rules apply to particular situations. "Keep your promise" applies only when I have made a promise. But the categorical imperative, as the imperative of morality itself, must apply to *every* situation. There must then be something common to every situation that makes it a potentially moral one. This common characteristic is that in every situation there is *some* moral rule, *some* objective principle, which applies to that situation, which makes the situation a moral one, and which expresses what I ought to do (or what I ought not to do) in that situation.

If applicability of some moral rule constitutes the common characteristic, then the categorical imperative as the supreme rule of morality must express a characteristic common to all moral rules, thereby granting to each particular moral rule its moral authority. According to Kant there is but *one* such common characteristic: *every moral rule commands universally.* Every moral rule is a *law,* for a law is a rule which commands universally. Every particular moral rule contains two elements: the action specified and the universality of application. This universality, the common element in every law, means that there are no exceptions to the command. Everyone in the same kind of situation must obey the law governing it. Everyone who makes a promise must keep it.

But there must be an infinite variety of situations, and it is logically possible that a different moral rule covers each situation. Must we know every moral rule there is? How can I know that my maxim coincides with the moral rule? There is only one sure way, says Kant. Only one law can consistently apply in any given situation, so *if my maxim could be thought of as the law for that situation,* without conflicting with any other law or norm of consistency, *then my maxim conforms to the law for that situation.*

There is, therefore, but one categorical imperative, which is: ACT ONLY ON THAT MAXIM WHICH YOU CAN AT THE SAME TIME WILL TO BECOME A UNIVERSAL LAW.

If I can consistently propose that my maxim be the maxim for everyone in the same situation, then my maxim conforms to the objective principle governing the situation. In so acting, I act morally. On the other hand, if my maxim proposes an exception to what is applicable to everyone, or if what I propose conflicts with another recognized moral maxim, then my maxim does not coincide with the moral rule applying to the situation. In so acting, I act immorally.

This then is the meaning of "acting morally": I act morally when I choose in such a way that my own principle or policy is one which at the same time applies to everyone in the same situation. If I can consistently (and honestly) will that everyone ought to do what I do, then my maxim must conform to the objective principle applicable to everyone. I thereby act as though *my* maxim were the objective law for everyone; I will *my* maxim to be the *universal law*.

Kant explicitly states that the objective principle is *not* itself a rule of action: it is rather a practical definition of what constitutes moral action.

Now if we can derive all imperatives of duty from this single imperative as their ultimate source of authority, we can at least explain what we mean by the idea of duty, even though we be unable (at this point) to decide whether what we mean by duty is anything more than an empty idea.

But we are understandably puzzled by his suggestion that all imperatives of duty (i.e., particular moral rules) can be derived from this single imperative, "as their ultimate source of authority." Does he mean that from this principle alone we can deduce our duty in any given human situation? Or does he mean that we can determine whether our maxim coincides with universal, objective law? Apparently the latter is closer to Kant's point of view. His examples (discussed below in Chapter 7) will present the situation of a man who already has a tentative maxim or who already contemplates a certain action. In them the categorical imperative will function as a standard for judging the moral status of the maxim. Only in this indirect way does the command of reason prescribe any particular activity.

What is the importance of the categorical imperative to the practical activity of morality? For Kant it is the *validating form* of moral action. Just as there is a form of the syllogism which "validates" certain arguments, so there is a "moralizing" form for human actions which "moralizes" the action. If the action is in the proper moral form, it is moral. This form of morality, as we learned in Section I, is universality. So the validating form of moral action is the categorical command of reason: Act only by that maxim which you can at the same time will to become a universal maxim, i.e., a law. Furthermore, when we understand the proper forms of the syllogism, we understand thereby what validity means. Likewise, we understand what morality means when we see how actions become moral by conforming to the objective principle of morality.

But understanding the meaning of a concept does not prove that there are actual instances to which it refers. Kant has stated more than once that the concept of duty might be empty; there may be no truly moral actions at all. Even more critical is the question whether moral action as such is even possible. The theory of determinism states that free human choice is but a delusion, since so-called free choices are but foregone conclusions, effects in a long causal chain. Kant has not yet argued for freedom of choice, nor against determinism. (We will have to wait for his examination of the real possibility of moral action until Section III.)

However, certain questions about the categorical imperative must be answered before we proceed to its justification. For example, how does Kant propose that we derive all our duties from one categorical imperative? Are there perhaps other formulations of this law of morality? How can we relate the idea of universalizing one's maxim to the idea of acting from duty? To answer such questions, Kant diverges from his main exposition. The explanation of the categorical imperative will be in two parts: (1) an ethical discussion of ways in which the categorical imperative may be used in moral situations (Chapter 7); and (2) an examination of the necessary foundation of the categorical imperative, particularly, the self-legislating will (Chapter 8). The next chapter, then, will consist of a discussion of the three variations of the "one" categorical imperative and the famous Four Examples. This part of Section II may be seen as a preview of Kant's later *Metaphysics of Morals*.

9. *Summary*

Kant has taken reason in its practical activity and derived from its function the same foundation for morality which he discovered in Section I. There he began with common rational knowledge about morality and discovered the underlying principle. Here he has taken practical reason as the source of action, and found in reason itself the standard for all moral action.

He first pointed out that every action called rational is one which is done from some principle or policy. Only a rational being can act from the idea of law, i.e., according to principle. Reason determines the principles; will is the capacity to act on them. Were we completely rational, every action would fully accord with reason; but since we are not, some actions do not conform to the principles recognized by reason.

When reason presents an action to the will as objectively necessary, but the will is drawn to something else, there arises a tension between reason and will called *constraint*. This constraint is expressed by an *imperative,* a command of reason, the chief feature of which is the "ought." "You ought to keep your promise" expresses the relationship between reason's command and a will which is not bound by natural necessity to follow reason.

How does reason recognize a certain action to be objectively necessary? Since there are two kinds of practical necessity, means–end necessity and objective (unconditional) necessity, reason presents these to the will in respectively distinct commands: a hypothetical imperative and a categorical imperative. The *hypothetical* imperative expresses only the necessity involved in willing the required means to some end. The necessity is analytic: the concept of "willing the end" contains the concept "willing the means." The necessity of a hypothetical imperative is one of practical consistency, not moral obligation.

The *categorical* imperative, on the other hand, commands absolutely, unconditionally. The necessity is one of moral obligation, not of means–end. It does not command an action as a means to something else but as something to be done for its own sake. Since it commands with necessity, it is an *a priori* command; but as its necessity is not mere practical consistency, it is nonanalytic; i.e., it is synthetic. The categorical imperative, then, is a *synthetic a priori command of practical reason.*

Being unconditional, the imperative of morality applies equally to all moral situations. One acts morally when he makes his own personal principle, his *maxim* of acting, coincide with the objective principle, the moral law. Now the common feature of every moral situation is the universality of the rule applicable to that situation. Thus one will act morally whenever his maxim coincides with the universality of the rule applicable to everyone in that situation. And since in any moral situation there is but one applicable rule, an agent is assured that his maxim coincides with the moral rule of that situation when he universalizes his maxim so that it can consistently apply to everyone in that situation.

Moral action can thus be defined as action which accords with the universally applicable rule. Only one imperative expresses this universal rule of morality: act according to a maxim which could consistently be made the maxim for everyone. Thus the categorical imperative: *Act only on that maxim which you can at the same time will to become a universal law.*

CHAPTER SEVEN

Part 3—The Three Variations of the Categorical Imperative

1. *Kant and Cicero*

The various formulations of the categorical imperative present us with a perplexing problem.[1] Kant explicitly states that there is only *one* categorical imperative, but he then presents three other formulations of it. Are they simply paraphrases of the one categorical imperative from different points of view, or is Kant formulating more than one categorical imperative?

To answer this question let us examine Kant's ethical debt to the Stoic tradition. In the first part of Section I, Kant says: "A person who deliberates, calmly, moderates his emotions and passions, and exercises self-control, seems to have all the essential elements of good character. These qualities were highly praised by ancient philosophers. . . ."[2] The ancient philosophers to whom he refers were the Stoics, whose cardinal virtues included calm deliberation, moderation and self-control.

In his *De Officiis,* Cicero proposed various principles by which a person could determine his duty. Christian Garve (1742–1798), a contemporary of Kant, had translated the *De Officiis* into German and included some commentary notes. Kant possessed a copy, which represented to him the "Popular Moral Philosophy" he mentions in the title and body of Section II. This part of

Section II can be taken as Kant's attempt to incorporate the principles of Cicero (*per* Garve's notes) into his *a priori* moral system. Such an application constitutes a brief "Metaphysics of Morals," i.e., a deductive quest for particular moral rules from a given *a priori* foundation.

Cicero sought a universal rule which would resolve the conflict between duty and interest. He discovered three, in fact, and each is used by Kant as a basis for a variation of the categorical imperative. The three rules suggested by Cicero are:

1. Live according to Nature, i.e., Nature as it would be under ideal conditions *(Convenienter cum natura vivere);*

2. Honor every man as a human being, *because* he is a human being *(Omnino hominem ex homine tollit);*

3. Live as a member of a universal society of rational beings *(Communis humani generis societas).*

There is an obvious parallel between these rules and Kant's three formulations of the categorical imperative, given here for comparison:

1. Always act on a maxim which you can will to become a universal law of Nature;

2. Always act so that you treat humanity, whether in your own person or in another, as an end, never merely as a means;

3. Always act so that your will by its maxims can regard itself as making universal law for a possible kingdom of ends (human beings).

The present chapter will examine the three formulations as variations of one general formulation. While Kant does not mention Garve or Cicero or Cicero's three principles, this interpretation[3] permits us to take Kant at his word that there is only *one* categorical imperative, which he later gives what he calls the "general" formulation. This general formulation serves as the direct or immediate ground of the good will. The other formulations, while they may be applied to moral situations in the same manner, are related to the good will only indirectly: they are ideas of popular moral philosophy subsumed under the general formulation. We might even think of them as illustrative variations of the one categorical imperative.

2. *The First Variation: A Universal Law of Nature*

The universal law of cause and effect constitutes the basis for what we call Nature, in the general sense of structure or form. Nature may be defined as the existence of things as they are governed by universal laws.[4] So we can express the imperative of duty in these words: ALWAYS ACT ON A MAXIM WHICH YOU CAN WILL TO BECOME A UNIVERSAL LAW OF NATURE.

For Kant, Nature is just the system of existing things governed by laws which describe patterns of events. These laws have two main characteristics. First, every law is *universal*, without exceptions. Secondly, each law is *consistent* with all the others. Nature does not work against herself.[5] The Nature which Cicero speaks of is an ideal nature, a Nature working consistently with Divine Mind to accomplish divine purposes.[6] The Stoic determined whether his proposed action was in accordance with duty by trying to see that his action agreed with the laws of nature. If he discovered an inconsistency, he would recognize that his proposed action was out of tune with Nature and thus would violate the moral law. If there was no inconsistency, then his action was in tune with the Divine purpose and conformed to moral law.

Kant adapts this idea to his own way of speaking: Always act on a maxim which you can will to become a universal law of Nature. What he does not say, but surely means for us to include, is that if we discover any inconsistency between our "naturalized" maxim and the laws of nature, then our action does not accord with duty. We can paraphrase this formulation of the categorical imperative as follows: Consider your proposed action as though it were a natural occurrence according to a law of nature. If there is no other law of nature inconsistent with the "law" exemplified by your maxim, then your action will be in accordance with duty.

2a. *The Four Examples*

In this section Kant describes four situations, each providing an example of a situation in which someone has a duty. These four examples are among the most famous in the history of philosophy. Kant uses the same four situations to illustrate each of the three variations of the categorical imperative. But it would be wrong to take them as argumentative examples: examples cannot validate a moral principle. Kant employs them to illustrate how we should apply the categorical imperative in its various formulations. We are perfectly free to take the concluding judgments as expressing Kant's personal ethical beliefs about right and wrong, but such a perspective has only a historical value; to place too strong an emphasis on his examples would distort his theory. Yet, for his purposes, the examples are excellently drawn. Each illustrates one of the four types of duty.

Before stating the duties, however, Kant tentatively divides duties into two kinds, with two further divisions within each kind. There is no point in arguing for this particular division, since it is used simply as a schematic device to give some order to the illustrations. Were it an essential matter, Kant would surely have argued more strongly for it.

We will now consider a few duties, examining duties both to ourselves and to others, as well as perfect and imperfect duties.*

> *** I will postpone the division of duties for the *Metaphysics of Morals* which I hope to publish. The division here thus may seem arbitrary, but will serve to give order to my examples. Briefly, by a *perfect duty* I mean one which allows no exception in favor of inclination; such duties may be to ourselves or to others. The schools do not use this division, but I do not want to argue this question here, since the examples will serve whether the division be granted or not.

The division of duties is as follows:
1. Perfect duty to self (example 1).
2. Perfect duty to others (example 2).
3. Imperfect duty to self (example 3).
4. Imperfect duty to others (example 4).

What is the distinction between a perfect and an imperfect duty? After the fourth example, Kant distinguishes between them on the basis of the difference between thinking and willing a certain end. But an examination of the examples themselves will offer another distinction: a perfect duty is *negative,* an absolute prohibition. It commands us always and everywhere to *avoid* the action being considered (e.g., suicide and making false promises). An imperfect duty, on the other hand, is *positive,* bidding us do something, but *not specifying the means to employ* (e.g., benevolence to our fellow man). The particular action depends upon many considerations of the situation (such as how much money the benevolent man has to give, or to whom he should give it).

The first example, then, is that of a perfect duty to oneself. The question is: may a man commit suicide?

**1. *Perfect duty to self.* Consider a man reduced to despair by a string of misfortunes; he is tired of living   422
but is yet sufficiently reasonable to ask himself whether
taking his own life would not be a violation of duty. He asks himself whether the maxim of his action could be a universal law of Nature. His maxim is: "From self-love, I will live by the rule to end my life when longer life seems likely to be miserable rather than satisfactory." Can this maxim of self-love become a universal law of Nature? At once we see that there would be a self-contradiction in a system of Nature that allowed self-love to justify the destruction of life when the purpose of self-love is to motivate us to make life better. Nature cannot exist in such a way. Thus the maxim cannot be made into a law of Nature; and consequently it conflicts with the supreme law of duty.**

The case is simple: a man whose future is one of pain, utter misery, even the loss of reason, asks whether he may legitimately end his life to avoid these horrors. He considers whether it could be a law of Nature that a man who foresees a life of misery may end his own life. But he also realizes that Nature has instilled in him an instinct for self-preservation. The self-made law is thus inconsistent with the actual law of Nature: self-love would lead to self-destruction at the same time that it leads to self-preservation. We must conclude, then, that suicide conflicts with morality, and that under no circumstances may a man take his own life without violating the moral law.

But we immediately think of heroes who have deliberately destroyed themselves for a cause (e.g., the man who throws himself on a hand grenade to save his comrades' lives). Would Kant say such deeds were immoral? Surely not. He speaks of one who is faced with a conflict between a duty and an interest. The maxim to take one's own life is based on a desire to escape pain and misery. The heroic soldier, on the contrary, is not trying to take his own life but to save the lives of others. However, if he performed his heroic deed because it offered a way of suicide without shame, the morality of his action is then thrown open to question.

2. *Perfect duty to others.* Another man finds himself forced to borrow money. He knows that he will be unable to pay it back, but he also recognizes that no one will lend him money unless he firmly promises to repay it by a certain date. He is tempted to make the promise, but he is still conscientious enough to ask himself whether or not it is unlawful and against duty to avoid his financial troubles in this way. If he decides to make the promise, his maxim would be: "Whenever I find that I need money, I will borrow with a promise to repay even though I know I will not be able to do so." We can allow that such a policy of self-love will be entirely beneficial to his future welfare. The question, however, is whether such an action is right. Let him put this policy into the form of a universal law of

Nature and ask: "What will happen if my maxim becomes a universal law?" At once he sees that his maxim could not be a universal law of Nature: it necessarily contradicts itself. For imagine a universal law of Nature that everyone who thinks himself in need would promise anything at all with no intention of keeping such a promise. Both the promise and the goal sought by it would be impossible. Who will believe such a promise? The very attempt would be taken as a ridiculous, laughable pretense.

This example has often been used as an argument that Kant needs consequences to determine the rightness or wrongness of an action.[7] It does appear, at first glance, that Kant is using the consequences of making false promises as the basis for saying that making such promises is immoral. But we must remember what Kant wants to illustrate. A proposed law of Nature allowing false promises would be inconsistent with the real law of nature. If a person decided to make such a promise and thereby raised making false promises to the status of a law of Nature, he would then be unable to make the false promise. The law of false promise-making would be self-defeating. A person makes a false promise assuming that his hearer will take it as made in good faith. But if the law of Nature rules that a promise made by a person in need of money would not be kept, to whom could such a promise be made? Surely there is an inconsistency in proposing an action which becomes impossible to perform at the same time that it is proposed. Since this would be the case in universalizing the maxim of making a false promise—as judged by the standards of the Law of Nature imperative—making a false promise must be judged immoral and it is our duty to avoid it.

3. *Imperfect duty to self.* A third man finds that he has a talent which, were it cultivated, would make him 423 a useful person in many ways. But he lives in comfortable surroundings and devotes himself to pleasures without trying

to develop and perfect his fortunate natural ability. Yet he asks himself whether his maxim of neglecting his talent, which surely agrees with his yen for pleasures, can also agree with what is called duty. He finds that a system of Nature could very well include a law that every man (like the South Sea Islander) could allow his talents to rust away while he devotes his life simply to idleness, enjoyment, and sex—in short, to a life of pleasure seeking. But this man cannot *will* that his maxim become a universal law of Nature, ingrained in our own nature as an instinct. As a rational being, he necessarily wills that all his abilities be developed; he must employ these abilities, given to him by Nature for any number of potential uses.

Here Kant is aware that there would be no rational inconsistency between a South Sea Island universe and the universe as it is. The inconsistency is found in the willing. What this means he will explain shortly.

4. *Imperfect duty to others.* A fourth man is prosperous but sees that others must live in dire distress. He could help them, but he thinks: "What is that to me? Let a man be as well off as heaven allows—or as well off as he can make himself. I ask nothing of him and envy him nothing. But I have not the slightest inclination to help him when he is in trouble." Now if this maxim became a universal law of nature, mankind could still exist and perhaps exist in a better condition than where everyone praises benevolence and goodwill, even practising them at Christmas, but at other times cheats, betrays, and violates the rights of his fellow man. While there *could* be such a universal law of Nature, yet it is impossible to *will* that such a law should govern universally as a law of Nature. A will which proposes such a law would contradict itself. Occasions can indeed arise in which a person would desire the love and sympathy of others; but by proposing such a law of Nature, he would have robbed himself of all hope of the help he wants.

Here, too, the inconsistency is in the willing and not in the realized state of nature. Kant now explains what he means by saying that the inconsistency is in the willing.

> These examples of what we may take to be actual duties are clearly derivable from the single principle. **424** The general canon for judging the moral quality of our actions is this: *we must be able to will that the maxim of our action be made a universal law.* Some actions (as illustrated by the first two examples) are such that we cannot even *think* the universalization of their maxims without involving a contradiction; and it goes without saying that willing such a contradiction would be impossible. Other actions (as in the latter two examples) do not involve that kind of contradiction, yet it is still *impossible to will* that the maxim be made a universal law of Nature for such a volition would be self-defeating. The first two maxims clearly conflict with strict or narrow (rigorous) duty; the second two maxims conflict with broader (meritorious) duty. And thus these examples of every kind of duty (perfect, imperfect, to self, to others) clearly show that duty must be determined by this one principle, not by reference to any object.

The first two examples (ending misery by suicide, and making a false promise) illustrate inconsistency between a universalized maxim and a law of Nature. We can call this an "objective inconsistency," because it postulates a system of nature with mutually opposing "laws": the "law" I will by universalizing my maxim *versus* the actual law of nature. The latter two examples (living the South Sea Island existence, and refusing to help one's fellow man) illustrate a "volitional inconsistency" which is brought about by my willing my maxim to be a natural maxim, when it is inconsistent with my genuine natural maxims. By "natural maxim" I mean one which we have by the very fact that we are human beings, e.g., the maxim to seek happiness. When Kant speaks of the "impossibility" of willing a volitional inconsistency, he does not mean that a person cannot choose to act from such a maxim, for obviously a person can and often does. But he cannot *consistently* will that his maxim be a natural maxim; a genuine natural maxim must cohere with all other natural maxims. For instance, it would be inconsistent for me to act from a maxim intended to make me miserable, for it is my natural maxim to seek happiness. By trying to universalize the maxim, I would make it into a natural maxim which would obviously conflict with my genuine natural maxim to seek happiness. Kant's criterion for moral maxims is consistency: either a consistency between the "naturalized" and actual laws of nature, or between the "naturalized" and genuine natural maxims.

In order to understand where Kant finds the volitional inconsistency in the third and fourth examples, we must recall Kant's assumption that Nature is purposive. Because man is a rational being with a purpose given him by Nature (the perfection of his rational nature in the good will[8]), he wills that purpose from a natural maxim. But when he chooses to waste his rational nature in a life of indolence, he is "naturalizing" a maxim which is inconsistent with his real natural maxim. Thus his maxim to spend his life as a South Sea Islander is immoral. Again, in many of our pursuits we depend on the assistance of others; we cannot know in advance that we will never need their help. When a man chooses to remain aloof from the needs of others, he proposes to "naturalize" a maxim which conflicts with his genuine natural maxim that he achieve his own purposes in life. By "naturalizing" his maxim that a rational being never assist another who is in need, he is cutting himself off from achieving possible future goals. The two maxims are inconsistent and thus his maxim not to help others is immoral.

But a moral transgressor does not test his maxim by the standard of universal law. What does happen when a person wills from a maxim which conflicts with his duty?

If we were to introspect when we transgress duty, we would find, of course, that we do *not* will that our maxim be made a universal law. Not only are we unable to will such a law but,

more to the point, we wish the opposite maxim to remain the general norm while we allow ourselves an exception "just this once," to follow our personal whims. But if we judged all cases from a single point of view, that of reason, we would find a contradiction in our own willing: we *objectively* will that a certain rule hold as a necessary universal law and at the same time we *subjectively* will that our own case be made an exception to the universal law.

As a matter of practice, however, we regard our action from two points of view: the one of a will which conforms in every way to reason, and the other of a will as it is influenced by desire. This avoids an open contradiction, producing instead a clash of desire against the law of reason. In this way the universality of the principle weakens to a general rule of conduct, allowing our maxim to reach a compromise with the practical law of reason. While we could never justify this ploy by an impartial judgment, we demonstrate that we do in fact recognize the validity of the categorical imperative, but at the same time allow ourselves (who still "respect" the law) a few minor, unimportant exceptions, which appear "necessary in this case."

Kant here expresses a valuable insight into the psychology of a transgression of duty. A person who fails to do his duty may still recognize the dutiful action as his *usual* obligation. When he recognizes an action as a duty, he recognizes the validity of a moral imperative; when he refuses to perform his duty, he makes an exception in his own case. He concedes that the moral law is usually binding but insists that the present situation has extenuating circumstances.

When a duty is refused, Kant suggests, there is another inconsistency. The transgressor proposes to make an exception to a law which is universally and unconditionally binding. When he allows such an exception, he rejects the law as a law. Yet in continuing to recognize his general obligation, he recognizes the law. Thus, says Kant, to transgress a duty knowingly is to act inconsistently; it is to acknowledge the universality of a law and yet deny its universality.

But at least we have proved that if duty is a meaningful concept which has true legislative authority over   425
our actions, duty must be expressed in categorical imperatives only, never in hypothetical imperatives. We have gone even further, showing clearly and precisely for every kind of situation what the categorical imperative contains, namely, the law of duty. But is there in fact such a thing as duty? We have not yet come far enough to prove *a priori* that there really is such an imperative, a practical law which of itself commands us absolutely and without any other motive, and that to obey this law is to do one's duty.

The categorical imperative is the *only* law of morality; no imperatives grounded in self-interest can command us unconditionally. But we have not yet proved that the categorical imperative *can* or *does* command us under moral obligation. We believe that it does, because we experience a feeling of constraint which we refer to as the call of duty. But duty must be proved *a priori*, not by any feeling. The next three paragraphs reaffirm that a valid morality must be *a priori*, expressed in categorical imperatives, and independent of any empirical elements.

But while we seek to prove that duty is real, we must at all costs avoid thinking that the proof can be based upon the particular characteristics of human nature. Duty refers to the practical, unconditional necessity of acting. The imperative of duty must then apply to a being only in so far as that being is *rational*, and this only can be its foundation as a law for the human will. Particular characteristics of human nature, such as certain feelings and propensities, and (if it be possible) even unique functions of human reason which would not necessarily belong to every rational being—any of these may produce a maxim for us, but not a law. They can provide a *subjective* rule for us to follow, given that we have the impulse and incentive, but never an *objective* law which can command us to act despite every natural propensity, desire, and feeling to the contrary. In fact, the less subjective motives support doing one's duty and the more they oppose it, the greater shines the sublime, inherent value of the command, for the conflicting inclinations do not in the slightest lessen the authority or validity of the law.

At this point our philosophy is in a critical position: it requires a firm basis, even though nothing in heaven or on earth will serve to support it. Here our philosophy must prove its virtue as absolute authority for its own laws, not as a delivery boy of laws whispered by some implanted sense or heaven knows what guardian spirit. While such laws are better than no laws at all, they cannot equal that law which only reason can dictate. Such commands of reason must be derived wholly   426
a priori in order to have any commanding authority; they cannot depend upon any human inclinations but only on the sovereignty of the law and reason's respect for the law. Without such a law, man is condemned to self-contempt and inward abhorrence.

Empirical elements, then, not only fail to assist the principle of morality, they even sully its purity. For in morals the proper and supreme value of the good will rests exactly on the freedom of its principle of action from all those contingent influences arising from experience. We cannot repeat the warning too often or too strongly—avoid the lazy, narrow-minded habit of looking for moral principles among empirical motives and rules. Weary human reason too quickly seeks repose on this pillow, to dream sweet fantasies in which it embraces no Juno but only a cloud. In such an illusion, reason substitutes for legitimate morality a bastard formed from limbs of varied heritage, resembling whatever one wants to see in it but bearing no resemblance to Virtue's true figure in the eyes of those who have once beheld her.*

* To see Virtue's proper form one must show morality "in the nude," stripping her of all trappings of sense and paste decorations of reward or self-love. How lovely she then appears, surpassing everything else that lays claim to our affections! Such a vision anyone can perceive with the slightest effort of reason—providing, of course, he is still capable of abstracting.

Kant has emphasized these points before, pointing out that we have not yet proved that morality can be justified. We cannot base morality on the nature of man as we know him by experience but must ground morality in reason alone. The moral law is most apparent when it conflicts with and not when it conforms to self-interest. Kant then raises a different question: do rational agents have a duty to examine their maxims by the standard of the categorical imperative? If so, what is the basis for their obligation?

The question then is raised: Is it necessarily a law that all rational beings judge their actions by maxims which they could will to become universal laws? Such a law must be connected entirely *a priori* with the idea of the will of a rational being as such. But to find the connection we must take a reluctant step into metaphysics, but not into speculative philosophy—rather into the metaphysics of morals.

In practical philosophy we do not seek reasons for what happens, but objective, practical laws for what *ought* to happen (even if it never does). We need not ask why this pleases or why that displeases, how a mere pleasant sensation differs from the pleasures of an acquired taste, or how the latter differs from the rational satisfaction of approval. We need not seek the bases of pleasure or displeasure, the sources of desires and impulses, or know how these join with reason to generate maxims. These are all questions of empirical psychology which we saw[9] belong to that part of the material philosophy of Nature which is based on empirical laws.

427

Our question here concerns objective practical law, involving how the will determines itself by reason alone, which it can only do *a priori*. Thus anything related to experience must be

discarded. Let us then inquire whether reason can determine its own activity.

We cannot determine by any kind of experience whether a rational being has an obligation to judge his maxim according to the categorical imperative. If we have an obligation to determine the moral status of our own actions—if we have a duty to make sure that our action conforms with moral law—this obligation itself must rest solely on reason. Our question, then, is not so much *whether* we have such an obligation—for if we do not, moral principles are pointless—but *how* reason makes such commands.

3. *The Second Variation: Humanity as an End*

Every action has a purpose. We do not act unless we act for some end; without a purpose, direction, or point for acting, we simply do not act. We walk in order to get somewhere, to exercise, to carry something. Actions which are pointless, or purposeless, are really not actions at all, but are more properly called *re*-actions, or bodily responses to feeling. We always do *something* and aim *at something*. What we wish to accomplish is called our purpose in acting, our goal—or in Kant's vocabulary, our *end*. Some ends are immediate, others are long range, and still others are ultimate. For example, a Christian attends Sunday worship with the immediate end to pray; his long-range goal might be the salvation of his soul and eternal bliss in heaven, while his ultimate purpose is to achieve a life of union with God. All of these can be his purposes for attending Sunday worship.

Once we achieve an immediate end, we set up another immediate end under the guidance of a long-range end. As steps in the achievement of long-range ends, immediate ends are not ends in themselves, but are intermediate ends, i.e., ends which are also means to further ends. In order to get downtown I must go to the first street crossing, then to the next, and so on. Each is an end, since I walk to arrive at that spot. But I do not wish merely to get to the first crossing; I seek that point only as a part of the way downtown. Only an end which is desirable in itself and for itself alone and *not* as a means to something else can be called an *end-in-itself*, or an ultimate end.

There are ends which a person seeks because they will satisfy his personal desires or needs. These are called *subjective*, or personal, ends. On the other hand, there may be some end which everyone ought to seek. Such an end would be *objective* since it would not depend on any desire to achieve it or need for it.

We think of the will as an ability to act self-determiningly according to the idea of certain laws. Only rational beings have this ability. That basis of self-determination which lies beyond the willing itself we call an *end*. If this basis comes from reason alone, then the end so derived holds for all rational beings alike. On the other hand, that action which may produce such an end we call the *means*. The subjective urge of desire is the *impulse* to act, and the objective reason for willing to act we call the *motive*.[10] Thus we can distinguish between *subjective ends* which arise from desires, and *objective ends* which rest only on rational, and hence universally valid, motives. Rules for acting are *formal* if they have no subjective ends; they are *material* if they have subjective ends based on particular desires.

Whatever material end a rational being arbitrarily chooses to produce by his action has value as an end only in relation to the particular kind of desire in the agent. Such a relative value obviously cannot be the foundation for a practical law which will be universally valid for all rational beings and all their volitions. Relative ends can generate only hypo-   428 thetical imperatives.

We must distinguish between a *subjective ground* and a *subjective end*, between an *objective ground* and an *objective end*. Every action has both a subjective ground and an objective ground, in that every action springs from some incentive and seeks to achieve some goal. The inner *desire*, the source of my wanting some object, is the subjective ground. The goal of the action, *achieving* the desired object, is the objective ground for which I act. "Ground," whether subjective (as the source of the purpose) or objective (as the object of desire), refers to the fundamental springs in any act of willing. "End," on the other hand, refers only to the result willed, not to anything in the act of willing. A subjective end is one which is sought because the agent desires it. Although the goal is sought through the action, it still remains a personal goal arising from some desire, making it a subjective end. Every subjective end, of course, is at the same time an objective ground of a particular act of will.

Kant calls all subjective ends *material,* since they are ends only in the context of a situation involving a person who desires them. Any principle of action (maxim) which is based on such a personal, subjective desire has imperative force only because the person actually desires to achieve the end. "If you want to be skilled in bowling, you ought to practice every day." The imperative, "Practice every day," has authority only to the extent that the agent actually desires to be skilled in bowling. Thus subjective ends can serve as the foundation for hypothetical imperatives only.

An *objective end,* on the contrary, is not dependent on desire (although, as an objective of the will, it would be an objective ground). But being independent of desire, yet worthy of being an end, it must have its value as an end *in itself*. That is, it must have intrinsic value and be desirable for its own sake; its value must be independent of particular situations and personal inclinations. In a word, it must be an end which all rational beings *ought* to seek simply because it is *a thing good in itself*.

But suppose there were something which by its very existence would have an absolute value all by itself. This would constitute an *end in itself* and could generate exact laws. Only in such an end could we find the basis for a practical law, that is, for a categorical imperative.

Such an end must be sought because of its own intrinsic worth. Its status as an end could not depend on its being desired by someone; it *ought* to be sought solely because it has intrinsic value. Such an end would provide the basis for a law for all rational beings in every situation, i.e., it would be the foundation for a categorical imperative.

Man is such an end. Man, or more generally, every rational being, exists as an end in himself. Whatever he may do, involving only himself or other rational beings, he must always be valued as an end, not merely as a means to be used at the whim of this or that will.

Objects of desire have at best a conditional value. Unless they be the basis of some desire or need, they have no value at all. But the inclinations which give rise to needs are themselves so far removed from absolute value that every rational being must wish himself completely freed of such desires. Thus any object which our actions may produce will have only a conditional value. Nonrational beings which exist in Nature independently of our wills have at best a value as means, and we refer to them as *things.*

But rational beings, on the other hand, we call *persons,* since by their very nature they exist as ends in themselves, never to be treated simply as things. A person is an object of respect; thus we cannot treat him in any arbitrary fashion. He is not simply a subjective end, as though his value rested solely on our desires; he is an *objective end,* one who exists in himself as an end. We cannot make him a mere means to some end substituted in his place. If a rational being be not such an end, nothing whatsoever has absolute value. But if everything has only relative contingent value, then there can be no supreme principle of practical reason.

The only object of intrinsic value is man as a rational being. He is thus an object of respect and can be seen as a valid foundation for a universal principle of action. In his first proposition of morality, Kant insisted that a rational being has intrinsic worth: the only absolutely good thing is the good will. The good will is grounded in reason, and whatever serves as the foundation of an absolute good is itself of intrinsic value. *All* rational beings, because they are beings who can reason, are objects having intrinsic value. Consequently, every man is an object having absolute value, for as a rational being he is the foundation of his own good will, which is the absolute good.

The intrinsic worth of a rational being does not depend upon his *having* a good will, for few men, if any, have such a worth. Rather it is because every man is a rational being and as such *could* have a good will, that we consider him a being of intrinsic value. A diamond in the rough is valuable because it can become a beautiful jewel, not because it already is one.

The first variation of the categorical imperative considered whether the maxim of the action could consistently be willed to be a universal law of nature. The second variation refers to the purpose or end of the action as an end of intrinsic value, and so as an objective end for every rational being.

If there be a supreme practical law, a categorical imperative for the human will, it must be derived from 429 **the idea that what is an end in itself is necessarily an end for everyone. From this we can conclude an objective principle for the will, that is, a universal practical law. The principle rests on this:** *rational nature exists as an end in itself.* **Now so far as I necessarily think of my own existence this way, the principle serves me only as a subjective rule of human action. But what is more, every rational being thinks of himself in the same way as I do, based on the same rational grounds that hold for me.* This makes the rule an objective principle and thus a supreme practical law from which we can derive all laws of the will. The practical imperative, then, is this:** ALWAYS ACT SO

THAT YOU TREAT HUMANITY, WHETHER IN YOUR OWN PERSON OR
IN ANOTHER, AS AN END, AND NEVER MERELY AS A MEANS.

* I state this proposition here as a postulate. Grounds for it will be
presented in Section III.

We see clearly the similarity between this variation of the
categorical imperative and Cicero's second rule: Honor every
man as a human being, *because* he is a human being. Just as the
first variation commands us to consider the maxim of our action
—no matter what maxim it may be—as a universal law of nature,
so this variation commands us to treat human beings—no matter
who or in what situation—as having unconditional value, not as
something which serves merely as a means to some personal
(subjective) end.

We cannot conclude, just because every human being views
himself as an end, that we *ought* to treat men as ends in themselves. A general truth cannot serve as the justification for a
moral law since we learn the general truth by experience,
whereas a moral law must be based on reason. But if man
necessarily views himself as an end—and always from the same
rational ground—then we can conclude that every man must
never treat himself or any other human being as a mere means.
Only in this way can the universal statement be shown to be
a priori and a valid ground for a moral law. However, it is one
thing to assert that every man necessarily sees himself as an end
in himself and quite another to prove it. The proof, however, will
be postponed until Section III (chapter 9), where Kant will
attempt to validate the ultimate principle of morality.

3a. *The Four Examples*

Kant again examines the four examples previously given, this
time from the standpoint of humanity as an end.

Let us see now whether we can derive particular moral laws
from this principle. Consider again our previous examples:

1. *Necessary duty to self.* A man thinking of committing suicide will ask himself: "Would my action be consistent with the idea of humanity as an end in itself?" If he kills himself to escape a painful situation, he uses a person (himself) as a mere means for keeping his life tolerable so long as he lives. But man is not a thing; he is not something to be *used* as a mere means. In all his actions and at all times, man must be considered as an end in himself. So I cannot mistreat the humanity of my own person by mutilating, ruining, or killing myself.*

* Certain questions, however, may arise in this matter, leading to confusion. For example, may I risk my life now in order to make my life safer in the future? We must leave the examination of such questions to ethics proper.

If rational nature exists as an end in itself, then I may not use it as a means to the achievement of some merely personal objective. It makes no difference whether it be my own rational nature or another's: the law holds alike for every being having a rational nature. I cannot act in any way which would tend to harm my rational nature. This applies not only to self-destruction, but also to less permanent harm, such as drunkenness and narcotic addiction.

Kant suggests two interesting questions, although he does not discuss them. First, to what extent may a man risk his life to save himself? The answer is by no means obvious and would depend upon the many factors of the particular situation. The second question, implicit in this example, is this: may a man mutilate himself if it does not harm his rational nature in any way? May a person offer one of his eyes to a blind man for some financial compensation? On the surface, at least, he is not involving his rational nature in such an operation. Perhaps it would depend on the motive: whether he gave up his eye in order to help the blind or just for the money. It does not seem to be a clear-cut case which can be decided by the categorical imperative alone.

2. *Necessary duty, or strict obligation, to others.* Anyone who proposes to make a false promise can see 430 immediately that he plans to use the other person as a mere means to an end which ignores the other person's value as an end in himself. The person I intend to exploit for my own benefit cannot possibly consent to being used in this way, and thus I cannot at the same time consider him as sharing the purpose of my making such a promise. This violation of the duty we owe to other men becomes more evident when we use examples of attacks against their freedom and property. Then we see patently that one who violates the rights of men intends to exploit the person of others as mere means, without any thought that they must always be valued as ends. They are rational beings who must themselves be thought of as sharing in the purposes of the action.*

---

* The trite rule, "Quod tibi non vis fieri, etc." (Do not unto others what you would not have them do unto you), cannot serve as a moral principle. Indeed, while it may be derived from our principle, it is limited by various restrictions. It cannot be a universal law, for it lacks a basis for duties to self as well as strict duties to others. One cannot even derive duties of benevolence from such a rule, for many a man would be willing for others not to help him so long as he was not obliged to help others. If this rule were a guide, the criminal could use it against the judge who punishes him, and so on.

Making false promises is clearly immoral, for one who makes such a promise is using another person solely as a means to his own subjective end. The same immorality attends slavery, racial discrimination, theft, unfair taxation, and poor wages—in brief, any action which treats another human being as a *thing* rather than a *person*.

The similarity of the second variation to the Golden Rule leads Kant to emphasize that the Golden Rule cannot be a valid principle of morality. In the above footnote Kant argues that this rule—"What you do not want done to you, do not do to another"—allows certain actions which are contrary to morality. The basic flaw, however, is that the Golden Rule is grounded in desire or aversion, not in reason alone, so it cannot serve as a principle of morality. Still it has a certain practical value: no man wishes to be treated as a mere means and so in common fairness should not treat another as he himself would not wish to be treated. But in the end, such a rule by itself has no moral validity.

3. *Contingent, or meritorious, duty to self.* It is not enough that our action not exploit the humanity of our own person as an end in itself, but more, the action must *harmonize* with the idea of humanity. Every human being has talents for self-improvement; these are grounded in Nature's purposes for humanity. If we fail to exercise our talents, we may not conflict with the continued survival of humanity as an end, but we surely do nothing to further it.

4. *Meritorious duties to others.* Every man seeks his own happiness as his natural goal. Perhaps humanity would survive even though no one helped others to become happy, as long as no one got in the way of another's happiness. But this would be only a negative kind of harmony with humanity as an end. A positive harmony requires each person to do as much as possible to promote the happiness of others. For since a person is an end in himself, then as far as possible *his* ends must become *my* ends too, if the idea of harmony with humanity as an end is to have any positive effect on me.

When Kant discusses the third and fourth examples, he again presupposes a purposiveness in nature. Every man, he assumes, naturally wills his own improvement and his own happiness; and nature intends each of us to develop our rational natures. Life on a South Sea Island would not, strictly speaking, harm my own rational nature. But it surely does nothing to improve it. Since my own rational nature naturally seeks its own improvement, then in neglecting to improve I am prostituting my rational nature to satisfy my desires for comfort and pleasure. By not improving myself, I act contrary to my duty to further the goal of rational nature.

To what extent can the goals of others become my own? Must I seek the improvement of another's rational nature as my duty in the same way that I am duty bound to seek my own improvement? No, says Kant. My duty to others is to promote their happiness. In Part II of the *Metaphysics of Morals* he distinguishes between the ends of nature and a natural end. A natural end is one which all men as human beings actually seek: happiness. But the end of nature for man is that which all men *ought* to seek: namely, the improvement of their own rational natures.[11] Our duty to others is to further their natural end, happiness, since each individual himself must be held responsible for improving his own rational nature. Hence Kant's dictum: "Seek the perfection of self and the happiness of others." But there is an obvious limitation to our duty to seek the happiness of others: we must not seek their happiness to such an extent that we fail to improve our own rational natures, nor to such an extent that we prevent others from seeking their own perfection. We cannot, for instance, ply a friend with gin to the point of drunkenness with the excuse that we are fulfilling our duty to make him happy. "Happy" he may well be, but he is in no condition to improve himself.

This principle—that humanity and generally every rational nature is an end in itself—is the supreme restriction on a man's activity. Being a universal principle, applying to all rational beings, it cannot be grounded in experience, since experience cannot inform us about every possible rational being. Furthermore, the principle does not propose humanity as a subjective end which men actually determine for themselves, but rather as an objective end, one which serves as the supreme limiting condition for all subjective ends whatsoever. The principle must then be derived from pure reason.   431

We have already noted that the idea of man as a being having intrinsic worth cannot rest on each man's conception of his own worth. Rather it rests upon the *necessity* which attends each man's conception, and such a necessity can rest only on reason. (This will be discussed in Section III.)

Rational nature is the supreme limiting condition on our freedom of action. Evidently Kant intends something similar to St. Augustine's famous precept: "Love God, and do what you will." In Kant's language, "Treat humanity always as an end, and do what you will." Kant does not intend the principles to spell out what life a man should lead; they command a man to lead his life whatever the particulars *in a moral manner*. And since morality is the control of inclination by a rational will obedient to universal law, it is surely immoral to relegate any rational will to the status of a mere means for the satisfaction of inclination.

The second variation of the categorical imperative does not forbid us to treat others as means; it forbids our treating others as *mere* means. Every time I trade at a store or deal with anyone for some personal advantage, I treat the person as a means to my advantage. The principle says: Never treat a person merely as a thing, but always treat him as a person.

4. *The Third Variation: The Autonomous Will in a Possible Kingdom of Ends*

This variation incorporates two concepts: *the autonomy of the will* and *the kingdom of ends.* Kant first develops the idea of the will as self-legislating (autonomous), and from this he constructs the concept of a kingdom of ends. He believes that each of these ideas can be related to one of the variations already presented. Given that the will elevates its maxims to the status of a universal law (first variation), it follows that the will is self-legislating; given that each rational nature is an end in itself (second variation), it follows that all rational wills together constitute a "kingdom of ends."

4a. *The Will as Self-Legislating*

According to the first variation of the categorical imperative, the objective basis for all practical lawmaking lies in the rule and its form, universality, which lets us conceive the rule as a law, even a law of Nature. The purpose of an action provides a subjective basis only. The second variation shows us that any rational nature which seeks an end is an end in itself. From these two variations we can deduce a third practical law for the will, a principle which is the ultimate foundation for harmonizing the will with universal practical reason. This principle is grounded in the idea that *every rational being has a will which makes universal law.*

From the standpoint of the will in its relation to the law, the basis for respect is the unconditional universality of the law. Because the moral law is a universal law, binding all rational wills, the will is constrained to obey. But from the standpoint of the will as the origin of its own choices, the will must recognize itself as an inherently valuable end in itself. Because every rational nature has inherent value, one's own will is an end in itself and must never be treated as a mere means.

Kant now combines the two ideas, that of a rational being and that of a will which makes universal law. The latter idea, that of a will making universal law, forms the first part of the third variation of the categorical imperative: *Always act as a being which makes universal law.*

According to this principle, we must reject any maxim which does not conform to the universal lawmaking of the will. Thus *the will is subject to the law in so far as it makes law for itself.* This is the only way it can be both subject and author of the law.

When I obey a command because it is given me by some particular person, then I do not obey the command itself, but rather the person who commands me. My motive may be self-interest or respect for authority, but it is not respect for law as such.[12] When a soldier obeys his commander from fear of being confined to the guardhouse, his motive is prudence. However, whenever I obey a command because it is the law, then *I must impose this command upon myself.* The *moral* necessity of obligation, expressed by the moral "ought," is grounded in *my own* reason, not in someone else's authority. One soldier may obey his commander because he considers it his moral duty to do so, while another may obey from fear of the consequences of disobedience. The first acts morally, because, although the command itself arose from another's authority, the soldier makes the command into a moral law binding on himself. The second soldier does his duty, but from prudence, since the incentive is not respect for law but respect for the commander's authority —perhaps fear would be more accurate in some cases. All actions done from duty are done from respect for a law given by a self-legislating will.

The first two variations of the categorical imperative—the first commanding us to conform our actions to the idea of a natural order or law, the second commanding us to treat every rational being as an end in himself—excluded from their sovereignty every element of motive based on desire. In no other way could they be categorical. But we only *assumed* that these principles are categorical imperatives in order to explain the idea of Duty. Our purpose in this section does not allow our offering an independent proof.

What could be done at this point, however, would be to show that the distinguishing mark of the categorical   432
imperative, as opposed to a hypothetical imperative, is a
will which acts from duty while renouncing all self-interest. And we have this mark shown in the third variation, in *the idea of the will of a rational being as making universal law.*

A will may be subject to a law from self-interest. But if the will makes universal law, we must conclude that it is free of any self-interest. For otherwise the will would require yet another law which commanded that the maxim of acting from self-interest conform to the idea of universal law.

The principle that every human will can make universal law

from its maxims* is a good basis for a categorical imperative, assuming we can prove it. Grounded as it is on the idea of making universal law, it excludes any basis of self-interest; and so of all possible imperatives this one only can be unconditional. Or better yet, let us turn it around: a categorical imperative, as a law for the will of every rational being, must command us to ACT ALWAYS ON A MAXIM BY WHICH THE WILL CONSIDERS ITSELF AS MAKING UNIVERSAL LAW. Only in this way can the practical principle and the imperative be unconditional, since the will which obeys them cannot find its motive in self-interest.

* I need not provide examples to illustrate this principle; those we have already used for the first two variations will serve here quite well.

Another way of expressing this part of the third variation is to say that an agent must never act in a manner in which interest would conflict with self-legislation. This does not forbid our acting from self-interest; such would be an intolerable rule and quite impossible to follow. But if an agent can act from duty at all, he can do so only as a rational being *who rules himself*. When he acts from duty *in opposition* to interest, he obviously recognizes the validity of the imperative on grounds other than self-interest. When his self-interest and his duty *coincide*, the question of conflict or ground does not arise. Yet even here the morality of the action must be judged by the moral imperative, not by self-interest. But when an action done from self-interest cannot also be done from self-legislation, then it violates the imperative of morality. Hence we can set up as a standard for moral judgment: *Always act as a self-legislating agent.*

Let us take Kant's footnote suggestions and see how this variation can be applied in the four situations. First we shall briefly discuss the first and third examples from the viewpoint of the self-legislating will. (Since the second and fourth examples involve our duties to other rational beings in a community of ends, they more properly apply to the second part of the variation and we shall examine them when we discuss the kingdom of ends.)

1. *Perfect duty to self.* A person contemplating suicide cannot consistently will to take his own life and at the same time act as a universal lawgiver, since in killing himself he is destroying the very source of the law. It is a moot law which by its very promulgation nullifies itself.

3. *Imperfect duty to self.* One who intends to live a life of ease on a South Sea island does not destroy the source of the law, true, but he cannot will that such a life be commanded by universal law. For by refusing to improve the talents of his rational nature he is legislating that the lawgiver limit his own ability to make law, namely, by remaining rationally undeveloped. Man's natural maxim to develop his intellectual capacities, evidenced by his natural curiosity, would thereby be opposed by the "naturalized" maxim that he remain ignorant, and this generates a volitional inconsistency. (Note that the question of limiting one's ability to make law is independent of how many laws a lawgiver actually makes. No lawgiver makes every law that could possibly be made.)

It is no wonder, then, that all previous attempts to find the principle of morality have failed. Moral philosophers recognized that man was bound to law by duty; but they failed to see that he is bound only to a universal law which is self-made and that he must conform only to a will which, while it is his own will, yet is designed by Nature to make universal law. So long as they saw man simply as subject to a law, whatever it might be, they insisted that this necessarily required some principle of self-interest as the spring or impulse to obedience. Not understanding that the will was the source of its own law, they concluded that something else had to constrain   433 the will to act in this or that way.

By following the path of such logic, they wasted all their efforts in finding an ultimate foundation for duty. Rather, they found only the (subjective) necessity of acting from self-interest, whether for oneself or another. But the resulting imperatives were at best conditional, incapable of being true moral commands.

I will call this moral principle the principle of the AUTONOMY OF THE WILL; all other principles which oppose it I will classify under *Heteronomy*.

By "heteronomy" Kant means a will acting through self-interest, willing nonautonomously.[13] No heteronomous principle can serve as a moral command but only as a general rule of prudence, expressed in a hypothetical imperative. Failure to understand that self-legislation (autonomy) is the foundation of morality has misled all previous attempts to discover the ultimate principle of morality. The above paragraph foreshadows the last part of Section II (Chapter 8) in which Kant discusses the "spurious" attempts to discover the ultimate principle in a heteronomous will.

4b. *The Autonomous Will in a Kingdom of Ends*

The idea that every rational being must consider himself as making universal laws by his maxims and must judge himself and his actions by this standard, provides us with another and very fruitful idea, namely, that of a KINGDOM OF ENDS.

By "kingdom"[14] I mean the orderly community of different rational beings under a common law. By law the universal validity of an end is determined, so if we abstract from the personal differences between rational beings, as well as their personal goals, we can conceive the totality of remaining ends as forming an orderly system: each rational being as an end in himself and as capable of proposing personal goals for himself. In this way, from the previous principles, we can derive the idea of a kingdom of ends.

Every rational being is subject to the same law which commands that he treat himself and all others as ends in themselves, not merely as means. This establishes an orderly system of rational beings under a common law—in short, a kingdom. And since this law defines how each rational being relates to every other as end and means, we can call such system a *kingdom of ends* (which is, of course, only an Ideal).

Kant thus introduces the idea of a kingdom of ends. This idea combines two familiar concepts: that of the autonomous will and that of each will as an end in itself. The principle here advocated is the ideal harmonization of all autonomous wills in a systematic, harmonious community. This ideal kingdom of ends has two distinctive features: (a) every member is himself the lawmaker by willing his own law; (b) every member has duties to every other member. But how can there be a kingdom in which every member makes laws for every other member? This would produce chaos, unless *every* member legislates *the same law,* for himself and others. And if, as Kant believes, every perfectly moral rational nature would will the same maxim in a given situation, then in the *ideal* community of ends, every member would legislate the same moral law. Though each in fact would command himself, the law would be the same for every person. Hence we have the complete third variation of the categorical imperative: *Always act as a self-legislating (autonomous) member of a kingdom of ends.* That is, always act according to a maxim which a rational being, living in a community of rational beings, would will autonomously for the benefit of every member in the community.

The positive command is that we act in such a way that all ends (both subjective and objective) are *harmonized.* Forbidden by this imperative is any action which would tend to prevent one's own perfection or another's happiness. From this point of view the relation of the third variation to the second is quite clear (see above, p. 161). Since *everyone* has duties to himself and to others, it is the duty of everyone to harmonize the performance of these mutually related duties.

A rational being belongs to the kingdom of ends as a member by making universal law for it, and at the same time being subject to its law. He is its sovereign when he makes the law without being under the influence of any other will. As a rational being he may think of himself as either a member or a ruler in this kingdom of ends (which has its basis in free will); but either way he must consider himself as making the law. He could not, however, think of himself as ruler simply because of the maxims of his will, but only if he sees himself as a completely independent being, without needs and possessing the absolute power corresponding to his will.

To speak of a sovereign in this kingdom of apparently equal and autonomous ends seems contradictory. In Part I of the *Metaphysics of Morals*,[15] Kant describes a sovereign as having many rights but no duties toward his subjects. The sovereign makes the law but is not subject to the law. In the *Critique of Practical Reason*,[16] he postulates faith in God, the stabilizing "sovereign" of the human kingdom of ends. Neither of these concepts, however, seems to fit here, where Kant says explicitly that every rational being may think of himself as both a member *and* as sovereign of the kingdom of ends. And while a human being must consider himself as a rational being, he would presume somewhat to think of himself as God, the Holy Will. Furthermore, a rational being must consider himself subject to the law, while the Supreme Lawgiver is not subject to it.

The only reasonable interpretation[17] of this bipolarity is that Kant is using the concept of the sovereign to emphasize the kind of laws that the "true" sovereign makes. Notice the characteristics of the sovereign: he is completely independent, he has no desires, and possesses absolute power. And *as sovereign* his sole function is the welfare of the state or commonwealth, both as a community and as a totality of individuals making up the community. In so far as he is sovereign he makes laws not to his own interest (for he has none) but solely for the good of the community. And this good can be defined as the harmonization of the goals of all rational beings composing the community.

Thus when a rational being, as a member and sovereign of the kingdom of ends, makes laws which bind all the members, including himself, these laws must have as their sole objective the welfare of all the members as rational beings. That is, the laws must treat all members of the kingdom of ends as ends in themselves and also seek to harmonize as far as possible the personal goals of all the members. This concept, then, serves as the guiding principle for making moral judgments. We might paraphrase the third variation of the categorical imperative in the following way: *Always act as the absolute and autonomous sovereign of a community of rational beings,* making laws in a completely disinterested manner, laws which will harmonize the goals of all the members, including your own. Any maxim which seeks personal advantage to the harm of the community is immoral; any maxim which is influenced solely by one's own desires or the will of others fails the test of being universal law. In brief, the principle commands us to act *as if* we were God, with supreme power to make laws that have as their object the welfare, happiness, and perfection of all rational beings, and yet to keep in mind that these laws apply to ourselves no less than to any other.

The second and fourth examples, postponed above, can now illustrate the application of the second part of the third variation.

2. *Perfect duty to others.* Anyone who accepts a promise from me assumes that the promise will be kept, and he may make his plans accordingly. Anyone who lends me money will have some future use for the money he expects me to repay. However, when I propose the maxim that when in need I will make a false promise, I propose a situation in which the legitimate expectations and plans of my creditor will be thwarted. Such a maxim impedes the harmonious realization of goals and purposes and so contradicts the law that my maxim should promote such a harmony. Thus my maxim is immoral.

4. *Imperfect duty to others.* As an autonomous and thus sovereign member of a kingdom of ends, I cannot put my own interests above the general welfare of the community. A situation, in which by my aid others can more effectively and harmoniously achieve their personal and rational purposes, puts me under obligation, as sovereign, to give such aid. But if my maxim permits me to refuse aid to others, then the maxim contradicts my natural maxim as sovereign; it allows me to act for my own interest, rather than the welfare of the community. When I, as sovereign, will my own purposes to the detriment of the community, I generate a volitional inconsistency. My maxim, therefore, is immoral.

The rational will is an end in itself because it is self-legistative, regarding itself as making universal law by its maxim. It acts morally when it acts out of respect for its own legislation, not from self-interest. But since all rational beings are equally self-legislative, their interrelating self-legislation forms a community based on a common law, which ideally tends toward the complete harmonization of all ends.

5. *Autonomy as the Basis of Human Dignity*

Traditional and historical conceptions of the sovereign have carried with them the flavor (and often the assertion) of the superiority of the sovereign. But Kant, while he insists that each rational member of a kingdom of ends is an autonomous sovereign, nevertheless emphasizes the equal value of all members in this ideal kingdom. There must be something about each member, then, which forbids our elevating any one man—whether oneself or any other—to a superior status. This characteristic is what Kant refers to as the incomparable *dignity* of rational nature.

What then is morality? Nothing but the relation between an action and that law which establishes a kingdom of ends. This

law, however, is grounded in the will of every rational being, and by it he commands himself always to act by a maxim which he would will to be a universal law. In other words, *the will can conceive of itself as making universal law through its maxim.* When a maxim does not already conform to this objective standard—that the rational will make universal law— the necessity of conforming one's maxim to this standard becomes a *moral* necessity, a *duty.*[18]

The practical necessity, or duty, of acting on this principle cannot rest on feelings, impulses, or desires. It must rest solely on the relation of one rational being to another, a relation wherein each rational will is taken to be a maker of universal law. Only in this way can the rational will be regarded as an end in itself. Reason, then, relates every maxim of the will, in so far as the will makes universal law thereby, to every other rational will; it even relates the maxim to the action of others which are directed at itself. It does so, not from any personal motive or desire for advantage, but from the idea of *the dignity of a rational being* as one who obeys no law except the law he himself makes.

In a kingdom of ends, everything has either a *price* or a *dignity.* Anything having a price can be replaced by something else with an equivalent value. But if its value is priceless, having no equivalent, we say it has a dignity. Those things which relate to general human desires or needs have a *market price.* On the other hand, things which we value not from need but from taste, for the immediate purposeless enjoyment we derive from them, are said to have an *aesthetic price.* But that which is the fundamental condition for all value must be an end in itself; its value is not relative, but inherent. Such is its dignity.

435

Everything for which we act has a value. This is obvious: were an object valueless, we would ignore it. So every end, by the very fact that it is an end, has some value or other. Ends may have a purely subjective value (e.g., "I just *like* it, that's all"), or an objective value (e.g., "This will relieve my headache"). If the valued object is such that something else will serve just as well, we say this end or object has a *price*. We value money, and we value ice cream; we exchange one for the other. The price of the money and the price of the ice cream are given a value-equivalence.

If the price can be stated in some financial equivalent (the most common price system of a society), then the object has a *market price*. But some values have no monetary equivalent, and among these we find aesthetic pleasures. We cannot say that the experience of hearing *Das Rheingold* is worth ten dollars. Everyone attending the opera may have paid that sum for a seat, but it does not follow that any person's enjoyment can be valued at ten dollars. Yet aesthetic experiences are equivalent to other experiences. For instance, I could perhaps enjoy *The King and I* just as much as *West Side Story* and more than *Das Rheingold*. This kind of value Kant calls an *aesthetic price*, a price of taste.[19]

That which has no equivalent in value we say is priceless. An end in itself, having an intrinsic objective value, is above price: it has a *dignity*. Moreover, one thing may have dignity because it is a thing of unqualified value (the moral will), while another may have dignity because it is the condition or foundation for that unqualified value (rational nature).

Now morality is the sole condition under which a rational being can be an end in itself, since only by conforming to moral law can a rational being be a lawmaking member of a kingdom of ends. Consequently, only morality and humanity—in that a human being is able to be moral—have dignity. Skill and hard work have a market price; wit, lively imagination and humor have an aesthetic price. But keeping one's promises and helping others, from principle rather than from inclination, have inherent value. Nothing in Nature or in art can take their place, for

their value does not consist in any effects they may produce nor in any resulting advantages or benefits, but only in the way reason conceives of them. That is, by the maxims of the will, these virtues exhibit themselves in actions even when there seems to be no chance of success.

Such virtuous actions do not depend on subjective attitudes or tastes in order to secure our immediate favor and approval; they require no intuitive feeling of satisfaction. These actions show the will which performs them to be worthy of immediate respect, and reason requires no further inducement in order to impose such duties on the will—in fact, using other inducements to impose a duty would be a contradiction. We thus evaluate reason's moral disposition as having dignity, a value infinitely beyond price. Nothing whatsoever can be held up to compare with it without violating its sanctity.

How can we justify such a lofty claim about the moral disposition or virtuous activity? By showing that it gives the rational being a sharing role in making universal law. His own nature as an end in himself makes him worthy for membership in a possible kingdom of ends. As an end in himself he makes universal law in a kingdom of ends, free of Nature's law, obeying only the law he himself makes by his maxim,   436 law to which he is himself subject. Nothing has value except by law. So the maker of this value-determining law must have a dignity, an unconditional and priceless value. Only the word "respect" conveys the esteem a rational being must have for the law and the lawmaker. *Autonomy is therefore the foundation of the dignity of human nature and of every rational nature.*

Such inestimable value is based on autonomy. Precisely because man is self-legislating, he is an end in himself. In making his own law, he is making law which is universally binding for every rational nature. Herein lies the essence of dignity. For whatever determines the value of everything else must itself be above value. Persons must be of greater value than any end they create by their interest. But the value of moral action is incomparably greater than anything in nature or art; only the good will, the source of the moral choice, has unqualified value. The autonomous lawmaking by the rational will is the basis for the incomparable value of a moral action. Hence, the autonomy of the rational will is the basis of man's incomparable dignity. *In the concept of autonomy,* we may conclude, *we find the ultimate foundation of all morality.*

6. *Summary*

Kant himself summarizes his discussion by relating the three variations to form a systematic triad of principles. He states explicitly that the three variations are only variations of the same law and that the difference is basically the point of view.

These three ways of expressing the principle of morality are basically variations of the very same law, and each one incorporates the other two. While there is indeed a difference between them, the difference is a matter of subjective emphasis rather than objective duty. The point was to relate more closely an Idea of Reason to direct perception, and by such an analogy bring this Idea closer to our feelings.

In the beginning of Chapter 3 we saw that every action involves three elements: the motive, the result, and the will. Correspondingly, the maxim of a moral action involves all three factors, and each of them emphasized by a variation of the categorical imperative.

All maxims have:
1. *A Form, which is the universality of the maxim.* Accordingly, the first variation of the moral imperative states: "Choose only that maxim which could hold as a universal law of Nature."
2. *A Matter, that is, an end.* The second variation, insisting

that a rational being by its very nature is an end in itself, states: "In every maxim rational nature must be the absolute standard which limits all merely relative and arbitrary ends."

3. *An Ultimate Source, in autonomy.* Thus the third variation: "All maxims, since they arise from autonomous lawmaking, must harmonize with a possible kingdom of ends, just as with a system of Nature."*

* From a teleological point of view, Nature is a system of ends. This theoretical ideal of a system of ends helps to explain why things happen the way they do. So morality can view the possible kingdom of ends as a system of Nature. As such it becomes a practical ideal for producing what is not yet actual, but which may become so if we act in accordance with this ideal.

We saw in Chapter 6 that the form of every moral maxim is its universality; the first variation is thus an analogy with the universal laws of nature. Furthermore, every action must aim at some desired objective; so the second variation insists that, whatever the value of one's personal goal, humanity has an intrinsic value which cannot be subverted to subjective values. To humanity all other goals must give first place. The third variation combines the "form-imperative" and the "matter-imperative." The first part of the third variation is derived from the universality of the form: that the self-legislation of the will constitutes its maxim as a universal law. The second part follows from the conception of the intrinsic value of human rational nature: that every rational nature is an end in itself, and that all actions ought to harmonize towards the accomplishment of all human purposes, both natural and moral.

At this point Kant introduces a second analogy, comparing the kingdom of ends to a system of Nature. He is careful to state that the moral kingdom of ends is *possible;* it is not, in theory, a nonsensical notion. It may indeed be an Ideal which we recognize will never actually come into being; yet it functions as do all Ideals, holding out a promise of a society in which all personal goals harmonize as completely as do natural purposes—

an ideal society which is never impossible, yet always just ahead of any particular resting place, urging us ever onward with the enticement of perpetual peace and a millenium of human paradise.

Here is a progression (similar to that of the *a priori* categories of speculative reason) from the *unity* of the form of willing (universality), through the *plurality* of the content (the objectives or ends), to the *totality* or complete system of the ends. However, when we are forming a moral judgment, we will do better to apply the strict formulation, that is, *the general formulation* of the categorical imperative: ALWAYS ACT ON THAT MAXIM WHICH CAN AT THE SAME TIME BE MADE   437 A UNIVERSAL LAW. Still, if we want to make the moral law acceptable, it will help to apply the above three variations to a single action. In this way we can relate the general formulation to our more natural moral perspectives.

If one wants the best method of moral evaluation, he should use the general formulation: universalizing one's maxim. It is the essence of the moral law *as law.* But Kant recognizes that this method can be too rigorous and unappealing to the average person. Thus in order "to gain a hearing for the moral law," he has presented the three variations of the general formulation. They are closer to the ways the average man thinks in moral situations. When we consider some of our customary standards of moral evaluation (e.g., "You ought to act according to your true self," "You ought to treat everyone as a human being," "You ought to try to make others happy"), we see how Kant views these variations.[20] He believes that the employment of any formulation of the categorical imperative will produce the same moral judgment. Hence the particular formulation is relatively unimportant from the aspect of reaching the correct moral decision. The three variations, as derivations from the general formulation, have practical use in moral decision, but no one of them states completely the essence of the moral law, though they all necessarily presuppose it—that is, the law of autonomy.

This "Metaphysics of Morals" contains many problems, some of which we have discussed, others of which we have ignored. For example, to what degree must Kant rely on the purposiveness of nature? Do his particular examples illustrate his point satisfactorily? Would three persons, each applying a different variation of the general formulation, necessarily arrive at the same conclusion as to his duty? We must leave these matters to higher criticism. But there are two corollary matters that require brief notice as a kind of afterview.

First, Kant does *not* give us an infallible method of discovering precisely what we *ought to do,* though he does provide a method for deciding what we ought *not* to do. The categorical imperative with its variations is not a guide to particular duties; it is a standard by which we judge whether or not what we propose to do is moral. The moral law commands us to *keep* our promises already made; it does not tell us when to make promises. The moral law then has a strictly *negative* function; but when I am faced with a positive action (e.g., "How should I promote the happiness of my children?"), the categorical imperative alone cannot provide the answer. I must judge which of the alternatives open to me can effect what I propose, and then which of these effective alternatives would fulfill the formal requirements of morality.

Secondly, how important is this "ethical interlude" to Kant's basic argument? Not very. True, he introduces the concept of autonomy here, but he takes it up later, and more emphatically. We can take Kant at his word that this part was included to "make the moral law more acceptable." It adds nothing essential to his main argument and it might even be an obstacle, since it may mislead us into taking the primary purpose of the *Foundation* to be the discovery of our particular ethical duties, rather than finding the supreme principle of morality. Even so, we would be philosophically poorer without this section, the most familiar passage of all Kant's writings; it is the most frequently quoted, the easiest to read, and the longest remembered. Without trying to diminish its genuine worth to moral philosophy, I have tried to present it in its proper perspective, namely, as an important but nonessential discussion of great interest and practical value. To paraphrase Kant's language, we could say that this part has its own inherent value, but not as a part of the *a priori* quest for the ultimate foundation and supreme principle of morality.

CHAPTER EIGHT

PART 4—Autonomy and Heteronomy

1. *Kant's Summary*

In this part of Section II, Kant summarizes his argument, showing in particular that each of the three variations of the categorical imperative is a *variation,* not an amending, of the general formulation.[1] This summary serves both as a review of the "ethical interlude," and also as a transition from the idea of the categorical imperative to that of autonomy. As such, little commentary will be required.

A. *The General Formulation*

We end where we began, with the idea of an unconditionally good will. The absolutely good will is incapable of doing evil; its maxims, when made into universal law, are never contradictory. So the supreme principle or law is this: ALWAYS ACT ON A MAXIM WHICH YOU CAN AT THE SAME TIME WILL TO BE A UNIVERSAL LAW. This rule alone guarantees consistency in the will and so is a categorical imperative, the supreme law for the absolutely good will.

B. *The First Variation: The Law of Nature*

In view of the analogy between the validity of the will (as

the law for possible actions) and Nature in its formal aspect (as the existence of all things in a unified system governed by universal laws), we can state the categorical imperative as follows: ALWAYS ACT ACCORDING TO A MAXIM WHICH YOU CAN AT THE SAME TIME CONSIDER TO BE A UNIVERSAL LAW OF NATURE.

C. *The Second Variation*: *Humanity as an End*

Rational nature's distinguishing characteristic is that it acts for an end. An end is the content of every act of will. The idea of the absolutely good will excludes any particular end which must be brought into being. As a thing good without qualification, the good will cannot be tied to any particular goal, for to do so would give the will only a relative value. The end proper to a good will cannot be *brought into* existence but must be *self-existent*. Such an idea can be expressed only negatively:[2] we must never act against this end, but in every act of will treat it not merely as a means but also as an end, as the originator of all conceivable ends, the possessor of a possible absolutely good will. Only by conceiving the unconditional end to be the absolutely good will itself do we avoid the contradiction of subordinating the good will to some other entity. The law can be stated in two ways: ALWAYS ACT ACCORDING TO A MAXIM WHICH HOLDS EVERY RATIONAL NATURE (WHETHER YOURSELF OR ANOTHER) AS AN END IN ITSELF; OR, ALWAYS ACT ACCORDING TO A MAXIM WHICH IS UNIVERSALLY VALID FOR 438 EVERY RATIONAL BEING.

To say that in using means to any end I must regulate my maxim so that it will be universally valid law for every agent is the same as saying that rational nature, as the originator[3] of ends, must be respected as the source of all maxims and never taken merely as a means. As such, rational nature must be treated as the ultimate standard for using any means: it must always be treated as an end also.

Kant's approach here differs from his discussion in Chapter 7, but his meaning is clear enough. Instead of arguing that rational nature has inherent value, he would have us think of rational nature as the orginator of all maxims and not merely as their object. That is, since rational nature is always itself the legislator through its own maxims, it cannot be considered solely as the object of a maxim, i.e., merely a means for another's purposes. What is an agent by its nature cannot be considered a mere object of action.

In his statement of the second variation Kant includes the idea of universality, the sole characteristic of all law. A comparison of the original statement of the second variation (in Chapter 7, Section 3, with the two statements expressed above will indicate the shift in emphasis from the concept of *human* nature as an end in itself (as the source of a possibly good will) to *rational* nature as the origin of all practical law. The shift in emphasis carries us further toward the concept of autonomy.

D. *The Third Variation: The Autonomous Will in a Kingdom of Ends*

It follows without question that every rational being must be able to consider himself an end in himself; and with regard to any law to which he is subject he must be able to see himself as making universal law. For the way he makes universal law through his maxims shows him to be an end in himself. It further follows that his dignity (prerogative) compared to mere things means that he must make his maxims accord with his own nature and that of other rational beings as legislative beings, i.e., as persons. In this way the world of rational being *(mundus intelligibilis)* may be seen as a kingdom of ends, since each person, as a member, makes his own universal law. Thus: EVERY RATIONAL BEING MUST ACT AS IF BY HIS MAXIMS HE WERE ALWAYS A LAWMAKING MEMBER IN A KINGDOM OF ENDS.

The formal principle of these maxims is: ALWAYS ACT AS IF YOUR MAXIMS WERE ALSO THE UNIVERSAL LAW FOR ALL RATIONAL BEINGS.

Here, as in the second variation above and implicitly in the first, Kant rephrases the general formulation after giving the variation in order to show the close relationship between the general formulation and its variations. When we consider a maxim as universal law, we see its analogy with the universality of the laws of nature (first variation). When we consider a rational nature, one inherently an agent, universalizing its own maxims, we conceive every agent as an end unto himself (second variation). And from the idea of every person legislating his own moral law, in common with every other rational being, we arrive at the community of persons as ends in themselves (third variation).

E. *The Kingdom of Ends and the Kingdom of Nature*

Consider the analogy between the kingdom of ends and the system of Nature. The former is based on maxims, or self-imposed policies, while the latter is organized by laws which describe causes from outside. By analogy, however, we can call the natural system a "kingdom" of Nature, in so far as Nature appears to be ordered toward rational beings as her end—even though Nature seems to work like a machine. If the maxims which the categorical imperative ordains as law for all rational beings were universally obeyed (as laws of Nature are), then the kingdom of ends would be a fact.

But even when a rational being conscientiously follows a maxim, he cannot reasonably expect all other rational beings to accept it. Neither can he expect that the orderly purpose of a kingdom of Nature will harmonize with his own efforts as a member of the kingdom of ends (which he himself creates) to promote his own happiness.[4] But the law still binds categorically: ALWAYS ACT ACCORDING TO THE MAXIMS OF 439 A UNIVERSAL LAWMAKING MEMBER IN A POSSIBLE KINGDOM OF ENDS.

Kant presents the kingdom of ends as analogous to a system of nature. If the universe were composed solely of rational beings, the kingdom of nature and morality would coincide. But men do not always act purely from reason and the universe is not a moral realm. The principle difference, which is obvious, is that the laws of nature are always obeyed, so to speak, while the laws of men and morality are often violated. The utopian felicity of a true kingdom of ends would come about if all men in every action obeyed the moral law, and if nature also harmonized with its purposes.

Herein lies a paradox, that respect for a mere idea—the idea of the dignity of man's rational nature, excluding any advantages or goals to be achieved—can serve as an inflexible command to the will. In fact, this very independence of a maxim from all influences of self-interest constitutes the sublimity of the maxim and makes the rational agent worthy of membership in the kingdom of ends. If this were not so, man would simply be subject to the natural law of his own desires. Even if the kingdom of Nature and the kingdom of ends were joined into one system so that the kingdom of ends were no longer a mere Ideal but an actuality, this kingdom would surely become a strong impetus to choice, but it would gain no greater inherent value. The sole absolute lawgiver [God] would still have to judge a rational being's worth on the basis of his ability to command himself to perform disinterested actions solely in view of the dignity of rational nature in man. Things do not lose their nature simply by changing their external relations; a man must be judged by his rational nature, not by how he may be related to other things, including the one who judges him—even though his judge be the Supreme Being.

The point of Kant's paradox is subtle, and in fact he is making two points. First, it is our daily experience that much of what we intend to accomplish does not happen for one reason or another, even when we try to do our duty. Even were the universe so fortuitous that all our moral intentions turned out successfully, our purposes would still not give our action moral value. Even though the good to be accomplished would have a strong influence on our choices, moral worth would still be based on the moral maxim to act as a self-legislating rational being. What is more (Kant's second point), the Supreme Being who judges us all will determine the value of our lives—our worthiness to be happy—according to how we sought to achieve a good will, not by how much good we accomplished in our actions. For the actual success of our moral intentions is accidental to the moral value of the will from which such intentions spring. The paradox lies in the moral principle that while our motive must be always to perform our duties, the actual performance of our duties is less important than our motive, at least in the matter of a man's moral worth as a rational being.

F. *General Conclusion: the Definition of Morality*

Morality can thus be defined as the relation of actions to the autonomy of the will, that is, to a will which by its maxims can make universal law. **Whatever agrees with autonomy of the will is *permitted;* what conflicts with it is *forbidden.* A *holy will* is one whose maxims necessarily agree with the autonomous law; such a will is absolutely good. But a will less than absolutely good is subject to autonomous law (i.e., moral necessity) by what we call obligation. A holy will, consequently, cannot have any duties, since duty is the relationship between a will which is not absolutely compelled to obey the law and the objectively necessary action which is its duty.**

We have finally arrived at the definition of morality. Necessity for any action must be grounded in reason; for moral reason alone can legislate that universal law which imposes practical necessity. Autonomy is the only condition by which reason determines its own universal law, which law in turn makes an action objectively necessary, i.e., obligatory. Consequently, we may define morality as the relationship of the self-legislating will to an action perceived as objectively necessary through its own self-legislation.

In the above paragraph, Kant shows that the moral law as expressed by the categorical imperative does not prescribe specific positive duties. Any action is morally permissible which is consistent with an autonomous will, that is, which is not in conflict with it. Thus I may indeed eat ice cream, dance, cheer at a football game, and ride a bicycle—unless any of these actions conflicts with some duty.

In view of all this, we can easily see how we think of duty as a subjection to law and still ascribe a kind of 440 **sublimity and dignity to the person who fulfills all his duties. His sublimity does not come from his being subject to the law, but from his being the law *maker*, who at the same time *subjects himself* to the law. We have seen also that neither fear of nor attraction to the law can give an action any moral value— only respect for the law can give that. Our own will, conceived ideally as acting under no other condition but making universal law by its maxims, is the proper object of respect. Thus, *the dignity of a human being consists simply in his ability to make universal law to which he is also subject.***

We do not find our dignity simply in being subject to the law, but *in being subject through our own legislation*. Kant here restates the essential conditions for the dignity of a human being. The rational human being has dignity because he is autonomous. The autonomous will, however, has two characteristics: it is the lawmaker and at the same time it is subject to self-legislation. The moral law is self-imposed but it binds under moral necessity nevertheless. Indeed, only a self-imposed necessity could qualify as moral obligation.

2. *Autonomy and Heteronomy*

AUTONOMY OF THE WILL IS
THE SUPREME PRINCIPLE OF MORALITY

Autonomy of the will is that which makes the will a law to itself, without regard for any objects of desire. Thus the principle of autonomy: ALWAYS CHOOSE ACCORDING TO MAXIMS WHICH YOU CAN THINK OF AS BECOMING UNIVERSAL LAWS BY YOUR

CHOICE. This practical rule is an imperative: the will of every rational being is necessarily subject to it. But we cannot prove this by a simple analysis of the concepts found in the rule, for the rule is a synthetic proposition. Proof would require that we go beyond knowledge of objects of choice to a critical investigation of the subject itself, pure practical reason; for if there be any synthetic proposition which commands us under necessity, we must be capable of knowing it purely *a priori*. Such a proof does not belong in this section. But we can show by a simple analysis of concepts that *the principle of autonomy is the sole principle of morality*. Such an analysis shows that the principle of morality must be a categorical imperative, and that such an imperative commands no more nor less than autonomy.

There is but one supreme principle, the autonomy of the rational will, but autonomy may be considered under two aspects:

1. From the viewpoint of the will *as subject to* its own law, the supreme principle is expressed as a categorical command of morality.

2. From the viewpoint of the will as *making its own law,* the supreme principle is expressed in the concept of autonomy. But in each expression, the supreme principle is grounded in the rational will, a will which makes its own law and which is subject to its own law.

Consequently we have two statements of the supreme principle, the first being the general formulation of the categorical imperative: *Act only on that maxim which you can at the same time will to become a universal law.* This emphasizes the universalizing of the maxim. The second statement of the supreme principle, given in the above paragraph, emphasizes the autonomy of the will: *Always choose according to maxims which you can think of as becoming universal laws by your choice.*

These two aspects also appear in the double meaning of "principle." In one sense, a principle is a *guiding rule,* a standard, such as we find in a "principle of logic." In this sense, the categorical imperative is seen to be the supreme guiding principle of morality, not in the sense of imposing particular duties, but as a standard for determining the moral status of particular maxims. In the second sense, a principle is a *foundation,* a *ground;* in this sense autonomy is the supreme principle or ultimate foundation of morality. Some moral philosophers stress the former sense, emphasizing ethical guidance. But Kant wanted primarily to establish the ultimate *foundation* of morality and so he emphasizes the latter sense.

Again Kant raises the question of the synthetic nature of the categorical imperative. By analyzing the concepts of will and law we cannot prove that the will is subject to the moral law, since subjection of will to law is not part of the meaning of will. But we *can* prove by such an analysis of concepts that the categorical imperative is the essence of moral law. Neither of these assertions is new. The first half of Section II (Chapters 5 and 6) is an analytical investigation showing that morality requires a categorical imperative. We know what this imperative must be if we assume that the will has the original capacity to act from duty. But analysis can take us only so far; we have not proved that the will has this capacity. Only by examining the will in itself (that is, by a critique of pure practical reason) can we determine that the will is subject to the law of duty and not merely to causal laws of inclination. Such an investigation must be made independently of experience: it must be purely *a priori.* The problem (not to be examined until Section III) still remains: to prove by a critical examination of practical reason that the will *is* subject to the law of duty, or, as Kant expresses the problem, to prove how a categorical imperative is possible.

HETERONOMY OF THE WILL IS THE SOURCE
OF ALL SPURIOUS PRINCIPLES OF MORALITY

Whenever the will seeks its law somewhere other than in the fitness of its maxims to be self-made universal law, that is, whenever the will seeks law in the objects of   441 choice rather than in the will itself, then the result will always be *heteronomy*. Whenever the will fails to give itself law, seeking instead the source of its rule in a desire for some objects or in some rational ideal, the derived imperative can only be hypothetical: "I ought to do this because I want that." But the moral (categorical) imperative says: "I ought to do this or that even though I want nothing from doing it." For instance, the hypothetical imperative might say, "If I want to keep my good name, I ought not to lie;" while the categorical imperative would say, "I ought not to lie, although I would never even be suspected of it."

The moral law, therefore, must completely ignore all objects so that they have no influence whatsoever on the will; in this way practical reason (the will) will not support some outside interest but rather will exhibit its ultimate authority as the supreme lawmaker. For example, I ought to seek the happiness of others, not because their becoming happy is any concern of mine (either from some desire or from some rational satisfaction), but simply because a maxim which conflicts with the happiness of others cannot at the same time be willed as a universal law.

Heteronomy is the opposite of autonomy, describing any principle which is not based on the autonomy of the will. Kant's position is unambiguous: whenever the will does not make its own law, then the will determines its actions from a heteronomous principle; if the will does not act from duty, then it must act from some inclination or self-interest; if the imperative directing an agent's action is not categorical, then clearly it must be hypothetical; and most importantly, unless the guiding principle of the will be self-imposed, it cannot produce a good will.

Kant overstates his case. It would be virtually impossible to ignore all objects to the extent that they have *no influence whatsoever* on the will. It is quite enough, even for Kant's own purpose, that the autonomous will allow no object to *exceed* (or even equal) the influence of the moral law. If objects had no influence at all, it would be impossible for me to perform my imperfect duties. How can I choose between giving a needy person bubble gum or a decent job if I am forbidden to evaluate the alternative results?

This particular passage, as well as others, leads some commentators to say that Kant would make it our duty to act from duty. But this is impossible, since it would lead to an infinite series of duties for each duty. I would have a $duty_1$ to keep my promise, and I would also have the $duty_2$ to keep my promise from $duty_1$. But since the second-order duty is no less than the duty to keep my promise, I would also have the $duty_3$ to keep-my-promise-from-$duty_1$ *from duty$_2$*. There would be no end to it. We can only conclude that we do not have any duty to act *from duty.* "Duty" refers to actions, not to motives.[5]

The matter in dispute concerns the necessary condition for moral credit. In order to receive moral credit for doing my duty, I must act without relying on inclinations of self-interest. I must perceive my action as my duty, as an act complying with universal law, and perform the action for this reason. Kant does suggest that we should try to act from duty, even if we do not have a duty to act from duty. It we reconsider his argument in Section I, that only the moral motive can guarantee moral credit, moral goodness demands that we strengthen the moral motive in every way possible. The more we act primarily from a sense of duty, the more likely we are to do our duty in situations which test the very core of moral fiber. On the other hand, the more we rely on inclination or self-interest to spur us to do our duty, the less likely we are to do our duty when self-interest conflicts with duty.

The will which rests on self-interest or desire is heteronomous. In fact, the will which rests on *any* ground but its own self-legislation is heteronomous. Such grounds Kant considers "spurious," invalid foundations for a genuine moral law. To climax his argument thus far, he now will examine four major attempts to base morality on a principle other than autonomy.

3. *Criticism of Invalid Moral Principles*

CATALOG OF ALL POSSIBLE PRINCIPLES OF
MORALITY DERIVED FROM HETERONOMY

Here, just as they do in all cases, philosophers who
have not made a critical examination of human reason   442
will try all possible wrong ways before they finally find
the one correct way. From this point of view, all principles are
either *empirical* or *rational.* Empirical principles are based on
the idea of happiness and are related either to a *physical sensation* or to a *moral feeling.* Rational principles are based on some
rule commanding perfection, being derived either from a *rational ideal* of perfection as a goal to seek or from the concept of
the Will of God as an independent, perfecting norm to guide
human choice.

Principles of morality must be grounded in either reason or
experience. The principles based on experience may be divided
into two subcategories:

    a. *Hedonistic,* based upon some kind of pleasure prin-
ciple; or,

    b. *Intuitive,* allegedly justified by a moral "sense."
Rational principles (other than autonomy) are either:

    c. *Idealistic,* derived from an abstract ideal of human
perfection; or,

    d. *Theological,* based upon some conception of God's will.
Kant's criticism of any empirical principle is easily anticipated:
none will justify the objective necessity of obligation—and
without obligation there is no true moral law. Rational principles
are empty and so have no practical value, even though from
them we may derive a conception of necessity.

3a. *The Search for Happiness: Hedonism*

Although Kant explicitly thinks of Epicurus as the typical
exponent of the hedonistic principle,[6] readers will probably

be more familiar with the modern equivalent, expressed in the utilitarian philosophy of John Stuart Mill (1806–1873). Mill is the best known of the moral philosophers who base morality on man's natural quest for pleasure and his search for a life of happiness. Mill defines happiness in the following statement: "Actions are right in proportion as they tend to promote happiness, wrong as they tend to produce the reverse of happiness. By 'happiness' is intended pleasure, and the absence of pain; by unhappiness, pain, and the privation of pleasure."[7] We determine the right action by calculating which alternative will produce the *"greatest happiness* (= pleasure) *for the greatest number."* Mill came to his conclusions because be believed some kind of pleasure principle to be the spring of all human activity. Kant strongly rejects the principle of hedonism.

I. *Empirical principles* **never provide the basis for moral law, for moral law must hold for all rational beings without distinction. But whenever man's** *human nature,*[8] **or the particular situation which affects human nature, is taken as the foundation for moral law, such a "law" lacks universality, and the unconditional practical necessity of law is missing. The worst of these empirical principles is that of personal happiness, not merely because it is false, but because:**

(a) experience belies the presumption that good conduct and happiness always go together;

(b) the happiness principle is no help to morality, since making a man happy and making him good are two quite different things, just as making him prudent and enlightened in his own self-interest is quite different from making him virtuous; but especially

(c) the happiness principle sets morality on a basis of self-interest, which undermines and destroys its sublimity; for such a basis eliminates any real distinction between virtue and vice —the only difference being how well we can calculate what is to our advantage.

Though Kant gives three arguments against the hedonistic principle, his primary objection is that we cannot conclude from the fact that all men *do* seek pleasure that they *ought* to seek it. Principles derived from experiences of human nature, even if universally true, cannot provide the unconditional necessity required by the moral law. For a moral law must command independently of inclination, desire, or self-interest; often, indeed, it commands us to act in direct opposition to the pleasure principle.

Kant, moreover, flatly denies that pleasure is the spring of all human action: it is just not true that every human action is done only to gain this or that pleasure.[9] But even if it were true, our common moral knowledge would lead us to reject hedonism as a basis for morality.

a. A person's happiness is often disproportionate to his moral character, particularly if happiness be defined as a state of well-being or pleasure.

b. We do not make a man good by making him happy; often just the opposite is the case, especially if happiness is equated with pleasure.

c. Pleasure is notoriously a bad motive to suggest as a moral standard, for it instills into a man a selfish outlook which is contrary to the moral attitude. Expediency is not morality nor is prudence always virtue; sometimes it is simply cautious greed.

3b. *The Moral Sense*

Although Kant mentions Francis Hutcheson (1694–1747) by name, the moral sense theory is popularly ascribed to David Hume (1711–1776), who believed the moral sense to be a kind of passional reaction to elements of a moral situation. Essentially, the moral sense theory is a kind of intuitionist ethics,[10] asserting that there is in human experience a special moral faculty analogous to the sense of sight. Hume[11] refers to it as a sentiment of approbation; Hutcheson specially calls it a moral sense.[12] For both, the moral feeling is an experience of the moral tone of a situation. A moral agent somehow "sees" or "feels" the moral character of an action. And just as with any organic sense, the moral sense can be trained to a high sensitivity, enabling a man to make acutely discriminating moral judgments. Nevertheless the moral sense judgments spring from experience, and are merely *a posteriori*.

Kant's basic opposition is the same: experience cannot be a foundation for necessity of any kind.

II. By contrast there is the *moral sense*, an alleged special feeling.* This is a theory without depth, appealing to thoughtless men who trust in their feelings, even in matters dealing with universal law. But feelings can differ almost infinitely from one person to another, and thus simply cannot furnish a uniform standard of good and evil. Furthermore, the theory ignores the fact that one man cannot validly judge others by his own feelings. Even so, the moral feeling is closer to morality and dignity, for it honors Virtue with direct and immediate satisfaction and esteem; unlike the happiness principle, it does not tell her to her face that her worth lies in her favors rather   443 than her beauty.

> * I classify the principle of moral feeling under the happiness principle because every empirical principle promises some benefit from agreeable results, either in an immediate satisfaction (e.g., pleasure), or in long-term gains (e.g., happiness). We must also, with Hutcheson, classify the principle of Sympathy (feeling for the happiness of others) under his assumed moral sense.

Feelings of whatever kind, says Kant, are subjective. Why should my feelings, or anyone's feelings for that matter, serve as the standard for moral judgment? The moral feeling *may* be a universal capacity in man, but experience shows that men's reactions to moral situations are frequently incompatible. Further, moral obligation, we know, must often hold counter to feeling. Nevertheless, Kant feels some affinity for this theory since it does emphasize the unique status of moral judgments and concepts and does not make morality a high-sounding name for expediency. Virtue is still admired for her own—albeit empirical —beauty.

3c. *The Ideal of Perfection*

Of the empirical principles of morality, one is based on self-interest while the other is not. The two rational principles are similarly paired. The concept of perfection is not grounded in self-interest, but the theological ideal is. Kant discusses the ideal of perfection first.

III. Among the rational principles, we first see the *ontological ideal of perfection*. But this concept is empty; as a standard for selecting from the limitless universe of possibilities that group of attributes which would be most appropriate for us, this concept is completely useless. Furthermore, when we try to use this ideal to distinguish what *is* from what *ought* to be, we usually end up arguing in circles by sneaking into the argument that very morality we are trying to explain.

The expression "ontological ideal of perfection" means roughly the idealized condition of a particular thing. The perfection of man, for instance, might be expressed as a man perfectly rational, perfectly moral, perfectly capable of all human operations. Plato espoused such a theory,[13] which holds up to our minds the concept of the Philosopher, the perfect man, whom we should imitate. But this ideal is vacuous. "Perfect" depends for its meaning on the kind of thing talked about, as well as on some conception of the ideal condition of such a thing. There are "perfect" apples, cars, wills, etc., but there is no meaningful content to the idea of perfection by itself. If I were to tell someone simply, "Be perfect," what practical rule could he derive from my command alone? If he has any positive conception of the characteristics of the perfect man, he did not get them from my bare mention of perfection. In some way he had to supply any concrete content from some other source of information. But if that is so, then the idea of perfection by itself is no help as a moral principle. We must still add moral content to it.

3d. *The Theological Principle: The Will of God*

Even though it is empty and thus useless, the concept of perfection is preferable to the concept of God's Will as the foundation of morality,[14] since the latter ideal is usually founded on personal concern for salvation, not on respect for moral law.

IV. Even so, the ideal of perfection is better than the *theological ideal*, which bases morality on the supremely perfect Divine Will. For we cannot know God's perfect Will directly, but must deduce it from other ideas, of which morality is the foremost. But if we do not deduce God's Will from other concepts (and this in itself would provide a most circular explanation), then the only idea we could have would be of a will which seeks glory for itself and dominion over others, a will characterized by awesome power and vengeance. Any ethical system based on this kind of will would contradict morality.

The nature of God's Will cannot be known. What is more, we have no *direct* insight into God's Will even as it is revealed in scripture. Kant does not reject the commands of God found in the Old and New Testaments; he simply rejects them as sources of moral law, since they cannot be known *a priori.* Even if God were to give me a direct command, the moral question still remains: ought I obey God's command? It is not self-evident that it is my duty to do what God commands, and thus the actuality of an expressed divine command still does not provide us with the *a priori* grounds for moral judgment. Whenever someone suggests that an action has been commanded by God, we pre-judge the command according to moral principles derived from some other source before we will agree with the original suggestion. For example, we would reject completely the suggestion that God commands us to sacrifice children as a form of worship.

Still, if I had to choose between the ideal of a moral sense and that of perfection in general, I would decide for the latter. While neither of these ideals undermines morality—though they are wholly invalid grounds for it—the ideal of perfection at least keeps the question of morality free from sensibility, bringing it to the control of pure reason. And while this does not solve the problem, it does preserve free from corruption the undefined idea of a will good in itself, until an answer to the question can be found.

I see no point in a drawn out refutation of the rest of the theories. Being such an easy task, doing so here would be superfluous. What is more, such a refutation presumably is well understood by those who must choose the official theory—persons in their charge simply would not put up with any hesitation in judgment.[15] But more important for us here is to recognize that all these principles propose nothing but heteronomy of the will as the ultimate foundation of morality. And so they necessarily fail to achieve their purpose.

Whenever we posit some object of desire as determining the rule which guides the will, we must judge the resultant rule to be heteronomy. Such an imperative is conditional: *"If* (or since) you want this object, you ought to do such and such," a rule which cannot be a moral (categorical) command. No matter how the object may determine the will—whether through desire (such as the happiness principle) or through reason as it considers objects of will in general (such as the principle of perfection)—such a will never determines itself by thinking of the action, but rather determines itself under the influence of some impulse which the expected results arouse. In other words, "I ought to do this because I want that." 444

But this demands a second law tying me as agent to the first imperative; that is, a law which not only commands that I desire such an object, but also that I will my maxim according to the moral standard. Whenever I consider an object which I can possibly obtain, my will is moved in a perfectly natural and human way; but this influence on my will depends on the *natural* constitution of *my* will. I might be moved by sensations, such as desire or taste, or by understanding and even reason. These impulses afford varying satisfactions as they move me to exercise my will. But as a consequence my natural constitution would determine the law, and such a law, since it can be known and proved only by experience, would be *contingent*. It could never serve as an apodictic practical rule, which the moral law must be. A law of this kind always arises from heteronomy of the will: the will does not make the law for itself, but accepts it from some external impulse arising from the particular tendencies of a responsive human nature.

Of any principle of morality we should ask the following questions. Does the principle base compliance on the satisfaction of some desire or on some interest of the agent? Does the principle rely on experience of any kind? Does the agent presuppose any other moral standard in using the principle? If the answer to any of these questions is yes, the principle is spurious, for its foundation is contrary to the idea of the self-legislation of the will. Of all these heteronomous principles, Kant prefers the ideal of perfection. But being an empty concept, representing merely the theoretical limit of human excellence, it has no practical value as a basis for moral law.

4. *Conclusion*

Kant concludes Section II with a precise statement of the supreme principle of morality.

Therefore, the absolutely good will, which must have a categorical imperative as its principle, will not be determined by any

particular object. Its essence contains only the general form of willing—autonomy. Thus: the sole basis for that law which the will of every rational being imposes on itself is THE FITNESS OF THE MAXIMS OF EVERY GOOD WILL TO BECOME UNIVERSAL LAWS, without recourse to some impulse of self-interest.

The ultimate foundation of morality is the good will, which is an autonomous will; and the supreme law of morality commands us to act as a good will acts, namely, in a way which recognizes the lawmaking of its maxims.

Kant's search for the supreme principle of morality, the ultimate ground of obligation, is now finished. The outline of his argument is this:

1. Only that which has absolute value in itself can serve as the basis of obligation, since only such an entity ought to be sought universally and unconditionally.

2. The good will is the only thing which has absolute value.

3. Thus the good will (i.e., the moral will) is the foundation of obligation expressed by the moral law.

4. One acts with a good will when he acts solely out of respect for moral law, without regard for self-interest.

5. As the basis of all obligation, the good will must be the source of its own moral law; for were it subject to some external law, it could be subject only through self-interest or natural inclination.

6. The good will imposes its own moral law on itself when it wills that the maxims of its actions could become universal law for itself and every rational being.

7. The supreme moral imperative, then, contains only the form of law: universality. The statement of this law is the categorical imperative.

Kant's argument then concludes with the statement: *"The essence of the absolutely good will contains only the general form of willing—autonomy."* Having begun with the concept of the only absolutely good thing, he has developed it by seeking its necessary foundation, finding it in autonomy. The moral will, the good will, the autonomous will—these are only different ways of conceiving the one ultimate basis of moral obligation. Further, morality imposes valid constraint on the will of a rational being if and only if the will has imposed *upon itself* the moral necessity of acting.

However, the categorical imperative has not yet been shown to be a genuine moral fact. It is one thing to analyze concepts; it is quite another to prove that there is something to which the concept applies. From an analysis of concepts we know, first, that autonomy is necessary *if* the will can truly act from duty, and second that *if* the will is capable of self-legislation, then it is subject to the moral law. But neither experience nor analytical reasoning can give us any information as to the actual validity of the moral law, since neither experience nor analytical reasoning can prove that the will has freedom of choice.

How this synthetic practical *a priori* proposition is possible, and why it is necessary, are problems which   **445 cannot be solved within the system of a metaphysics of morals. We have not solved them, nor have we even claimed to have a solution. We simply showed that by developing the commonsense concept of morality, we found autonomy of the will inextricably connected to it—indeed, we found that autonomy is the very basis of morality. Thus anyone who takes morality to be real and not a mere fantasy must at the same time admit this principle of autonomy. Section II, then, like Section I, has been an analytical investigation.**

If we are to prove that morality is no mere fantasy—which is surely proved if the categorical imperative and autonomy of the will are true, i.e., are absolutely necessary *a priori* principles —we must show that a synthetic use of pure practical reason is possible. However, we cannot do this *without first undertaking a critical investigation of the faculty of reason.* In Section III, then, we shall outline the main steps of such an investigation, which will suffice for the purpose of this *Foundation.*

Although we have *discovered* the ultimate foundation of morality in the autonomy of the will, we have not yet *proved* that the will of man is actually self-legislative. Section III, then, will be devoted to an examination of this fundamental issue of morality, the freedom of the will. For if the will of man is not free, then moral obligation is truly a mere fantasy. If Kant can prove the real, and not merely theoretical, possibility of human freedom, he will have shown the real authority of the categorical imperative, and to that extent the validity of the moral law .

SECTION III

FINAL STEP FROM
A METAPHYSICS OF
MORALS TO A CRITICAL
EXAMINATION OF PURE
PRACTICAL REASON

CHAPTER NINE

PART 1—Freedom and Autonomy

1. *The Concept of Freedom*

Until we have some clear understanding of the meaning of "freedom"—even though it may be a limited understanding—we cannot embark upon the theoretical examination of practical reason's moral authority. We have already seen that moral law and the concept of duty presuppose human freedom of choice. If man be simply the unwitting pawn in a cosmic game of casual determination—that is, if all his choices are necessarily determined by his desires, and thus all his imperatives hypothetical—then moral law and moral character are fictitious and cannot possibly relate to any reality. On the other hand, if the rational (human) will is free, then morality is a genuine practical law. Consequently, in order to determine whether morality is a valid law for the human will, we must, as a first step, prove that freedom itself is a valid concept.

Let us begin by trying to clarify the meaning of freedom. Morality imposes a valid constraint on the will of a rational being only if the will *imposes* this constraint *upon itself*. To say that the will imposes constraint upon itself is to say that a person *freely*, on his own, determines his duty and chooses to do it. Choosing and performing one's duty is an example of what we would ordinarily call a free action. However, there are two philosophical views which deny the existence of any such free actions. They are *determinism* and *libertarianism*. These views can be characterized and contrasted with Kant's view of free action by considering what we might call the "causality" of an action. In every action there is some agent who performs the action. Consider then the possible kinds of causality which can be attributed to any action, particularly with regard to the agent's involvement in such causality.

1. If an action is caused by some set of conditions over which the agent who performs the action has *no* control, we shall say that the action has *dependent causality*, i.e., the causes of the action are not dependent on the agent but, on the contrary, the agent is totally dependent on the conditions which obtain at the time he performed the action.

2. If an action occurs for which there is no cause at all, we shall say that the action has *no causality*.

3. If an action is caused by a set of conditions over *some* of which the agent *does* have control, we shall say that the action has *independent causality*.

In this regard, determinism can be defined as the thesis which holds that human actions have only dependent causality. Libertarianism can be defined as a theory which holds that at least some human actions have no causality. The determinist position seems to follow logically from the general law of causality, that for every event there is a set of conditions which together are the cause of that event, and actions are a species of event. If the determinist position is true, there are no free actions, and so, for Kant, there is no situation in which morality validly imposes a constraint upon the will in the form of a command of reason.

One might think that to deny the determinist thesis is to espouse the libertarian thesis, affirming that free actions are those for which there are no causes at all. But this will not do. First, it is doubtful that there are any free actions in this sense—

indeed, it seems absurd to suggest that there are. Secondly, even if there were free actions in this sense, it would not help Kant's theory. Such free actions would simply be events that happen quite independently of anything else, including an agent's choices. However, morality *essentially* involves a relationship of some kind between one's will (his ability to choose) and his actions.

This is not the place to argue the competing theses. For one thing, each side affirms a basic truth. Determinism is correct to insist that the causal law is universal; libertarianism is correct to assert that human awareness confirms free choice. If Kant simply ignores the argument for determinism, he will thereby fail to justify human freedom, and if he fails to justify human freedom, he cannot validate the moral law. He identifies free actions with those actions, if any, which have independent causality. This would not be inconsistent with the universal law of causality, but obviously it conflicts with the determinist thesis. To justify this identification, Kant examines first the concept of freedom.

THE CONCEPT OF FREEDOM
IS THE KEY WHICH EXPLAINS THE AUTONOMY OF WILL

If a living being is rational, then he has *will*, which makes him a kind of cause. And if such a will is *free*, 446 then he can exercise his causal power without being determined to his choice by causal influences outside the will itself. Opposed to freedom is *natural necessity*, which is the exercise of choice under the determining influence of outside causes. Natural necessity is the only mode of choice for non-rational beings.

A rational will is a *cause* and so in some way must relate to the law of causality, as the determinists claim. But as an *independent* cause, capable of exercising some control over some of the causal conditions, the will escapes the dehumanizing causal "natural necessity" which would rob a person of his freedom of choice. A second important element in this definition is the uniting of free choice with rationality: a man has free will if and only if he is a rational being. However, to say that freedom is undetermined causal power does not define freedom in any positive way.

This definition by itself, being negative, contains no insight into the essence of freedom. But from the negative definition we can derive a positive conception of freedom which is much richer and more fruitful. The concept of causality involves the idea of *laws* which command that, whenever we determine something as a cause, we must also include something else—its effect. Thus, since will makes a rational being a cause, freedom of will cannot be separated from law; will cannot exercise a lawless freedom, even though it may act independently of the laws of nature. Will, as the ground of free causality, is subject to the immutable *laws of freedom,* laws of a special kind. Otherwise a free will would be an absurdity.

Will is a cause, but if it be free, then *it is not at the same time an effect,* as is the case in natural causal necessity. Certainly every cause is related to some effect, and the relation of cause to effect is expressed as one of *law.* If we wish to avoid the absurd position of claiming that a free will acts in accordance with no law whatsoever—no maxims, no subjective principles or policies, in a word, acts for no reason at all—then we must conclude that free will is subject to law. The difference between a free will and a determined will does not lie in one being free from law while the other is inexorably ruled by law, but rather it must lie in a difference in the kinds of law. A determined will is one which is wholly ruled by natural causal necessity, the laws of nature; a free will must be ruled by a different kind of law, a law of freedom.

In the very idea of law there is contained the idea of necessity, so that a free will is still subject to a kind of necessity, even when it exercises free choice. The necessity, of course, is moral necessity, not causal necessity. Furthermore, if will is a cause, it must cause something. The effect of choice will be an action of some kind. (Perhaps we should say that the effect of choice is the *initiation* of action, for sometimes we are unable to do what we set out to do. So long as this point is kept in mind, action can be said to be the *usual* effect of choice.)

The difficulties raised by this idea—of will itself as a cause of human action—become clear when we consider that a human action is not solely an act of will but is also an overt natural event, and as such is subject to the law of causal natural necessity. This puts us in what seems to be an inescapable difficulty: if the will be free, then according to the laws of freedom it causes actions which, as effects in the natural universe, are events caused by prior events outside the will. To put it more pointedly, an action caused by a free will is an action which is caused by something else. Not that any event is uncaused, rather that every human action, being an event, seems to require *two* unrelated causes, either of which should alone be sufficient to bring about the event. And yet, to eliminate either involves conclusions which commonsense and freedom refuse to allow.

A third point, that the free will is a rational will, requires further discussion. Where does reason play its part in human choice? In Section II, Kant identified will as practical reason itself, yet here he speaks of will as a distinguishable factor in human choice. Perhaps we should note a distinction which Kant makes in the German between *Wille and Willkür*, both translated as *will*.[1] *Wille* refers to will as the source of maxims, be these maxims autonomous or heteronomous. In this sense, will is the same as practical reason. *Willkür* refers to will as the spontaneous faculty of choice. Since *Willkür* is spontaneous, it is free in the sense that it is not determined in its exercise, although spontaneity does not mean autonomy.[2] In brief, *Wille* (practical reason) supplies the principles, *Willkür* (free choice) chooses according to them. These two aspects of will do not refer to different "parts" of the will, but to distinguishable activities of will. Spontaneous, undetermined choice *(Willkür)* may be exercised autonomously or heteronomously, depending on whether the maxims of will *(Wille)* be self-legislative or otherwise. In either case, spontaneous will *determines itself*, even though it may do so according to maxims other than the moral law.

Natural necessity, as we have seen, is a heteronomy of efficient causes: no effect can possibly come into being unless its efficient cause was moved to activity by yet another determining cause. What else then can freedom of the will be but *autonomy*, that which makes will to be its own law? But to say that will is its own law in all its choices is to assert nothing less than the rule that will ought always act on a maxim which at the same time contains will itself as the ground of universal law. Now this is precisely the formulation of the categorical imperative, the supreme principle of morality. Thus a free will is exactly the same as a will which is subject to moral law. 447

To assert autonomy as the law of freedom, Kant says, is to assert nothing less than the law commanding will to regard itself as the foundation for moral law. But at the same time, it is surely to assert a great deal *more*. That the will can make its own maxims does not mean that it must base its own law upon its nature as rational will. We can hold that a free will must be subject to self-legislated moral law without having to agree that a free will is itself the basis for such moral law. In fact, while traditional moral theory has insisted on free will as a necessary condition for morality, moral philosophers before Kant sought the ground of moral law in something outside the will, e.g., in man's natural end, God's Will, or human desire. In order to justify our joining the concept of a spontaneous will to the idea of autonomous law based on will itself, we must find something which relates both to freedom and the categorical imperative of morality.

If we assume freedom of the will, then by a mere analysis of this concept we can derive morality together with the rule of morality (the categorical imperative). But the rule of morality—that an absolutely good will is one whose maxim at the same time contains itself as the ground of universal law—is a *synthetic* proposition: no such maxim can be discovered by an analysis of the idea of an absolutely good will. We can construct such synthetic propositions only when the two ideas are joined to each other through *a third idea* in which the original two are both found. Through the positive conception of freedom we can discover the third idea; but this idea cannot be Nature as the world of appearances, as it is with physical causes.* We cannot yet explain what this third idea is, which we can derive *a priori* from the concept of freedom; nor can we give an understandable account of how the concept of freedom can be legitimately derived from pure practical reason, that is, how a categorical imperative is possible. Further prepration is required.

* In thinking of physical causality we join the idea of something as the cause to the idea of something else as the effect.

Here Kant formulates the method he will use to justify freedom of the will, and thus will's subjection to moral law. His problem, briefly, is this. We know from analyzing the idea of free will that such a will is subject to the law of morality, expressed in the categorical imperative. We also know from analyzing the idea of a good will that such a will acts according to the moral maxim, i.e., out of respect for law. But an analysis of concepts does *not* tell us that the good will which acts out of respect for law is a will which obeys the law of autonomy. Now the categorical imperative expresses a command of reason to a will in this way: "In order to be a good will, act according to a maxim which conforms to the law of autonomy." But reason can only exercise such command authority if it *has* the authority, or in Kant's terms, if we can relate the idea of a law of autonomy to the idea of a good will and, furthermore, establish this relationship *a priori*—for only an *a priori* relationship could give reason the authority to command the will categorically, unconditionally, under moral necessity.

We can relate these two ideas, Kant suggests, if we can find *a third idea* which relates *a priori* to the other two ideas. That is to say, this third idea will relate *a priori* to the idea of a good will, and will relate *a priori* to the idea of a self-imposed law of autonomy. In order to illustrate this method, let us consider the idea of two points in space and the idea of the shortest distance between them. No analysis of either idea alone will include the other idea. But if we include a third idea, that of a straight line, then the first idea can be related to the second: a straight line between two points in space is the shortest distance between two points in space (a synthetic *a priori* proposition).³ The present search is for some idea which will relate the good will to the autonomous will, an idea which relates to both *a priori*, but to neither simply by an analysis of concepts (for this would simply restate the original problem in other terms).

Although he does not tell us at this point what the third idea is, Kant does say that we can discover it through the positive idea of freedom, that is, through the idea of a will subject to the law of morality. We already know that this third idea will have to be consistent with that of free will subject to autonomous law. But at this point in the argument the search for the third idea would be premature: we must first prove to our satisfaction that freedom is a real possibility, not simply a fiction of the imagination. For if freedom be only a fantasy, then any discovery of such a connecting third idea would be at best a mere logical game, having no practical validity whatsoever. On the other hand, if freedom can be proved a real possibility, then it will become most important to determine whether or not the absolutely good will derives its law from its own nature or from some standard outside itself, since whatever that standard may be, it will serve as the fundamental and supreme principle of morality. To justify this principle, then, we must prove the genuine possibility of freedom.

2. *Freedom as a Presupposition*

WE MUST ASSUME THAT
THE WILL OF EVERY RATIONAL BEING IS FREE

It will not do to give just any reason for claiming that we have a free will; furthermore, we must offer sufficient evidence for claiming that *all* rational beings have free will. For since morality can subject us to law only as we are rational beings, it must be valid as law for all rational beings. Since morality must be derived solely from the concept of freedom, we must prove that the will of every rational being is free. We cannot find such a proof in certain alleged experiences of human activity, for our proof must be *a priori*—we must prove freedom of the will for all rational beings as such—and experience simply cannot provide us with such an *a priori* proof. 448

In Kant's introduction to the proof of freedom, the emphasis on the inadequacy of experience for an *a priori* proof must be kept in mind, for it may appear that Kant's proof is based upon nothing more than man's introspective awareness of his freedom of choice. But this is not so: the proof is based upon the relation of rationality to a free will. Man is a moral agent because he is a rational being. This then must be the basis of the proof, for only by proving that a free will is necessarily related to rationality can Kant prove the universality of free will, and thus prove that every human being is subject to the moral law.

PROOF:

Any being which cannot act except in a subjective conscious-ness of freedom is by this very fact really free in a practical sense.

That is to say, every law inseparably bound up with freedom is a valid law for such a being as much as if his will were proved free in itself by a conclusive theoretical argument.*

But every rational being possessing a will is aware of freedom and is conscious of acting as a free agent.

For by having will he has practical reason, that is, reason which acts as the causal agent regarding its objectives. Now we cannot conceive of (theoretical) reason consciously allowing its judgments to be made for it by something other than itself; in such a situation reason would simply conclude that its judgments had been due not to reason but to impulse. Reason must regard *itself*, not something outside itself, as the source of its principles.

Thus in its practical function—as the will of a rational being— reason must regard itself as free.

That is to say, only through the subjective consciousness of its own freedom can the will of a rational being (his practical reason) be the source of its own principles (maxims); and consequently, from this practical point of view, every rational being must have free will.

---

* I assume that the subjective consciousness of freedom which rational beings must be aware of when they act will suffice for our present purpose. In so doing we avoid having to provide a conclusive theoretical proof of the objective reality of freedom. Even if such a proof were found to be inconclusive, the same law which commands a being who is really free commands equally the being who cannot act except in a conscious awareness of his own freedom. We can thus avoid the burdensome theoretical question.

This proof may be disappointing at first. We have what appears to be just that appeal to the psychological experience of free choice which Kant warned against in the foreword to the proof. Our disappointment is understandable. We expected a theoretical proof, in metaphysical language, for the actuality of freedom, but we find only an apparently weak argument for the mere *possibility* of freedom. We can justifiably demand an accounting: where is the core of the proof?

As arguments go, the proof is a rather simple one: two premisses leading to a conclusion. Rephrased, the argument is:

(P1) All beings which must act with a subjective awareness of acting as free agents are beings which, in a practical sense, are really free agents.

(P2) All rational beings which possess will are beings which must act with a subjective awareness of acting as free agents.

(C) Therefore, all rational beings which possess will are beings which, in a practical sense, are really free agents. Q.E.D.

When put in this way, there is no doubt that the conclusion follows logically from the premisses. The burden of proof then falls upon proving each of the premisses true, for unless we can prove the truth of the premisses, the truth of the conclusion remains in question.

But two important aspects of this proof must be clarified before the premisses can be examined. First, since the conclusion is a synthetic proposition, at least one of the premisses must be synthetic, for from two analytic premisses only an analytic conclusion may be derived. Secondly, and of utmost importance, the proof is *not* a proof from speculative reason. Kant has already shown the impossibility of knowing anything about free will through theoretical metaphysics.[4] He would hardly have violated the emphatic doctrine of the first *Critique*. Rather, the proof is based upon *practical reason;* Kant does not try to prove that freedom of will can be known, but that freedom of will is *necessary in action.* We may not know by logical proof that the will is free, but we can know by acting that we *must act* as free agents. Hopefully, this important distinction will become clear during our examination of the premisses themselves.

The First Premiss: *"Any being which cannot act except in a subjective consciousness of freedom is by this very fact really free in a practical sense."*

We begin with the idea of a being who views himself as a free agent whenever he chooses to act. This introspective consciousness, however, is only a subjective awareness, not objective knowledge; being subjective, it does not provide the ground for a theoretical certainty about the actuality of freedom. But *if* the subjective consciousness of freedom is *necessarily* the agent's way of viewing himself when he chooses to act, then *he must think of himself as a free agent,* even though he may not know whether this thought has any objective basis in reality. Furthermore, he cannot escape being aware that, as a free agent, he is bound by any laws which determine that freedom. Thus, Kant will argue, any being which *necessarily* acts in this subjective awareness of freedom is subject to the moral law, whether or not freedom can be proved by a metaphysical argument. The first premiss is true analytically.

The Second Premiss: *"Every rational being possessing a will is aware of freedom and is conscious of acting as a free agent."*

In matters of theoretical judgment, reason must see itself as the author of its judgments; for if reason felt that some other impulse were the source, then reason would not consider that a judgment had been made at all, strictly speaking. For instance, suppose I have an irrational fear of the dark. I go into a room which is well-lit, and I see no one else present nor anything in the room which could harm me. Suddenly an electrical failure plunges the room into blackness and my reaction is an overpowering feeling of terror. Looking back, I cannot say that I judged that I was in danger, for I knew there was no danger. Nevertheless, I clearly *felt* in danger because of my fear of darkness. What happened is easily understandable: I did not make any judgment at all; my emotions simply responded to a stimulus. So too in human choice. If I choose to act, intend to act, and initiate an act, then I regard the activity as resulting from *my* agency, aimed at *my* goals. If I feel compelled by some outside force to move in a direction not of my choosing, I simply conclude that I had not acted at all: I had merely *re*-acted to some compulsion. This is the heart of my sense of responsibility; I feel responsible only for actions of which *I* am the agent. Nevertheless, I could be deluded in believing I am the cause of my actions since it is possible that subconscious desires or compulsions force me to my "choice." How can we prove that belief in free agency is justifiable? And even more, how can we prove it *a priori*? Morality, based as it is upon freedom, stands or falls on the *a priori* validity of awareness of freedom in acting. Unless we can establish *a priori* its validity, the second premiss will at best be an introspective judgment; we might still *appear* to ourselves as free agents, but our empirical belief would carry no moral weight whatsoever. The crux of the proof lies in the second premiss.

3. *Why Should I Be Moral?*

As he frequently does, Kant briefly summarizes what progress has been made. Once again he raises the fundamental question: Can reason be practical? That is to say, can reason by itself, through its influence alone, cause human action?

CONCERNING OUR INTEREST IN MORTALITY

We have finally shown that a meaningful idea of morality must be established on the idea of freedom, yet we have not actually proved that we, as human beings, are 449 really free. We saw only that *if* we wish to regard a rational being as conscious of his inherent causal agency—that is, as having a will—then we must grant freedom to human nature. On these same grounds we must grant to every being having reason and will the same freedom, namely, the capacity of exercising his causal power in the consciousness of freedom.

From the presumed idea of freedom, we derived the awareness of a law of action, namely, that we must always act on subjective rules of action (maxims) which can at the same time be objective rules, the universal law which we ourselves enact. But why should I as a rational being put myself under this law, and in so doing put all other rational beings under it as well?

I cannot allow that some interest makes me do so, for then we would have no categorical imperative. But, on the other hand, I must *take* an interest in this matter and try to answer these questions. For the purely rational being, who finds no obstacle whatsoever in acting solely from reason, "I ought" necessarily leads to "I will." But for us human beings, influenced by nonrational, sensuous motives, not always acting as reason alone dictates, the objective necessity of "I ought" does not always lead to the subjective necessity of "I will."

In the second paragraph above, Kant seems suddenly to have changed the subject. He began with a summary of the argument —and a very subtle, difficult argument it is—but then he asks a different question: assuming that I *do* have free will, why should I obey the moral law? This question is weighty and of crucial importance to every man, but it hardly seems relevant to the problem of freedom.[5] What follows is a discussion of the inestimable value of the moral law and its influence on the will.

Have we, in this idea of freedom, simply assumed the moral law of autonomy, because of our inability to prove by some other argument that the law is real and objectively necessary? Even were this so, we still would have made a great advance, for we would have determined the principle much more exactly than anyone had ever done before. But we would have gotten nowhere in proving that it is valid or that we are subject to it through some practical necessity. We could not satisfactorily explain how our universally valid maxim could be a law which is the limiting condition of our actions; nor could we determine the basis on which we judge the value of acting under such conditions—a value so great that no other can equal it. We could not make clear to anyone why a man would find his own personal worth in such actions, a worth in comparison to which a pleasant or painful existence means   450 nothing.

Sometimes we do take an interest in a personal quality without thereby having any interest in the external situation connected with it, except of course that by having the quality we then can profit from the related situation if reason should approve of it. Thus being worthy of happiness can be our goal, even though we do not make happiness itself our motive for acting. And yet we judge this to be so only on the above assumption of the supremacy of the moral law (which we acknowledge when we act in the consciousness of freedom by detaching ourselves from any empirical interest).

The vital question, "Why *should* I be moral?" can be read in two ways: what's in it for me? and, what is there about the moral law that I should obey it? The answer to the first question has already been given in Section I.[6] Morality is my only guarantee of becoming worthy of happiness. If ever I expect to find complete happiness, I had best convince myself that the moral life is a necessary condition for such happiness, even if it be not a sufficient condition. That is to say, while the moral life does not itself guarantee complete happiness, I will never reach complete happiness unless I live a moral life.

The second question is the critical one; what is there about the moral law that I should obey it, especially when I may want to do something else?

But why should we detach ourselves from such interests? Why should we view ourselves as free to act but still subject to certain laws? Can we find a value in ourselves alone which would make up for the loss of everything which we commonly think necessary for happiness? We cannot yet anwer these questions, nor do we understand how a person can act this way. In short, we must ask: *how does the moral law place us under obligation?*

Kant defines happiness[7] as the sense of well-being attending the fulfillment of all desires. The difficulty of his question lies in the apparent conflict of saying, on the one hand, that obeying the moral law is necessary in order to be worthy of happiness and, on the other, that obeying the moral law frequently prevents us from fulfilling those desires which seem necessary for happiness. How can we feel obligated to obey a law in order to be worthy of happiness when obeying that law may prevent us from being happy? Is there a contradiction between our moral purpose and our natural purpose? This would violate the axiom that Nature has ordained everything to its proper end.[8] Or could it be that the contradiction is only apparent, that we must take different points of view on each matter, the moral point of view and the natural point of view? And if this indeed be the case, where can we find the basis for making the distinction?

4. *The Dual Point of View*

The argument is becoming rather complicated. Let us step back for an overview of the situation thus far. Kant has offered a proof which purports to show that the human experience of acting in a conscious awareness of freedom is sufficient to establish the validity of the moral law. The second premiss of the proof states that human consciousness of freedom is sufficient ground for the practical acceptance of freedom. This premiss has not yet been proved true. Kant is aware that any justification of the second premiss presupposes the very possibility of free will. Should freedom be a logical impossibility, then the human experience we look to is only an illusion of freedom.

In fact, Kant has undertaken to solve *three* distinguishable problems: (1) proving that the idea of human free will is not logically impossible but rather is consistent with causal necessity, which rules the world of appearances. Once he has solved this problem, he can then move on, (2) proving that our conscious awareness of acting as free agents is sufficient justification for accounting ourselves to be really free, at least in a practical sense. Given this practical (if not metaphysical) proof of freedom, Kant can take the final step, (3) proving that the moral maxim of the absolutely good will must be the self-imposed, self-grounded law of autonomy. In order to confirm the law of autonomy as a valid moral law binding every human will, Kant must show that the experience of freedom is necessarily an agent's view of himself when he chooses to act. But in order that this experience can even be suggested as evidence for human freedom, Kant must meet the determinist's objection and prove that human freedom is really (not merely logically) possible. Thus the first step in this complex justification of the moral law will be to prove that human freedom is possible; the second step will be to prove that every human agent must think himself free; and the final step, that every human agent is bound by the law of autonomy.

Now let us return to Kant's discussion. Having considered the question, "Why should I be moral?" Kant returns to the main line of his argument by reviewing the two ways in which the idea of freedom and the idea of moral law have been related. He suggests that each idea has been used to justify the other, which, if true, would be an obvious fallacy.

I frankly admit that we find a circular argument here, which seems impossible to avoid. We presuppose our freedom from determining efficient causes so that we may think of ourselves as subject to moral law, as ends in ourselves. And then we maintain our subjection to moral law because we have presupposed freedom of the will. Freedom of the will and self-legislation of moral law are concepts which refer to exactly the same thing: autonomy. Consequently, we cannot use one concept as the foundation for the validity of the other. However, we can use them for the logical objective of showing how two different conceptions of the same subject, autonomy, can be combined into one concept —reducing them to the lowest common denominator, so to speak.

Obligation would be an empty concept, unrelated to anything real, if we could not freely choose to do our duty. By accepting our awareness of obligation as genuine, we recognize our freedom. Freedom, on the other hand, will be an empty idea unless we establish its practical necessity. The statement of the problem does seem circular: if we are free then we have duties, and if we have duties then we must be free. The problem becomes even more difficult when we see that each idea, freedom and obligation, is identified with the same idea of autonomy. If we are free to choose, then we ought to choose according to the laws of freedom, which are the laws of autonomy; and if we have a duty to act, we are obligated under the laws of morality, which again are the laws of autonomy. In short, I have a duty to obey the laws of autonomy because I ought to choose according to the laws of autonomy. This statement is not simply a truism, as though we are saying merely that duty is duty. As Kant points out, there are two different concepts here, free agency and moral obligation, both related to the concept of autonomy. The circle in the argument consists of using the idea of free agency to justify moral obligation, and then using our recognition of moral obligation to justify the idea of free agency. When we describe free agency as an agency subject to autonomy, we emphasize the agent's independence from outside determining causes, his *freedom from* laws of natural causal necessity. On the other hand, when we describe moral obligation as an agency subject to autonomy, we emphasize not the agent's independence from natural causality but his *subjection to* the laws of practical reason. Because the agent's freedom from natural causality subjects him to the law of morality and because his subjection to the law of morality presupposes his freedom from natural causality, we seem to be caught in a circular argument.

There may be a way to escape this difficulty, however. Could it be that when we think of ourselves *a priori* as agents exercising a free causality we *take a different point of view* from that of seeing ourselves as others see us, namely, as agents exercising a determined causality?

In order to escape the charge that we are arguing in a circle, we must show that one of the two ideas, free agency or moral obligation, has its own independent basis for validity. Because the two ideas support each other, we need only to find an independent justification for one of the ideas. Kant will try to justify free agency, since it is the necessary condition for moral obligation. He will argue that when we regard ourselves as agents, we take a different point of view from the one we take of ourselves as beings in a universe of time, space, and causality.

What I now propose needs no subtle reflection; even the most ordinary intellect can grasp it, even though it 451 may do so in a rather obscure form (sometimes referred to as "having a feeling"). To wit: whatever impressions we receive, such as sensations, which do not arise from our own design, give us knowledge of objects *only as we are affected by the impressions*. What the object may be like in itself we have no way of knowing. Consequently, no matter how clearly we attend to such impressions, *we can obtain only a knowledge of the objects as they appear to us*, never a knowledge of things in themselves.

Perhaps we first recognize this simply by noting the difference between ideas which we passively receive and those which we ourselves make up in imagination. But once we make this distinction, we have to allow that "behind" the appearances, so to speak, lie things in themselves, which do not appear to us at all. This we must admit, even though we recognize that in knowing them only by the way they affect us and lacking any other way of knowing them, we can never reach any knowledge of what they are in themselves. But this much lets us make a rough distinction between *a world of sense impressions* (things as they appear to us) and *a world of thought* (things as we may think about them). The universe we sense may appear differently to different observers, depending on what impressions each may receive; but the world of thought must be the same to all, since it is the foundation (in objective reality) for the world of appearance.

The doctrine stated so simply here—that we know objects only as they appear to us through our sense impressions—is central to Kant's whole theory of knowledge, and forms the basic premiss for his rejection of all metaphysical knowledge. Kant argued that there are collections of impressions which we accept as factually informative and then again those which we classify as simply imaginative, but that the distinction between the two cannot be decided simply by collecting more impressions; rather, the final judgment as to which collections ("manifolds") of sense impressions are factually informative lies in the laws of pure reason, those *a priori* laws which establish the necessary conditions for veracity.

Kant's theme here, as in the *Critique of Pure Reason,* is the inability of the human mind to know objects in the world except through perception. What objects may be unperceived we simply cannot know, for all our knowledge comes to us through impressions: through impressions of sense when we know objects in nature, or through introspective impressions when we know our own inner selves. Commonsense and a kind of instinctive realism lead us to assume that things exist more or less as we perceive them (why should they be otherwise?), that this underlying existence accounts for the order and regularity of our impressions, and that in turn we can affect external objects by our own activity. Nevertheless, these assumptions remain at best matters of reason, not facts of knowledge.

We may even insist, as did René Descartes (1596–1650), that surely we have direct knowledge of ourselves as we really are, as rational beings. But Kant rejects even this kind of direct knowledge.

No one can know his own objective nature, not even through introspective inquiry. He does not make himself what he is, nor does he have any *a priori* knowledge of his own nature in itself. And since the only knowledge he does have is through introspective experience, it follows that he knows himself only as his nature *appears* to him, according to the way his conscious-

ness is affected. And yet behind this appearance of himself—which consists of a complex of introspective impressions—he must necessarily posit something to support these impressions, namely, the ego, the self in itself.

In Kant's view, all impressions, both those of spatial objects and those of introspection, are ones which occur *in time.* But time, he argues (in the *Critique of Pure Reason*), is not itself an impression; rather it is one of the *a priori modes* of perceiving, inescapable and necessary for all perception. The element of time is something *added* by mind to the content of all impressions, making it necessary that everything (as we perceive it) have temporal characteristics. Thus we can know ourselves only as we perceive ourselves in time; we cannot know ourselves as we might exist unperceived even by ourselves (e.g., as God might know us).[9] Furthermore, since we know the self only as an introspective appearance, this sensible self is subject to all the laws which govern the world of sense impressions, particularly the laws of psychological causal necessity. The self as we perceive it, as we know it, lacks freedom.

Yet here too, even more than with objects in space, common-sense posits some core of existence which underlies all our introspective impressions—the self as it exists in itself.[10] While it is one thing to lack knowledge of things as they exist unperceived—or in Kant's terms, as they exist in themselves—we are surely free to *think* about things in their unperceived existence. The laws of nature which apply to objects in space and time cannot apply to the unperceived universe; they apply only to our experiences. The world of sense impressions is the world as we know and experience it, conforming in every way to laws of nature. The unperceivable world of thought, independent of the laws of nature, is unknowable—but thinkable.

Thus from the standpoint of mere introspection and receiving impressions of himself, a man must see himself as belonging to the sensible universe. But from the standpoint of his possible spontaneous agency (of which he is aware *immediately,* not through sensations), he must see himself as belonging to the world of thought. But this is all he knows of that world.

The thoughtful person must conclude that he takes one or the other standpoint regarding everything which 452 confronts him. Even nonintellectuals understand this, though they commonly try to find something behind the scenes, so to speak, some invisible, spontaneous agency. But they soon muddle the whole attempt by trying to make the invisible visible, i.e., an object of sense. Nothing at all can be learned this way.

Just as we may think of objects as they might exist unperceived, in themselves, so we may think of ourselves as beings which exist in ourselves—even though, once again, there is no way of acquiring any knowledge of ourselves as, say, we may exist in God's eye. But since the laws of natural causality apply only in the world of sense impressions, then we may indeed *think* of ourselves as *free, spontaneous agents in the world of thought,* choosing according to the laws of freedom, undetermined by the laws of causal natural necessity. Thus, we can see everything, including (and especially) ourselves, *from two points of view:* (1) as beings in the world of sense impressions, and thus subject to the law of causal necessity; and (2) as beings in the world of pure thought, subject only to the theoretical and practical laws of pure thought. But, as Kant points out, while this is recognized by most people—at least as a practical principle if not a theoretical one—only our experience in the world of sense impressions provides us with any knowledge of the self. Psychology is a legitimate science; metaphysical speculation about the self is not. Nevertheless, this dual point of view proves free will to be *a logical possibility,* and thus solves Kant's first problem.

If this view of the self as a being in the world of thought were optional, one we might take or leave as it suited us, then human freedom would be a logical possibility merely. But Kant must prove freedom to be a practical fact, which he can prove by showing that we *must* view the self as a being in the world of thought—that we have no option. His next step, then, is to explain why we must so see ourselves.

There is in every man a real faculty which sets him apart from everything else, even from himself so far as he is affected by objects. This faculty is *Reason,* a purely spontaneous activity of the mind which surpasses even the activity of the *Understanding.* The latter is likewise a spontaneous activity of mind and so differs from the faculty of *Sensibility,* which acts only in response to impressions passively received. But the Understanding, while it does produce its own ideas, can employ them solely for combining sensible impressions according to certain rules, thereby uniting the impressions in one act of conscious awareness. Except for this, the Understanding cannot think anything at all. But Reason, on the other hand, exercises its pure spontaneity (through what I call the pure Ideas) by going far beyond the sensible universe. Its primary function is to distinguish the sensible universe from the universe of thought and thereby set down limits for the exercise of the Understanding.

Kant here distinguishes three functions of intellectual activity.[11] *Sensibility* is the mind's capacity to perceive the impressions of inner and outer sensation through the *a priori* modes of space and time. Mind receives impressions and as it does so, one might say, spatio-temporalizes them. *Understanding* is mind's capacity to receive impressions from sensibility, combine them according to *a priori* principles of knowledge, and judge whether the combined impressions are genuine experiences of the sensible world. Since it operates according to its own *a priori* laws, understanding is a spontaneous faculty to the extent that its judgments are not determined by any casual necessity. On the contrary, judgments of causal necessity are products of understanding. However, understanding cannot judge objects or events which cannot in some way be perceived, for its sole function is to deal with sense impressions. It may produce its own *a priori* laws, but they are restricted in their application to the world of sense impressions; any attempt to use them in the world of pure thought must fail and finally end in contradiction.[12]

The third function of intellect is *Reason*.[13] Reason's legitimate function is to consolidate the judgments of experience produced by understanding, so that the more or less disconnected items of factual information can be systematically related to form a unified whole which conforms to the patterns offered in the Ideas. Since Reason organizes only the products of a spontaneous function of intellect (understanding) rather than the impressions of sensibility, Reason's activity is not limited to the world of sense impressions. It can escape the restrictions of time and space and seek to know things which may exist beyond experience, such as the existence of God, the creation and limits of the universe—and freedom of the will. Unfortunately, when it reaches beyond the products of the understanding, it cuts itself off from its only available tie to reality, perception. In such an attempt, Reason inevitably blunders, either by taking principles from understanding and using them ouside the context of sense impressions (e.g., using the principle of causality to explain the origin of the universe), or by using the pure Ideas in the world of sense impressions (e.g., using the Idea of freedom to characterize the self as it appears to us through introspective perception). Each of these two ways of misusing Reason leads ultimately to contradictory conclusions.

Reason's legitimate function, Kant argues, is regulative, not constitutive; that is, Reason cannot discover truth, but it can establish rules (in conformiy with its Ideas) by which understanding must organize empirical knowledge. For instance, Reason rules that the Universe be a consistent totality in which no law conflicts with any other. This conception, we may recall, was the underlying premise for the first variation of the categorical imperative. We do not know this to be factually true, but we still regulate our experiences in such a way that an experience which suggested an inconsistency in Nature (e.g., a man who could walk through solid brick walls) would be judged illusory.

Reason's ability to think independent of the restrictions of the sensible world of space and time has a most important bearing on morality: if we can think independently of sensibility, then *to that extent* we are free of space-time-causal restrictions. In particular, we can think of ourselves as existing in a world which cannot be perceived but can only be thought. Indeed, we *must* think of ourselves in this way.

It follows that every rational being, *as an intelligence*, must see himself as a member of the world of thought, not simply as a member of the sensible world through his lower faculties. Thus he has two points of view from which he must see himself and determine the laws governing how he acts: (a) as a member of the world of sense impressions he is ruled by the laws of Nature (heteronomy); (b) as a member of the world of thought he is subject to laws which are neither laws of Nature nor derived from experience, but based solely on reason.

Reason cannot view itself simply as a link in a causal chain. Every being which thinks—and this includes every human being —*must view himself as a spontaneous intelligence.* Of course, we also look upon ourselves as members of the world of appearances, but we cannot take the empirical view as our only perspective, even though it alone gives us what factual information we have about ourselves. We must also consider ourselves as members of the world of pure thought, not only in the realm of theoretical reason but especially in the realm of practical reason. From the standpoint of the world of pure thought, reason *must* view itself as a free agent—and thus subject to the moral law.

Because he is rational, a member of the world of thought, man cannot conceive what it would be to exercise his will except in the consciousness of freedom. For 453 freedom is nothing more than willing independently of the determining causes in the sensible world; reason cannot but regard itself as independent in this way. The idea of freedom is inseparably connected to that of autonomy, and autonomy to the idea of universal moral law. Ideally, the moral law is the foundation for all rational activity, just as the law of Nature serves as the foundation for all appearances.

Because he is a thinking being, man exercises his faculty of Reason, which is recognized to be a spontaneous activity. In order to do so, man must see himself as a being in the world of pure thought. From this standpoint he can exercise his Reason generally, his practical Reason in particular, independently of those laws which apply only to the world of sense impressions; that is, he can choose in the conscious awareness of his freedom. Now to act in this manner (as we say in the proof above) is to act subject to the law of freedom, which is nothing other than the law of autonomy, the supreme moral law. Therefore, in order to be a thinking agent, man *must* view himself as free and thus as subject to the moral law of autonomy.

Kant has found his "third idea": that of the rational self as a spontaneous member of the world of pure thought. It proves the possibility of human freedom and thus solves the first of Kant's three problems, as we noted above. Furthermore, the idea of the self as a spontaneous member of the world of pure thought is a necessary presupposition for holding that the human will can become a good will. If the good will is possible only as a member of the world of pure thought, then the good will must be subject to the laws which govern the world of pure thought. Thus *if* membership in the world of pure thought is necessarily a rational being's way of conceiving himself, the good will must be subject to the law of autonomy and Kant's third problem will have been solved. By his "third idea" of the world of pure thought, Kant has established the conditional validity of the second premiss of his proof for freedom. But his premiss is still only *conditionally* valid. We must take one final step before we can rest from our difficult journey. We must prove that Reason's point of view has an *a priori* basis, that it is not simply another frustrating misrepresentation of Reason. This last step will be the principal subject of our final chapter.

Another problem also has been solved, namely, the problem concerning the circular argument.

This allays the suspicion raised above, that we might be arguing in a subtle circle by deriving autonomy from freedom, and then deriving freedom from the moral law (autonomy). That is, there was some question that we posited the consciousness of freedom in order to justify the moral law, and then used the consciousness of the moral law to justify freedom. This would have meant that we were unable to find a ground for moral law —for while congenial minds would readily allow that our begging the question was a formally correct argument, they surely would not concede that we had thereby proved anything. But now we see that when we are conscious of being free agents, we have made ourselves members of the intelligible world, recognizing autonomy of the will and how it leads to morality; whereas when we are aware of obligation, we think of ourselves as members of *both* the sensible universe and the universe of pure thought at the same time.[14]

While we may think of ourselves simply as members of the world of pure thought, we cannot think of ourselves simply as members of the sensible world. The awareness of freedom always accompanies our thought, sometimes obscurely (when we study objects of natural science), sometimes purely (when we analyze moral concepts and principles), and sometimes in between (when we are faced with moral conflict). but we are never without the awareness of freedom. Now we can better understand Kant's definition of constraint as the relationship between a human will and the law of practical reason. To be aware of constraint is to feel the influence of two opposing forces, those which influence us as members of the world of sense impressions and those which influence us as members of the world of pure thought.

5. *Summary*

Freedom of will is the fundamental and necessary condition for morality, for unless we can choose independently of the laws of natural causality, we cannot meaningfully be judged subject to the moral command of reason. But to have freedom is not to be independent of all law; freedom is the ability of a rational being to choose according to the laws of freedom, which laws are those of practical reason, expressed in the categorical imperative. Since the validity of the moral law stands or falls on the possibility of freedom, it becomes crucially important to prove that will is indeed free and that a free will is subject to the law of autonomy.

The proof hinges on the necessity of the relationship between rationality and freedom, that in its exercise of rational will, a person must think of himself as a free agent.

1. All rational beings have will, which is the ability to exercise causality in the universe. This ability may be either spontaneous (free) or determined by natural causal necessity.

2. If a rational being, in the exercise of his will, *necessarily* acts in the subjective awareness of acting as a free agent, then in a practical sense he is truly a free agent. Although we cannot prove freedom by a deductive metaphysical argument, we may still be able to prove that every rational agent is a free agent *in his willing*, if we can only show that in acting he cannot but see himself as a free agent, and hence subject to the moral law.

3. In order to prove that a rational being must act as a free agent to himself, we must show *a priori* how the idea of a rational will is related to the idea of a will which necessarily thinks of itself as a free agent. Only in this way can we justify the conclusion that

a rational agent must *always and necessarily* act as a free agent, and thus as a moral one.

4. We need some interconnecting idea, one which relates directly to the idea of acting as a rational being *and* to the idea of acting as a free agent. The third idea cannot be discovered in either of the two ideas by an analysis of concepts, for that would beg the question of the relationship. We shall have to validate this third idea on independent grounds.

5. A rational being acts in the subjective awareness of itself as a spontaneous activity, especially in its function of Reason. Thus as rational beings we can take a dual point of view of ourselves: (a) as members of the world of sense impressions and thus subject to the laws which govern this world, especially the law of causal necessity; and (b) as members of a world of pure thought, acting independently of the laws of causal necessity, and thus subject to the laws of freedom. Since Reason, as a distinguishable function of intellect, does not relate directly to sense impressions, Reason can conceive itself, both in its theoretical and practical exercise, as a spontaneous faculty, determined not by the laws of causal necessity but only by the laws of freedom.

6. In Reason's ability to view itself as a member of the world of pure thought is found the third idea which relates rationality to freedom: a rational being can regard itself solely as a member of the world of pure thought, subject only to the laws of pure practical reason, which are the laws of morality.

One final step remains, to show an *a priori* relationship between choosing in the awareness of free choice and acting as a moral agent subject to the law of autonomy, and to show this relationship by relating both of these ideas to the "third idea" of the self as a member of the world of pure thought. If the relationship be simply assumed, then we have merely assumed the validity of the moral law and have failed to prove that rational beings have moral obligations. If the relationship be a judgment causally determined by some introspective experience, it cannot serve as the *a priori* foundation for the validity of the moral law, and the awareness of obligation becomes nothing more than another natural feeling wholly without moral status. Only by justifying the proposition, "All rational beings which possess will are beings which *necessarily* act in a subjective awarenes of themselves as free agents," as a synthetic *a priori* proposition of practical reason, can we ultimately establish the validity and authority of the supreme moral law. That final task now lies before us.

CHAPTER TEN

PART 2—The Validity of the Moral Law

1. *The Justification of the Categorical Imperative*

Kant's final task is to prove *a priori* that the point of view from the world of thought is valid for a being with will; that is, that a rational being *necessarily* takes that point of view when he wills. Without an *a priori* justification of autonomy, Kant's carefully wrought system of morality will collapse into heteronomy; and the necessity of moral obligation based on autonomy will turn out to be nothing more than causal necessity of desires and inclinations. We cannot rely on the merely logical possibility of autonomy. We must provide an *a priori* defense of the categorical imperative by proving that the point of view from the world of pure thought is necessary, at least in a practical sense. But how can we *prove* that every rational being with a will must conceive of himself as a member of the world of thought and so subject to the law of autonomy? Does a man, simply because he is a rational being with a will, necessarily conceive himself subject to the law of freedom, duty-bound by the categorical imperative? This is the crucial question which yet remains to be answered.

HOW IS A CATEGORICAL IMPERATIVE POSSIBLE?

Because he is a thinking being, every rational being counts himself as a member of the world of thought; and because he self as an efficient cause in that world of thought, he k of his causality as the exercise of will. On the other he is also aware that he is a member of the world of sense impressions, in which his actions seem to be merely events in a causal sequence. If we ask how the will, as a causal agent in the world of thought, can produce these actions, we cannot find any answer since we have no knowledge of that world; rather, all causal explanations must rely on appearances in the world of sense impressions (e.g., desires and inclinations). If I were simply a member of the world of thought, all my actions would conform completely to the law of autonomy (the supreme principle of morality); or if I were simply a member of the world of sense impressions, all my actions would conform completely to the natural causality of desires and inclinations—in short, to the law of heteronomy (the natural principle of happiness).

But the world of thought contains that reality which undergirds reality and law in the world of sense impressions. 454 As a thinking being, I can think of my will only as a member of the world of thought, and so I must recognize that the law which governs the world of thought, which is the law of autonomy, governs my will directly. At the same time that I know myself as a member of the world of sense impressions (and subject to laws of natural causality), I must also think of myself as subject to that law of reason which, in the world of thought, contains the idea of freedom. *Thus the law of the world of thought becomes an imperative for me, and actions which conform to this law become my duties.*

In this argument Kant seeks to prove that a rational being necessarily conceives himself subject to the categorical imperative. Let us examine a more detailed statement of his argument.

K1. The world of thought is the objective reality which supports the sensible reality of the world of sense impressions.

K2. Since laws of appearance govern the world of sense impressions, laws of thought must govern the world of thought.

K3. Every time I exercise my will I must think myself to be a member of the world of thought.

K4. Thus, every time I exercise my will, I must think myself subject to the law governing the world of thought, the law of autonomy.

K5. Therefore, every time I exercise my will, I must think myself subject to the law of autonomy, expressed in the categorical imperative.

K6. Therefore, the categorical imperative is valid as a law governing my will. Q.E.D.

Thus Kant completes the argument of the *Foundation*. Not only is the categorical imperative possible, he has argued, but it governs all human activity by imposing moral obligation. The good will, the only absolutely good thing, is within the grasp of every man. If the argument is satisfactory, Kant has proved the validity of the moral command of reason by showing that a free will is subject to *a priori* law. We cannot then avoid a careful, critical analysis of this crucial argument.

2. *How Good is Kant's Proof?*

To begin with, we can determine that the conclusion K6 follows from K5, for if I must think of myself as subject to the categorical imperative, then it does govern my will and so is valid for me as law. Furthermore, we can see that K5 follows from K4, for if the law of autonomy is the law governing the world of thought and if I must think myself a member of that world, then I must think myself subject to that law. In addition, K4 follows from K3, for if I must think myself a member of the world of thought whenever I will, then I must think myself subject to the laws of the world of thought. If K1 is true, then K2 must be true (or so Kant believes), for law must have some foundation for its validity and necessity other than itself.[1] He believes that if there is law in the world of appearances—and there is—then it should be "supported" by a law in the world of objective reality. Now, if I am a member of this objective world, I am subject to its laws and whenever I will I must think myself a member. In exercising my will I necessarily think myself a member of the world of thought, and this thought relates the concept of law in the world of pure thought to the concept of my being subject to that law. K3 is the statement of Kant's "third idea," which carries the argument from K2 to K4, and so to the conclusion, K6.

Unfortunately, analysis of this argument reveals three weaknesses. The first is that the fact of law in the world of sense impressions does not demand a basis in *law*. True, every law demands some ground or other, but only an existent reality of some kind; the reality need not itself be a law nor even be governed by law. As a consequence, we cannot deduce K2 from K1. A second and more serious difficulty is that we cannot even assert K1 with any assurance: we do not know at all what "supports" the world of appearance. We can *think* of the objective world as a foundation for the world of sensible appearances, but the thought does not permit us to assert that such a world exists and even less than it "supports" the world of appearance. Without K1 and K2, however, we have no grounds for thinking ourselves subject to any laws of the world of thought. Even if we prove *a priori* that every time I exercise my will I must think myself a member of the world of thought (which K3 asserts), we have not thereby proved that we must think ourselves governed by any kind of law. K1 and K2 were necessary to establish the validity of the law in the world of thought but, since they fail to do so, the validity of such law and our subjection to it are still unproved. The third fault is that the argument simply assumes the truth of K3. But as we saw clearly at the close of Chapter 9, K3 is the crucial premiss of the proof for freedom of the will. It also expresses Kant's "third idea," without which we cannot establish a necessary connection between exercising our wills and acting as moral agents subject to the law of duty.

Kant's argument, which set out to prove this connection necessary, actually assumes it as a premiss: *thus his argument begs the question and is a failure.*

Since the remainder of Section III shows clearly that Kant was aware of his failure to prove the validity of the moral law, we can legitimately ask why he bothered to present an argument at all. The first and most probable reason is that he wished to point out as accurately as possible the focal problem and the impossibility of solving it. Indeed, the remainder of the *Foundation* is a kind of apologetic explanation of this impossibility. Secondly, since Kant does insist that K3 is a necessary presupposition, so far as it connects willing with moral obligation, he may have wished to suggest indirectly that this *synthetic* union of the two ideas cannot itself be proved, but rather is an ultimate synthetic principle of a system which can be deduced analytically from it.

But the most troublesome aspect of his proof, which Kant apparently does not appreciate, is that by begging the question in his argument, he does not even justify our taking the synthetic connection as a *necessary presupposition.* The validity of the moral law rests squarely on the supposed connection between the fact of willing and law in the world of thought. We can still question whether morality is a sham, a mere stage setting creating the illusion of a good will without its substance. As a defense, let us ask another question: *could* Kant have given an argument which, although it would not prove the objective reality of the moral law, at least would prove that the law of autonomy is valid as a necessary practical law, which for practical reason would be all the proof we require? I believe he could have; and in light of comments he makes later in this section, I will outline briefly how such an argument might be developed.

The categorical imperative is possible because the idea of freedom makes me a member of the world of thought. If this

world were the only world I belonged to, all my actions *would* invariably conform to the autonomy of the will. But I also perceive that I am at the same time a member of the world of sense impressions—and so my actions in the world of sense impressions *ought* to conform to the law of autonomy. This categorical "ought" presents us with a *synthetic a priori practical proposition*: the idea of my will as influenced by sensuous desires is joined to the idea of that same will as a pure, self-directing member of the world of thought. In the idea of the autonomous will we find the ultimate law of reason which governs the will as it appears in the world of sensuous influences.*

* This is similar to the way in which concepts of the understanding, which in themselves are only the forms of law in general, are joined to our immediate impressions of the world of sense and, in this way, make up the synthetic *a priori* propositions which structure all our knowledge of the universe.

We find the key in the sentence: "This categorical 'ought' presents us with a *synthetic a priori practical proposition*." This suggests that a person who understands the practical implication of the moral "ought" does in fact recognize a ground for this "ought," a ground which cannot be derived from the world of sensuous desires. A world governed solely by laws of causal necessity cannot produce a meaningful "ought." If my whole realm of thinking were derived only from the world of appearances, any understanding of the moral "ought" as indicating a possible alternative to natural causal necessity would be utterly impossible. Thus *by the mere fact that I can understand the meaning of "ought," I must necessarily take the point of view of myself as a member of the world of thought, and thus as a free agent whom the "ought" commands.* Should I simply choose this point of view as an imaginative option, I would not thereby recognize an "ought" of moral law; but since I do understand and recognize the "ought" *as a moral imperative,* I must necessarily see myself subject to the laws of freedom.

The cardinal issue in this argument is not any recognition of a law necessary for a world of thought, nor the mere awareness of acting as a free agent. Rather, it is the assertion of free subject to law as a necessary precondition for an understanding of the moral term "ought." Let us put the argument into a rigorous form.

L1. If all understanding came solely from the world of sense impressions, no rational being could understand the implications of the moral "ought."

L2. Every rational being who understands the implications of the moral "ought" necessarily takes a point of view different from that of the world of sense impressions.

L3. Anyone who takes the point of view other than that of the world of sense impressions with its law of causality necessarily thinks himself an agent who can act *independently* of the law of causality: he thinks of himself as a free agent.

L4. Since "ought" signifies the will's awareness of its relationship to an objectively necessary action, *which only a law can determine,* a rational agent must think of himself subject to whatever law determines the action to be objectively necessary: that is, he must think himself subject to the law of freedom expressed in the categorical imperative.

L5. Therefore, any rational human being who understands the implications of the moral "ought" necessarily thinks himself subject to the categorical imperative.

L6. Therefore, the categorical imperative is a valid moral law for anyone who understands what "ought" means.

The advantage of this argument lies in its initial premiss, unspoken in the argument: that we do in fact understand what "ought" means. In order to understand this at all we must think of ourselves in some special way, a way quite different from our membership in the world of causal necessity. But once we think of ourselves as independent of this sensuous world, the categorical imperative becomes a valid command of reason, since *some* law must relate the will to an objectively necessary action, and the only law which remains is that principle which commands the will to act as a free agent—the law of autonomy. The law is therefore valid, not because we have proved that human beings have free will, but because we have proved that *we must think ourselves free agents subject to the law of free agency.* More proof than this we cannot ask, could not find—and do not need. The moral law is valid for all practical purposes; but then it is valid, since it need be valid only for practical purposes.[2]

Of course, we are still creatures of desire, subject as well to the laws of natural inclination, which exert at times an almost overwhelming influence on our wills. Yet no matter how compelling the pull of desire and inclination, so long as we exercise our reason when we act, we are subject to the law of morality. Moreover, we are always aware of this, Kant insists; no matter how debauched we may be, we still respect the moral law.

The practical use of ordinary human reason supports this argument. No one, not even the most hardened criminal—assuming that he uses his reason in other ways—will fail to wish that he could be a person honest in his purpose, faithful to good maxims, sympathetic and generally benevolent, even when it takes great sacrifice, disadvantage, and discomfort. His desires and inclinations prevent him from acting in that way, but he would like to be free of those impulses which weigh so heavily upon him.

Man shows here that he takes himself in thought to a realm in which his will is free, a world totally different from the sensible world of desire. He is aware that he could not gratify his desires in the world of freedom, nor would such a world satisfy his genuine or imaginary needs: this anticipation would destroy the supreme position of that very idea of freedom which makes him wish for virtue. He could only expect to become a person of greater inner worth. The idea of freedom forces him to transfer himself to membership in the world of thought, a world in which he is free from the natural   455 causality of the world of sense impressions. In this world of freedom he becomes aware of a good will which by his own admission stands judge over the bad will he has as a member of the sensuous world. Even while he transgresses the moral law he recognizes its authority. The moral law is his own will as a member of the world of thought; by thinking of himself at the same time as a member of the world of sense, he thinks this law as an "ought."

In more modern terms, so long as a man knows the difference between right and wrong he somehow wishes that he were virtuous, even when his life and habits show not the least evidence of it. He still respects the law and the good will as having an unqualified value, even though he knows well that living by the moral law in pursuit of the good will could not gain him the satisfaction and pleasures which his life of immorality occasionally offers. As long as a man must believe that he acts from his own choosing—whether or not this be so—he must respect the law expressed in the moral "ought."

3. *The Dialectic of Practical Reason*

The essential proof, for better or worse, has been given. The remainder of Section III examines two related questions, the one regarding the conflict between the two points of view and the other explaining why an absolute theoretical proof of freedom is not possible. The first question asks: how can two entirely different sets of laws, both governing the will, be equally valid for the same act of will?

THE EXTREME LIMIT OF PRACTICAL PHILOSOPHY [3]

Every man thinks of himself as a free agent. This way of thinking leads us to judge that some actions *ought* to have been done, even though they were not done. The idea of freedom cannot be derived from experience; experience may reveal demands which conflict head-on with the *a priori* commands arising necessarily from the idea of freedom, yet the commands of freedom still hold. On the other hand, it is equally necessary that everything that happens should be completely determined by natural causal law; thus the causal law is also *a priori*, since it involves the idea of necessity. Experience confirms the idea of Nature as a system, because experience (as knowledge of objects given through sensations and interrelated by universal laws) necessarily rests on the validity of such *a priori* laws. Freedom, then, is only an Idea of Reason which cannot substantiate its own objective reality. Nature, on the other hand, is a concept of the understanding, which *can* prove itself objectively valid by its application to and confirmation by events in experience.

We have seen in Chapter 9 that the understanding produces knowledge of the natural universe by ordering sensations to conform to fundamental *a priori* principles. These principles have already been proved valid by an appeal to reason (in the Transcendental Deduction of the first *Critique*) and confirmed by experience. Ideas of reason, on the other hand, have no such justification and cannot be proved valid as principles of knowledge. How can it be then that an unjustified Idea of practical reason can take precedence over a thoroughly justified concept of the understanding?

From this there arises a dialectic of reason: the freedom we attribute to the will seems to contradict Nature's   456 causal necessity. For scientific knowledge, reason relies on the idea of natural causal necessity, since only in this way can it explain facts of experience; but for the sake of its own agency reason must rely solely on the idea of freedom, since only with this idea can practical reason (will) be considered a cause of action.

Neither the cleverest philosophy nor commonsense can argue freedom away. But if the idea of freedom should contradict either itself or Nature, the already established *a priori* validity of Nature's causal necessity would take precedence and the idea of freedom would have to be abandoned. Since we cannot abandon the idea of freedom any more than that of natural necessity, we must demand that moral philosophy somehow avoid the apparent contradiction between freedom and natural necessity in human action.

This contradiction would be forced upon us if, when we choose to act, we think ourselves subject to natural causality *in the same way and in the same relationship* as we consider ourselves free agents. The inescapable task of theoretical philosophy must be to explain how this contradiction is illusory: that the illusion arises when we *fail* to take a different point of view and affirm a different relationship between the agent and his action when we think of the agent as free, and when we think of him as a part of Nature and subject to her laws.

Furthermore, philosophy must explain not only how we can regard a single agent from both points of view at the same time, but why we *must* do so. For if we could not explain why we must *necessarily* take both points of view, the mere fact that both could be combined without contradiction would not give us sufficient leave to trouble theoretical reason with such an embarrassing difficulty. Theoretical philosophy must do its duty, however, in order to clear the way for practical philosophy. The philosopher has no choice but to erase the apparent contradiction. If he should leave the theory alone, it would be a *bonum vacans*, an abandoned dwelling, which a fatalist might rightly occupy, driving morality from its domain as an unwarranted intruder.

But this would not bring us to the border of practical philosophy. In solving the above controversy, practical 457 philosophy can play no part; it only insists that theoretical philosophy pull free from the tangles of theoretical questions, so that practical reason itself may find peace and security from outside attacks which might contest the ground on which it wants to build.

The dual point of view saves us from contradiction: the two sets of laws, natural causality and freedom, do not conflict so long as we continue to take both points of view. The two worlds have no point of contact whereat the law of one world could suddenly become applicable in the other. But practical reason, since it operates from both points of view, cannot itself explain or justify them. That is the task of metaphysical (theoretical) reasoning. In the following paragraphs, Kant reviews the operation of will in this dualistic situation of agency.

Even common reason claims title to freedom of the will, based on its awareness and assumption of reason's independence from purely subjective causal influences, all of which belong to sensation and combine to form the world of appearance. When a man thinks of himself as an intelligent being with a will (a causal agent), he puts himself into a system of causal relationships entirely different from that other system of sensible appearances to which he also belongs, one in which his outward actions are determined by natural necessity. There is no contradiction at all in saying that an object as it appears in the sensible world is subject to laws governing appearances, and that the same object as it exists in itself may be independent of those laws.

Consequently man does and must think of himself as existing simultaneously in both systems: on the one hand, he is conscious of himself as a being influenced by sensations, so he is subject to the laws governing appearances; on the other hand, he is conscious of himself as an intelligent being, a member of a world of thought which is independent of the laws governing appearances. On these grounds man claims to have a will which can ignore desires and inclinations, and by doing so can—indeed must—think of its actions as results of its own agency. He is the cause of his actions because he is an intelligent being; through his actions he produces effects according to the principles governing the world of thought, which principles he knows only by pure reason, independently of experience.

Furthermore, since he conceives his own true nature as an intelligent being only by considering himself in the world of thought—for he knows his own *human* nature through experience—these principles rule him directly and categorically. Not even the allurements, influences, and temptations of the entire natural world of sense impressions can weaken in the least the laws governing his will as an intelligent being. He does not even hold himself responsible for these influences and desires for they do not arise from his true nature as will; he is responsible only for letting them influence his maxims to the ex-   458
tent that he violates the rational laws governing the will.

If knowledge of the world of thought is impossible, can practical reason find there the foundation for its law? Would this not constitute an illegitimate inference for reason to make, one which would end in an antinomy, an unavoidable contradiction, of practical reason? No, Kant would reply, for our idea of the world of pure thought is a *negative* idea, containing in itself only the characteristic of being independent of causal necessity. It gains positive value when we think ourselves as members of this world.

Practical reason does not overstep its limitations by thinking itself in the world of thought, although it would do so if it tried to enter this world through intuition or sensation. As a mere negation of the world of sense impressions, the world of thought does not give reason any laws which govern the will. The only positive element we find there is that the negative characteristic of freedom is joined with a positive one, the will as a causal agent. The will is the ability to act according to principles which comply with the essential condition of rational causality: that is, principles or maxims which have the validity of universal law.

But if practical reason tried to find an object of will (a motive) in the world of thought, it would exceed its limitations and pretend to be acquainted with something which it actually cannot know at all. The idea of a world of thought is simply the point of view outside the world of sense impressions which reason must take in order to think of itself as practical. Such a point of view would be impossible if the influences of sense impressions completely determined man. As is, this point of view is necessary in order for man to be aware of himself as an intelligent being, a rational cause, following the dictates of reason, and acting freely.

This point of view certainly involves the idea of an order and system of laws different from that of a mechanical world of sense impressions; it necessitates the idea of a world of thought populated by rational beings existing as things in themselves.[4] But this point of view gives us nothing more than the formal condition of the world of thought, namely, that maxims of the will be valid as universal law and thus conform to the will's autonomy, which is the only way will can consistently exercise its freedom. For any law which aims at some object is heteronomous, a law of Nature which applies only in the world of sense impressions.

Practical reason cannot legitimately look to the world of thought for some incentive or goal to aid the will in complying with the moral imperative. Not only is such a quest impossible —the world of thought cannot be an object of such knowledge— but further, even if it were possible, by finding such an incentive or goal, reason would thereby negate the law of morality and nullify the moral motive, which is to act for duty's sake alone. Paradoxical as it may seem, the moral law is valid *because* practical reason cannot know the world of thought.

4. *How Can Reason Be Practical?*

To ask how reason can be practical is to ask how a human will, living in a determined universe of appearances which is governed through and through by laws of causal necessity, can be a free agent in its activity. But in order to explain how reason is practical, we require a set of laws which govern the will, by means of which we can give the explanation demanded. But the only law we know in the world of thought is the law of freedom, which *presupposes* the freedom of will and consequently cannot in turn explain this freedom. A presupposition, however necessary it may be, cannot justify the principles which require it; on the contrary, the presupposition itself must be justified by those principles. *Because* we must think of ourselves as members of the world of thought, we must presuppose freedom as the foundation for this world; otherwise we could not even conceive of this world in any meaningful sense. Or to put it briefly: any will which thinks of itself as an agent must presuppose that condition which makes agency possible, namely, freedom.

If reason tried to explain *how pure reason can be practical*, it would certainly exceed its limitations. But this is the same as trying to explain *how freedom is possible*. In order to explain anything, we must subsume it under some law whose object can be experienced. But freedom is a mere idea; we cannot explain its objective validity by some law of Nature or through some possible experience. No example or analogy will help us to comprehend or even imagine how freedom is possible. *The idea of freedom has only one kind of validity: it is a necessary presupposition for a rational being which is aware of its own will* as the ability to determine itself to act as an intelligent being according to laws of reason, independently of desires which are subject to Nature's direction. But if we cannot explain freedom by the laws of Nature, we cannot explain it at all.

But we can still *defend* freedom by refuting the arguments of those who claim a special insight into the essences of things and boldly assert that freedom is impossible. We can show them that the apparent contradiction which they point to rests on their thinking of man as necessarily an object of appearance, so that the laws of Nature can explain human activity. When they consider man as an intelligent being, they should likewise think of him as a thing in itself—but no, they persist in making him an object of appearance there as well. According to this view, to say that man's will is a free cause in a world of determined natural causes is an obvious contradiction. But if they are reasonable and are willing to reconsider, they must grant that things in themselves must exist "behind" the appearances as a hidden support; and when they recognize that the laws which govern appearances cannot be extended to govern things in themselves, the apparent contradiction fades away.

The impossibility of proving that the will is free has one beneficial result at least: no one can prove that will is *not* free. The attempts by determinists to deny genuine freedom have for the most part relied on the law of cause and effect, according to which every event, whether physical or psychical, is what it is because some prior states or events were what they were. Objective freedom, they claim, is simply a self-contradictory idea, that a being subject to causality can act independently of causality. Of course, implicit in this argument is the singularity of the determinist's point of view; he sees the will simply as an object in the world as we know it, the world of appearances. From this point of view alone the will appears completely determined. It is only when we also think of ourselves as members of another world that freedom becomes possible—yet we know nothing else of this other world. Consequently, there is nothing else known which could possibly conflict with freedom in the world of pure thought.[5]

If I know the world of thought only as a world in which I think myself a free agent, then nothing in this world can attract me, nothing can influence my will, nothing can appear as an incentive, nothing can interest me—*other than the law itself.* And yet interest seems to demand some basis other than its own mere existence. Why do I find this interest in moral law? How is it that I find a deep satisfaction in obeying the call of duty, particularly when duty commands me with no promise whatsoever of satisfaction of any kind?

Just as we find it impossible to explain freedom of the will, so too we find it impossible to locate and explain the kind of interest* we take in moral law. But we do take an interest in it, relating this interest to a moral feeling. Some moral philosophers have mistaken this feeling for the standard of our moral judgments; rather it should be seen as a *subjective* effect of the law on a will whose objective principles are found in reason alone.

460

* Interest makes reason practical; it is a cause which determines the will. Only rational beings can take an interest in something; irrational beings merely feel sensuous impulses. When the objective validity of the law suffices to determine the will, we say that reason takes a direct, pure interest in the action. But when reason can determine the will only by an appeal to some object of desire or to a particular feeling in the agent, we call this an indirect interest. Since reason by itself cannot discover any such object or feeling outside of experience, indirect interest is merely empirical, not a pure, rational interest. The logical interest which reason takes in unifying the many objects of experience into a meaningful system cannot be a direct interest, but must rest on the presupposition that some purpose will be served by the exercise.

If reason alone can command a rational will (which is influenced by sensuous desires) to act as it ought to act, then reason must be able to instill a feeling of pleasure or satisfaction in the performance of duty. This means that reason must be able to arouse sensuous influences in support of its own principles. But we simply cannot explain *a priori* how a mere idea which is completely empty of any empirical content can arouse a feeling of pleasure or displeasure. This presents a special instance of the general law of cause and effect and can be known not *a priori*, but only through our experience of the relationship between two objects in appearance.

How then can we hope to explain why the universality of the maxim as moral law can interest us? We would have to explain how a pure idea of reason, which gives no object to experience, can produce an effect in the world of experience. And this is impossible for human intelligence. One thing we do know: the law is not valid because it interests us; this would be heteronomy, basing practical reason on a sensuous feeling, which will never produce moral law. Rather, *the law*   461 *interests us because it is valid,* because it arises from the will of intelligent being, which we take to be our own true nature. In this way, *whatever characterizes the will in the world of mere appearances is necessarily subordinated to the true nature of the will in itself.*

Could it be that the interest we find in the moral law conveys to us in some unfathomable way a feeling of true rationality, of progress towards the achievement of a good will, which we somehow recognize as the truly unqualified good? Certainly when we obey the call of duty we find a deep, intangible satisfaction which can exceed even the most intense earthy delight —and yet we cannot explain it.

5. *The Limits of Practical Reason*

Granted that the idea of freedom is a presupposition of practical reason, is there possibly some line of reasoning which might help to establish the validity of this idea as a presupposition? For example, in what sense can we call the idea of freedom a *necessary* presupposition? Is its necessity as a presupposition anything more than a merely logical relationship? And would some other presupposition serve as well?

Thus the question, "How is a categorical imperative possible?" can be answered to the extent that we can state *the only presupposition which makes it possible: the idea of freedom.* We can also see how this presupposition is a necessary and sufficient condition for the practical exercise of reason, convincing us of the validity of the categorical imperative and of the moral law.

But human reason cannot possibly prove the truth of this pre-supposition.

Once we grant this presupposition—that an intelligent being has free will—autonomy necessarily follows as the sole formal condition for determining this will. The *possible* truth of this presupposition can easily be proved by theoretical philosophy, since it involves nothing contradictory to the laws of natural causality which connect appearances in the world of sense impressions. But what is more, we can prove its *practical necessity*: freedom is an unconditional principle which *must* be presupposed by any rational being aware of its own causality as will acting independently of desire; that is, we presuppose the idea of reason as the underlying condition for all our acts of will.

The idea of freedom is undoubtedly a logical possibility; it is not self-contradictory, nor does it contradict any other known truth—so long as we adhere to the two points of view. This is a merely negative appraisal of truth, however; it is a minimum condition which every judgment must meet before any further consideration will be given it. From a practical standpoint, on the other hand, freedom can be proved as a necessary pre-supposition for every exercise of rational will. This does not mean that a person is forced to acknowledge the truth of free will simply because he wills. Rather, free will must be assumed at least implicitly by a person who wills, because if he thought of himself as a mere effect, he would *not* think of himself as a causal agent and so he would not bother to will at all. Willing demands a ground in freedom (as its *ratio essendi*), even though it does not demand that the fact of freedom be recognized as a necessary truly. We do not assume free will in order to prove that man exercises will; on the contrary, willing is a datum of experience, but it is a datum totally unexplainable by means of causal necessity. Consequently, either our capacity to will is absolutely unexplainable or we must presuppose freedom as that condition which explains our ability to will.

That freedom is compatible with the given experience of willing does not prove freedom true, but only that freedom is the
sole presupposition which can make willing possible—or else we
hold the datum itself to be a hallucination. Common sense,
however, forbids our classifying as hallucinatory an experience
as universal and commonplace as exercising our capacity to will.
Therefore, from the fact that I will, reason demands that I will
as a free agent, demands that freedom be presupposed as the
objective reality which "supports" my capacity to will—even
though reason cannot prove that freedom is a fact of objective
reality. If I will, I necessarily will *as if* my freedom were a
proven fact; unless I will under this implicit assumption, I do not
will at all. On this basis, then, because I will as a self-conscious,
rational being, freedom must be a necessary presupposition of
practical reason.

But if we seek to answer the question: (a) how can pure
reason be practical without relying on motives drawn from
somewhere else; or (b) how can the bare principle of the universal validity of all its maxims as laws (surely the only way
pure practical reason gives commands) arouse a purely moral
motive and interest without depending on some object of desire;
or, to put it simply, (c) how can pure reason be practical?—
then human reason fails completely and all the effort and work
of looking for answers is futile.

I would again waste my time if I tried to find out how
freedom itself is possible as the causality of a will. I   462
would have to abandon the empirical basis for explanation—but it is the only one I have. Yes, I could gambol about
in the world of thought, the world of pure ideas, for I do have
good ground for these ideas. But I have not the least knowledge
of the world, nor can I ever hope to gain any, no matter how
hard I exert my natural powers of reason. The world of thought
is only an abstract idea which remains after I have eliminated
all sensuous influences on the will. This idea permits me to

keep the moral motive distinct from the world of appearances, showing that it does not contain absolutely everything, that something more must exist outside it.

Yet of this "more" I have no knowledge at all. Once I exclude all material content from pure reason which frames this ideal, taking away all its knowledge of objects, I have left only its form, the practical law that all its maxims must be universally valid. By conforming to this ideal, reason can be related to a world of pure thought as a possible efficient cause which governs the will. No other motive is allowed except this idea of a world of thought in which reason itself provides the motive. But how to explain it any further is the very problem we cannot solve.

I cannot doubt that I am exercising my will when I will. The exercise of will is a fact of experience. Freedom must be presupposed as the necessary condition to account for it. But I am wasting my time if I try to explain how the mere idea of freedom can produce an event in the world of sense impressions, particularly an event which cannot be explained by means of freedom and yet cannot be explained without it. This is the paradox of free will: the causal laws of the world of appearance cannot explain will, since through causal necessity no explanation of will is possible, and yet causal necessity is the only way we have for explaining events. On the other hand, the experience of willing cannot be explained without the presupposition of freedom; but the idea of freedom cannot further explain how a rational agent can will, since the idea of freedom does not involve a system of causal laws. That the idea of freedom is a necessary presupposition for a rational will may justify the validity of the moral law, but it explains no fact of human experience whatsoever.

We have thus reached the limit of all moral inquiry. Yet it was important that we find this limit: (a) so that reason would not look to the world of appearances for some understandable but empirical supreme motive, one that would destroy morality; and (b) so that reason would not uselessly flap its wings in the vacuum of transcendent ideas we call the world of thought, unable to move except into a world of fantasies. Moreover, the idea of a world of pure thought to which we and all intelligent beings belong—while we belong at the same time to the world of sense impressions—gives us a basis for a *rational faith*. Although we know nothing about it, this ideal universal kingdom of rational ends in themselves can arouse in us a lively interest in the moral law. We can become members of that kingdom only by living strictly by the maxims of freedom   463 *as if* they were laws of Nature.

Kant's idea of a rational faith in an ideal universe of rational ends can lead to a form of Absolute Idealism. The reasoning might run something like this. If we believe that the will of every rational being is free, then each person becomes an autonomous member of the world of thought by his very willing. This world of objective reality is governed by laws of freedom, which are the laws of Reason. Thus all men are ends in themselves in a universe governed by Reason, and when they seek to conform their maxims to the law of autonomous reason, they join their own finite minds and wills harmoniously to Absolute Reason, which is superior to the collective whole of finite beings. Thus through reason and will we can come to partake of the Absolute Reason which governs the objective world of thought.

The weakness in this kind of argument lies in inferring from what is at best an ideal that the ideal is a reality. True, a man may find a certain meaning in existence by thinking that he unites himself to Absolute Mind when he performs his duty; nor would this conflict with the moral motive. But we must keep in mind that this is an *interpretation* of human existence, not a known fact. The ideal may make life more positively meaningful than concepts like "worthiness of happiness," but it cannot posit a goal which can take precedence over the moral objective of achieving the good will.[6]

CONCLUSION

A theoretical philosophy of Nature points to the absolute necessity of a First Cause of the universe. A practical philosophy of freedom also points to an absolute necessity, but only the necessity of the laws governing the actions of rational beings as such. All reasoning follows the basic rule that knowledge be pursued to the awareness of necessity, otherwise it is not rational knowledge. But a basic limitation on this reasoning prevents our knowing the necessity of what exists, what happens, or what ought to happen, unless we presuppose some *condition* for what exists, happens, or ought to happen. Reason then looks to higher and higher conditions in its search for satisfaction, continuously seeking the *ultimate unconditional necessity* in knowledge. It finds itself forced to *assume* this unconditional necessity without being able to prove it or fully understand it, and is content simply to find some idea which fits the presupposition.

Reason seeks the unconditional condition. In metaphysics the unconditioned is represented by the Uncaused Cause of all existence. In moral philosophy it is the absolutely supreme principle which is not derivable from some more remote principle. Human reasoning, however, is wholly incapable of reaching the unconditional condition, either of theoretical or moral metaphysics: the intellectual instinct which sends human reason on its quest keeps it unceasingly searching. Built into reason is the need for an explanation of everything by means of the conditions necessary for this or that to exist or happen. The ideal goal of this rational instinct is ultimate discovery, that ultimate condition necessary to everything else, but itself unconditioned by any higher necessity. There is only one fault in all this: reason would not recognize the unconditioned condition if it found it. Implanted in Reason is the instinctive restlessness to search for the unconditioned condition—but no means is provided for recognizing such a condition. Consequently, no matter what is presented to reason as a condition, reason must seek the condition for this condition, and the condition for *this* condition, and so on. Thus when we hear the statement, "The universe was caused by God," we feel a familiar and irresistible urge to ask, "Yes, but what caused God?" while at the same time we recognize the impatience and frustration, the necessity and absurdity, of asking such an impossible question. If we believe God to be the First Cause, we must accept this belief as a necessary presupposition, itself unexplainable, but which explains finite existence. Freedom, too, is a necessary presupposition, forced upon us by our inability as human beings to explain rational will, and our inability to justify freedom.

We cannot criticize our deduction of the supreme principle of morality for failing to explain how the unconditional practical law is absolutely necessary (as the categorical imperative must be). The fault lies in human reason itself; and yet we cannot blame reason for being unwilling to explain the moral law by an appeal to some conditional interest, for any such law would not be moral—it could not be the supreme law of freedom. And so while we cannot comprehend the unconditional practical necessity of the moral imperative, we can at least explain *why* we cannot comprehend it—which is all that we can ask fairly of a philosophy which tries by its principles to reach the very limit of human reason.

6. *Epilogue*

In the final estimate, Kant's work has been both a success and a failure. He succeeded admirably in showing the necessary elements, the fundamental principles, and the ultimate ground which can constitute a genuine metaphysics of morals. But he failed in the end to prove that his metaphysics is not an illusion of human reason, one having a certain internal coherence but no genuine effectiveness in human affairs. The failure cannot be imputed to Kant's inadequacy as a moral philosopher. As he analysed the compexities of human reasoning, he concluded that some questions were beyond man's capacity to answer. The question of whether or not freedom is real was one of them.

One advantage of writing a commentary is that the writer has the chance to say the last word, and I will briefly exercise this irreverent advantage. Kant's failure, it seems to me, lies not so much in reason's inability to find the truth of freedom as in Kant's asking a question which needs no answer. When I employ a system of logic erected on the principle of contradiction, I cannot legitimately ask whether the principle can be proved valid or not. A man reasons by the chosen principle or he does not reason at all, in any intelligible sense. This is the essence of the supplementary proof for the validity of the categorical imperative that I presented earlier in this chapter. It simply cannot seriously be questioned whether the moral law is valid for any rational being with a will. Merely to be aware of one's existence is enough to "prove" the moral law valid, for morality is nothing more than a formalized definition of what it means to act as a rational being. A human being is duty-bound because he is a human being.

NOTES

1. Kant's Moral Revolution

1. Jacques Maritain, *Moral Philosophy*. (Scribner, New York City, 1964.) p. 95.

2. A 633=B 661. Quotations from the *Critique of Pure Reason* are taken from N. Kemp Smith's translation (Macmillan, London, 1956).

3. As Kant does, I use "condition" in the sense of a necessary prerequisite, as in "Good behavior is a condition for parole." Sensations must meet the conditions set down by pure reason in order to be acceptable as meaningful experiences.

4. See the example in Plato's *Republic*, Bk. I, 331 E.

2. The Purpose of the *Foundation*

1. Chap. 1, Sect. 4.

2. Epicurus to Menoeceus. Reprinted in A. I. Melden (Ed.), *Ethical Writers* (New York, Prentice-Hall, 1955), p. 145.

3. A recent version of this theory is found in John Stuart Mill's *Utilitarianism* (1863).

4. I should point out that the *Metaphysics of Morals* has lately received considerably more attention, reflected not only by good translations but also in commentaries and articles.

5. This matter will be discussed in depth in Chap. 7, Sect. 1.

3. The Propositions of Moral Value

1. Although the question is of considerable importance, no discussion will be found here regarding the many possible meanings of *good*. Kant does not discuss this question in the *Foundation*, and I am content to rely on the reader's understanding of the ordinary distinctions made.

2. In the *Nicomachean Ethics*, Aristotle treats this problem from a different point of view: how can a man perform just deeds unless he is

already just? "The doer is just or temperate not because he does such things but when he does them in the manner of just and temperate persons [i.e., with the right disposition or motive]." (1105 b)

3. Cf., J. S. Mill's *Utilitarianism,* Chap. 2, for a statement of this view.

4. Cf., *Critique of Pure Reason,* the First Antinomy (B 455 to B 462), and the Solution (B 545).

5. In the *Critique of Pure Reason,* Kant does admit that this principle is an analogy. (Cf. B 425) To present it in the argument here as an axiom, however, without any qualification, does seem somewhat unwarranted.

6. A poignant example of this facility to "perceive" an obligation in a factual situation is found in Arthur Miller's *Death of a Salesman,* where Linda says of Willy Loman, her husband: "He's not the finest character that ever lived. But he's a human being, and a terrible thing is happening to him. So attention *must* be paid" (my italics).

7. This is reflected in our frequent interchanging of *ought* and *must* when speaking of obligation. Thus, "You ought to repay Smith the ten dollars," is often equivalent to, "You must repay Smith the ten dollars."

8. This entire discussion centers on duty *as recognized.* A person may easily omit doing something he ought to do, objectively speaking, yet be unaware that he ought to do it. Duty, as a moral concept, has moral implication only when the agent is aware of it. However, to examine this complex problem here would take us too far afield.

9. W. D. Ross, in *The Right and the Good* (Oxford, 1930), suggests, through a calculus of motives, that mixed motives may produce actions in such a way that "the value of the action is greater than if it had been done from duty alone." Cf. pp. 168–173.

10. Such parallelisms are frequent in the Bible; Psalms is a treasure house of them. E.g., "O Lord, my heart is not proud, nor are my eyes haughty." (Ps. 130)

11. In this paragraph Kant again anticipates. He had mentioned the moral maxim before defining *maxim.* Here he speaks of the formal rule of reason. Since he will soon explain what he means by this, analysis here is unnecessary.

12. In Section III (Chap. 9 below), Kant will explain that a free will is "determined" by laws of freedom, expressly rejecting any suggestion that a free will is arbitrary in its choices.

13. *Pflicht ist Notwendigkeit einer Handlung aus Achtung fürs Gesetz.* Literally: "Duty is the necessity of an action out of respect for law." To translate it, "Duty is the necessity of acting out of respect for

law," or, "Duty is the necessity of an action performed from respect for law," is neither an accurate translation nor an accurate interpretation of the third proposition. My reading, *Duty is an action which, out of respect for law, I acknowledge as necessary for me to perform,* while it certainly goes beyond the letter of the text, expresses what Kant intends by the third proposition, which a literal version cannot convey.

14. The German word is *Achtung.* H. J. Paton translates it by "reverence," but others agree on "respect." Reverence suggests something Kant did not mean, namely, an awareness of *superior* value. But he cannot mean that the law is superior to my will, since it is precisely in my practical reason (my will) that the law is grounded. The law is not superior to man; as Jacobi observed, "The law is made for the sake of man and not man for the sake of the law." To recognize unqualified value is not to recognize superior value.

15. See Kant's comment on the law of love, pp. 61–62.

4. The Form of Law: Universality

1. Cf., A. E. Ewing, *Ethics* (New York, Free Press, 1965), p. 57f, for an intuitionist's view of this same example.

2. H. J. Paton, *The Categorical Imperative,* p. 194.

3. David Hume, *An Inquiry Concerning the Principles of Morals.* See Section 9, "Conclusion," for a summary of Hume's position.

4. A classic use of this argument is found in Milton's treatise on divorce.

5. Prologue to Section II

1. Cf. Chap. 1, Sect. 2, above.

2. David Hume, *An Inquiry Concerning the Principles of Morals.* Appendix I.

3. See above pp. 24–25.

6. Practical Reason and Its Imperatives

1. See Chap. 1, Sect. 3, for a review of the distinction between speculative and practical reason.

2. Cf., Plato's *Meno,* 77B et seq.

3. Compare this to Kant's distinction in the *Prolegomena* between judgments of perception (valid only for the subject) and judgments of experience (universally valid). Pt. II, Sect. 18–20.

4. This raises the interesting theological question of whether Jesus, as Son of God, could have chosen other than the good. How was He tempted? If He experienced the call of duty, was His will then not completely good? But if He could not know the constraint of duty, how was He truly man? Fortunately, I need not discuss the problem here.

5. Compare Aristotle's distinction, *Nicomachean Ethics,* Bk. 6, Chap. 12 (1144a).

6. In his First Introduction to the *Critique of Judgment,* Kant makes the following observation:

Let me here correct a mistake I made in the *Foundation for a Metaphysics of Morals.* After I had indicated that the imperatives of skill command only conditionally, related as they are to a goal which is merely possible (i.e., conditional, or problematic), I called such commands "problematic imperatives." But this expression is contradictory. A better expression would have been "technical imperatives," imperatives of art. Thus the pragmatic rules, the counsels of prudence, become technical imperatives, since these also prescribe conditionally, being related to an actual and subjectively necessary goal. (Prudence, you see, can be considered as the use of free agents, particularly one's own natural powers and desires, as means to some further goal.) But we retain the distinct classification of "counsels of prudence," because the goal which we seek from others and ourselves —happiness—is no merely arbitrary goal. In such imperatives of prudence we require not only the means to the goal (happiness) but indeed some definition of the goal itself. In technical imperatives, on the other hand, we can assume that the goal is clearly understood.

7. Kant's treatment of *means* in his discussion of the hypothetical imperative is not very thorough. When he says that willing the end analytically includes willing the means, he fails to distinguish between the following senses of *willing the means:* (a) willing *all* of the means, or only some of them; (b) willing one among alternatives; (c) willing the *best* means. Such a distinction is not essential to his discussion but it arises whenever one tries to construct examples to illustrate what Kant means by the analytic means–end relationship.

8. This passage serves to show again that happiness is not the goal of reason. Since human reason does not know exactly what happiness is, it cannot judge accurately whether its choices will or will not lead

to happiness. It would be poor arrangement by Nature if man's rational goal in life could be achieved only by a lucky shot in the dark. Another note of interest is that the particular suggestions which Kant lists as empirical counsels—"diet, frugality, courtesy, restraint, etc."—are prudential maxims of Stoicism and give us an insight into Kant's own ideas on what constituted the Good Life. (Cf. Chap. 7, Sect. 1.)

9. Cf., above, Chap. 1, Sect. 5, p. 14.

7. The Three Variations of the Categorical Imperative

1. See the discussion in Chapter 1, Section 2. Kant begins his discussion with no indication that he is doing anything more than continuing the investigations of the previous chapter. Later, when he resumes the investigation (Chap. 8), he summarizes the long interlude as though he had never written it. A. R. C. Duncan believes that the long discussion is a later addition, something of a second-thought attempt to "gain a hearing for the moral law." (*Practical Reason and Morality*, Chap. 11 in particular.) A list of some important discussions on the variations will be found in the bibliography at the end of this chapter.

2. See above, p. 43.

3. Cf., "'Kant and Greek Ethics (II)," Klaus Reich, *Mind*, Vol. 47, Oct. 1939, for a detailed treatment of Kant's debt to Cicero. My own debt to Duncan and Reich will be obvious.

4. Cf., Kant's *Prolegomena to Any Future Metaphysics*, Pt. II, Sect. 14. Also, *Critique of Pure Reason*, A 216.

5. Such consistency is one of the most persuasive arguments for an intelligent and providential Creator of the universe. See Thomas Aquinas' fifth argument (*Summa Theologica*, I–I, Q. 3), and Hume's rebuttal of the "Argument from Design," as it is often called (*Dialogues on Natural Religion*, Bk. 2). Kant agreed with Hume that the Argument from Design is inconclusive (*Critique of Pure Reason*, A 620–630).

6. The Stoics believed in a positive divine influence (*Nous*) which guided the affairs of men and nature. The Stoic rules commanded men to live in a manner attuned to the Divine rational influence. They held this to be the meaning of the precept to "act conformably to Nature."

7. Cf., J. S. Mill, *Utilitarianism*, Chap. I.

8. See Kant's argument for this point in Section I above, pp. 47 ff. For a different interpretation of how the inconsistency appears in

willing against duty, see Julius Ebbinghaus, "The Interpretation and Misinterpretation of the Categorical Imperative," *Philosophical Quarterly*, Vol. 4, 1954, 97–108, especially Part II. Ebbinghaus emphasizes the natural goal of happiness as the locus of the inconsistency in willing.

9. In the Preface. See above, Chap. 2, Sect. 1, and the summary graph on p. 22.

10. This sentence is not clear. The various translations differ quite noticeably:

Beck: "The subjective ground of desire is the *incentive*, while the objective ground of violation is the *motive*."

Paton: "The subjective ground of a desire is an *impulsion;* the objective ground of volition is a *motive*."

Abbott: "The subjective ground of desire is the *spring*, the objective ground of the volition is the *motive*."

Falk: "The subjective ground of desire is the *motive*, while the objective ground of volition is the *reason*."

Kant uses "subjective" and "objective" in a different sense than usual, more like "point of departure" and "aiming point." We might paraphrase the sentence in question as follows: "The originating source of desire is called an incentive (which may be a need, drive, etc.); the objective insofar as it is proposed to be achieved by acting is called the motive (or purpose, or end)." Kant sees desire as the origin of many motivating impulses, and the motive as the objective toward which the impulse aims.

11. Consider the following passage:

IV. ENDS WHICH ARE ALSO DUTIES

They are: (a) The perfection of self and (b) the happiness of others. We cannot twist these around so that the same person will have duties to seek his own happiness and the perfection of others.

Surely all men, by their very natures, seek their own happiness. But it would be meaningless to list this end as a duty, for how can it be one's duty to pursue that which he cannot help but seek? Duty involves a constraint between the will and an end chosen in opposition to natural desire. It is absurd, then, to argue that man *ought* to seek his own happiness with all his might.

Similarly, it is wrong to think myself duty-bound to promote the perfection of others as though it were my own end. The perfection of each man as a person consists simply in his ability to establish his own ends and determine his own duties. How then could I be duty-bound to do for someone else what no one but he himself can do? (*Metaphysics of Morals*, Pt. 2, Introduction, Sec. 4, p. 385.)

12. The same holds when we obey civil laws except that instead of personal authority, we respect legislative or statutory authority.

13. The words *autonomy* and *heteronomy* are derived from the Greek: autonomy from *autos* and *nomos*, meaning self-law or law imposed upon oneself; heteronomy from *heteros* and *nomos*, meaning another's law or law imposed from without. Kant's use of such terms is obvious.

14. Kant's word is *Reich*. Beck translates it as "Realm," while Abbott and Paton prefer "kingdom." The difference is minor since Kant is not speaking of any particular form of government but rather of a community of individual rational beings under a common law. Cf. Paton, p. 187f.

15. Sec. 49, (p. 317, Ak. ed.).

16. Bk. II, Chap. 2, Sect. 5 (pp. 123–132, Ak. ed.).

17. My interpretation of this obscure passage is, I admit, not universally shared. But most commentators do not comment at all on this question as it appears here. I have avoided reading it in light of Kant's later writings, because (a) it is not clear that such interpretation by hindsight is correct, and (b) it requires a theistic premiss. My reading requires neither, but makes sense of what Kant says in the *Grundlegung* (although I do not insist that it is how Kant meant to be understood).

18. Kant concludes this paragraph with the following sentence: *"Duty does not bind the sovereign in a kingdom of ends, but only the members, and all of them in the same manner."* This sentence seems clearly inconsistent with everything Kant has said about the sovereign in a kingdom of ends as subject to his own law—unless here he means God, the Sovereign of Heaven. But no groundwork has been laid for this remark and, since it involves the difficulties I have already mentioned in Note 17 above, I take the liberty of excising it from the main body of the text.

19. I have translated *Affectionspreis* as "aesthetic price," there being no good English equivalent of the German. "Affective price" conveys little meaning to the modern reader.

20. The common imperatives given here are basically the three Stoic rules discussed in the beginning of this chapter.

8. Autonomy and Heteronomy

1. In this recapitulation Kant takes a slightly different approach. This suggests that the ethical discussion of the three variations was written separately from the core of the *Foundation*.

2. Kant seems to overlook the need of positive action in imperfect duties to ourselves and to others. As we saw in the third and fourth examples, duty requires more than the mere negative avoidance of treating a rational being solely as a means; we must also work positively for our own perfection and the happiness of others.

3. Kant's term is *subject*. I avoided using this term because its technical meaning is unfamiliar and, without a precise explanation, might confuse more than clarify. The use is similar to Aristotle's (Cf. *Categories*, Chap. 5, 2a).

4. That is, one cannot have the duty to seek the perfection of others or his own happiness. Cf., note 11, Chap. 7.

5. On the other hand, "moral worth" applies to motives, not to actions. Compare the second proposition of moral worth (Chap. 3, Sect. 2).

6. Cf. *Critique of Practical Reason*, Bk. 1, Chap. 1 (p. 40, Ak. ed.).

7. Utilitarianism, Chapter 2.

8. Exemplified by Aristotle's *Nicomachean Ethics*.

9. Cf. Henry Sidgwick, *The Methods of Ethics* (Chicago, 1962), 7th Ed., Bk. 1, Chap. 4, for a classic refutation of the universal dominion of the pleasure principle.

10. Recent advocates of intuitionist ethics are G. E. Moore (*Principia Ethica*, 1903), Sir W. David Ross (*The Right and the Good*, 1930), and A. C. Ewing (*The Definition of Good*, 1947).

11. *Inquiry Concerning the Principles of Morals*, Appendix (Bobbs-Merrill, Indianapolis, 1957), p. 107.

12. *An Inquiry Concerning Moral Good and Bad* (1725), Introduction, *ad fin.* (*British Moralists*, ed. Selby-Bigge. [Bobbs-Merrill, Indianapolis, 1954] Vol. I, p. 72.)

13. Although Kant had specifically in mind Christian Wolff's *Universal Practical Morality*. See above, Chap. 2, p. 29.

14. This view in Kant's day was represented by Christian August Crusius (1715–1775), who espoused the somewhat Leibnizian position that God had implanted in the human mind certain rules and concepts which gave man an intuitive insight into God's preestablished harmony in the world.

15. Kant apparently takes a tongue-in-cheek dig at the Prussian ministry of education, which had the power to authorize selected theories as official doctrine. That such administrators usually lacked the basic intellectual background for making such distinctions emphasized all the more the danger of their doing so, especially as a matter of national domestic policy.

9. Freedom and Autonomy

1. For the distinction between *Wille* and *Willkür* I am indebted to Professor John Silber's discussion in *Ethics*, Vol. 73, 1962, and in his introductory essay to Kant's *Religion Within the Limits of Reason Alone* (New York, Harper, 1960). I assume responsibility for any variance from his treatment.

2. See Henry Sidgwick, *Methods of Ethics*, 7th Ed. (Chicago, 1962), pp. 511–516.

3. The example indicates how two ideas may be related by a third. It also illustrates how their relationship is *a priori*, but one must be familiar with Kant's transcendental doctrine of space to see the *a priori* connection. Cf., *Critique of Pure Reason*, B 37 *et seq.*

4. *Critique of Pure Reason*, The Paralogisms of Pure Reason, especially B 425.

5. I confess that Kant's purpose in this shift of approach escapes me. By distinguishing here between acting *from* interest (i.e., heteronomously) and *having* an interest, he yields no insights into the problem at hand but rather offers a paradoxical parallel which only muddies the development of his argument. This point, moreover, has already been discussed in Section II (Chap. 6, p. 110) and will be discussed again at some length in Chapter 10.

6. See above, Chapter 3, p. 43.

7. Cf. Chapter 3, p. 60.

8. See pp. 46–47.

9. To the complaint of the scholar of the Kantian *Critique* that I am not precise in my discussion here, I can only apologize with the excuse that I did not mean to be. The precision appropriate to a learned seminar on Transcendental Logic would here be unnecessary and pedantic.

10. While we may have some privileged access to ourselves that is denied to others, it consists not of a different kind of knowledge but only of private experiences unavailable to others.

11. These functions, while distinguishable, do not occur separately. In fact, Kant warns strongly of the danger of converting a distinction for purposes of analysis into a real distinction.

12. This is Kant's famous doctrine of the Antinomies of Pure Reason. See *Critique of Pure Reason*, especially B 531–535.

13. Kant uses three terms—Sensibility, Understanding, and Reason—in rather rigid senses. Here Reason (with a capital *R*) refers to the third, organizing function of mental activity.

14. In the *Critique of Practical Reason,* Kant gives the following solution to the problem of circularity:

> To avoid having anyone imagine that there is an inconsistency when I say that freedom is the condition of the moral law and later assert that the moral law is the only condition under which freedom can be known, I will only remind the reader that, *though freedom is certainly the* ratio essendi *of the moral law, the latter is the* ratio cognoscendi *of freedom.* For had not the moral law already been distinctly thought in our reason, we would never have been justified in assuming anything like freedom, even though it is not self-contradictory. But if there were no freedom, the moral law would never have been encountered. (Translated by L. W. Beck, Bobbs-Merrill, Indianapolis, 1956, p. 4, note.)

10. The Validity of the Moral Law

1. We might seek the basis for objective law in the world of thought itself, but (a) this would not help us in the present instance, because the "fact" of the objective law is itself in question, not its source; and (b) the question involves other metaphysical problems, such as God's purpose and intention in creating a rational being.

2. To anyone familiar with Kant's doctrine of the *Critique of Pure Reason,* my argument will seem to require some intuition of freedom in order that the conceptual appreciation of "ought" be validated. Someone may point out that Kant, even in the *Grundlegung* (see pp. 247–48 above), explicitly rejects such an intuition of practical reason. I am convinced that in this respect Kant was wrong, and that without some foundation in practical reason—a "Transcendental Aesthetic of Practical Reason"—Kant's theory cannot support the *a priori* moral law.

3. The rest of Section III comprises a self-contained capsule version of Kant's doctrine of the impossibility of metaphysical knowledge. Relatively little reference is made to the main topics of the *Foundation.* Perhaps Kant again included an essay which fitted in very well but had been written independently. So far as I know, no one has suggested a "patchwork theory" for the *Grundlegung,* although (as I have noted here and there) there is some evidence to support it.

4. That is, in contrast to objects of appearance. As things in themselves, rational beings would exist free of the determining influences of the causal necessity found in the world of appearances.

5. We must remember that this is at best a polemical argument, useful for debating purposes. Kant would not wish the categorical imperative to rest on such a slender base as the logical impossibility of disproof. However, this device very effectively rebuts the arguments of the determinists and so removes at least that barrier from the path of reason's inquiry.

6. The reader interested in further pursuit of the idea of rational faith is urged to examine Kant's *Religion Within the Limits of Reason Alone,* translated by T. M. Greene and H. H. Hudson (Harper, New York, 1960). See also Paton's brief comment on rational faith, *op. cit.,* p. 256.

ADDITIONAL READINGS

For a detailed and thorough discussion of the various topics in the *Foundation*, the reader is advised to consult H. J. Paton's *The Categorical Imperative*. Those desiring more advanced interpretation and criticism are directed to the readings marked with an asterisk. Publication details will be found in the Bibliography following.

SOME GENERAL SURVEYS OF KANT'S THEORY

Copleston, F., *A History of Philosophy*, Vol. 6, Chap. 14.
Encyclopedia Brittanica: "Kant."
Ewing, A. C., *Ethics*, Chap. 4.
Körner, S., *Kant*, Chap. 6 and 7.
MacIntyre, A., *A Short History of Ethics*, Chap. 14.
Philosophical Encyclopedia, s.v., "Kant."

1. Kant's Moral Revolution

* Caird, Edward, *The Critical Philosophy of Immanuel Kant*, Vol. 2, Bk. 2, Chap. 1.
Copleston, F., *A History of Philosophy*, 6, Chap. 10 and 11.
* Duncan, A. R. C., *Practical Reason and Morality*, Chap. 1–3.
Körner, S., *Kant*, Chap. 1.
* Paton, H. J., "The Aim and Structure of Kant's *Grundlegung*," *Philosophical Quarterly*, 8 (1958), 112–130. A review of Duncan's work listed above.
——, *The Categorical Imperative*, Chap. 1.
* Silber, John R., "The Context of Kant's Ethical Thought," *Philosophical Quarterly*, 9 (1959), 193–207, 309–318.

2. The Purpose of the *Foundation*

* Gregor, M. J., "Kant's Conception of a 'Metaphysics of Morals'," *Philosophical Quarterly*, 10 (1960), 238–251.
Ross, W. D., *Kant's Ethical Theory*, Introductory chapter.

3. The Propositions of Moral Value

* Dietrichson, Paul, "What Does Kant Mean by 'Acting from Duty'?" Reprinted in *Kant: A Collection of Critical Essays*, Ed., Robert P. Wolff, 314–330.
* Duncan, A. R. C., *Practical Reason and Morality*, Chap. 4.
Paton, H. J., *The Categorical Imperative*, Chap. 2 and 3.
Ross, W. D., *Kant's Ethical Theory*, 8–36.

4. The Form of Law: Universality

Paton, H. J., *The Categorical Imperative*, Chap. 5–7.

5. Prologue to Section II

* Duncan, A. R. C., *Practical Reason and Morality*, Chap. 5.
Paton, H. J., *The Categorical Imperative*, Chap. 8–10.

6. Practical Reason and Its Imperatives

* Duncan, A. R. C., *Practical Reason and Morality*, Chap. 6–7.
* Ebbinghaus, Julius, "Interpretation and Misinterpretation of the Categorical Imperative," *Philosophical Quarterly*, 4 (1954), 97–108. Reprinted in *Kant: A Collection of Critical Essays*, Ed., Robert P. Wolff, 211–227.
* Kant, *Critique of Practical Reason*, Trans. Lewis W. Beck, 17–33.
* Kolenda, K., "Professor Ebbinghaus' Interpretation of the Categorical Imperative," *Philosophical Quarterly*, 5 (1955), 74–77.
Paton, H. J., *The Categorical Imperative*, Chap. 11–12.
* Singer, Marcus, "The Categorical Imperative," *Philosophical Review*, (1954), 577–591.
* Williams, T. C., *The Concept of the Categorical Imperative*.

7. The Three Variations of the Categorical Imperative

* Duncan, A. R. C., *Practical Reason and Morality*, Chap. 11.
* Haezrahi, Pepita, "The Concept of Man as End-in-Himself," reprinted in *Kant* (see above), 291–313.
* Harrison, Jonathan, "Kant's Examples of the First Formulation of the Categorical Imperative," *Philosophical Quarterly*, 7 (1957), 50–62, reprinted in *Kant* (see above), 228–245.

* ———, "The Categorical Imperative," (A Reply to Kemp's Criticism), *Philosophical Quarterly*, 8 (1958), 360–364, reprinted in *Kant* (see above), 246–258.
* Matson, W. I., "Kant as Casuist," *Journal of Philosophy*, 51 (1954), 855–860, reprinted in *Kant* (see above), 331–336.
  Paton, H. J., *The Categorical Imperative*, Chap. 13–17.
* Reich, Klaus, "Kant and Greek Ethics (II)," *Mind*, 47, Oct. 1939.
  Ross, W. D., *Kant's Ethical Theory*, 43–65.

8. Autonomy and Heteronomy

* Caird, Edward, *The Critical Philosophy of Immanuel Kant*, Vol. 2, Bk. 2, Chap. 2, 159–222.
* Duncan, A. R. C., *Practical Reason and Morality*, Chap. 8.
* Gahringer, Robert E., "The Metaphysical Aspect of Kant's Moral Philosophy," *Ethics*, 44 (1954), 277–291.
* Kant, I., *Critique of Practical Reason*, translated by L. W. Beck, 36–42.
  Paton, H. J., *The Categorical Imperative*, Chap. 18.
* Schrader, George, "Autonomy, Heteronomy, and Moral Imperatives," *Journal of Philosophy*, Vol. 60, 1963, 65–77.

9. Freedom and Autonomy

* Beck, Lewis W., *A Commentary on Kant's Critique of Practical Reason*, Chap. 11.
* Caird, Edward, *The Critical Philosophy of Immanuel Kant*, Vol. 2, Bk. 2, Chap. 3, 223–255.
* Duncan, A. R. C., *Practical Reason and Morality*, Chap. 11.
  Paton, H. J., *The Categorical Imperative*, 19–23.
  Ross, W. D., *Kant's Ethical Theory*, 66–96.
* Silber, John R., "The Ethical Significance of Kant's *Religion*," Introductory essay in *Religion Within the Limits of Reason Alone*, translated by T. M. Greene and H. H. Hudson, lxxix–cxxxiv.

10. The Validity of the Moral Law

* Caird, Edward, *The Critical Philosophy of Immanuel Kant*, Vol. 2, Bk. 2, Chap. 4, 256–267.
* Kant, Immanuel, *Critique of Practical Reason*, trans. by L. W. Beck, 74–92.
  Paton, H. J., *The Categorical Imperative*, Chap. 24–26.

SELECTED BIBLIOGRAPHY

I. Kant's Ethical Works in English

A. *Grundlegung zur Metaphysik der Sitten*

Abbott, Thomas Kingsmill, *Kant's Critique of Practical Reason, and Other Works on the Theory of Ethics* (Longmans, London, 1889). Reprinted in Library of Liberal Arts edition (Bobbs-Merrill, Indianapolis, 1949), entitled *Fundamental Principles of the Metaphysics of Morals*.

Beck, Lewis White, *Kant's Critique of Practical Reason and Other Writings in Moral Philosophy* (University of Chicago Press, 1949). Reprinted in Library of Liberal Arts edition (Bobbs-Merrill, Indianapolis, 1959), entitled *Foundations of the Metaphysics of Morals*.

Paton, H. J., *The Moral Law: Kant's Groundwork of the Metaphysics of Morals* (Barnes and Noble, New York City, 1961).

B. *Kritik der Praktischen Vernunft*

Abbott, Thomas Kingsmill. (See above.)

Beck, Lewis White. (See above.) Reprinted in Library of Liberal Arts edition (Bobbs-Merrill, Indianapolis, 1956), entitled *Critique of Practical Reason*.

C. *Metaphysik der Sitten*

Ladd, John, *The Metaphysical Elements of Justice; Part I of the Metaphysics of Morals* (Bobbs-Merrill, Indianapolis, 1965).

Ellington, James, *The Metaphysical Principles of Virtue; Part II of the Metaphysics of Morals* (Bobbs-Merrill, Indianapolis, 1964).

Gregor, Mary J., *The Doctrine of Virtue; Part II of the Metaphysics of Morals* (Harper, New York City, 1964).

D. *Other Works*

Beck, Lewis White, *Perpetual Peace* (Bobbs-Merrill, Indianapolis, 1957).

Greene, T. M., and Hudson, H. H., *Religion Within the Limits of Reason Alone* (Harper, New York City, 1960).

Infield, Louis, *Lectures on Ethics* (Harper, New York City, 1963).

II. Books

Beck, Lewis White, *A Commentary on Kant's Critique of Practical Reason* (University of Chicago Press, Chicago, 1960).

Caird, Edward, *The Critical Philosophy of Immanuel Kant* (Glasgow, 1909).

Duncan, A. R. C., *Practical Reason and Morality: A Study of Immanuel Kant's Foundations for the Metaphysics of Morals* (Nelson, London, 1957).

Gregor, Mary J., *Laws of Freedom* (Barnes and Noble, New York City, 1963).

Jones, William T., *Morality and Freedom in the Philosophy of Kant* Oxford University Press, New York City, 1940).

Körner, S., *Kant* (Penguin, Baltimore, 1955).

Paton, H. J., *The Categorical Imperative: A Study in Kant's Moral Philosophy* (University of Chicago Press, Chicago, 1948).

Ross, Sir William D., *Kant's Ethical Theory: A Commentary on the Grundlegung zur Metaphysik der Sitten* (Oxford University Press, New York City, 1954).

Teale, A. E., *Kantian Ethics* (Oxford University Press, New York City, 1951).

Williams, T. C., *The Concept of the Categorical Imperative* (Oxford University Press, New York City, 1968).

Wolff, Robert P. (Ed.), *Kant: A Collection of Critical Essays* (Doubleday, Garden City, 1967).

III. Articles

(Those articles marked with an asterisk are reprinted
in the Wolff collection of essays noted above.)

Chroust, A. H., "About a Fourth Formula of the Categorical Imperative," *Philosophical Review*, 51 (1942), 600.

* Dietrichson, Paul, "What Does Kant Mean by 'Acting From Duty'?" *Kant-Studien*, Band 53 (1962).

* Ebbinghaus, Julius, "Interpretation and Misinterpretation of the Categorical Imperative," *Philosophical Quarterly*, 4 (1954), 97–108.

Ewing, A. C., "The Paradoxes of Kant's Ethics," *Philosophy*, 13 (1938), 40.

Gahringer, Robert, "The Metaphysical Aspects of Kant's Moral Philosophy," *Ethics*, (1953–54), 277–291.

Gregor, M. J., "Kant's Conception of a Metaphysics of Morals," *Philosophical Quarterly*, 10 (1960), 238–251.

Haezrahi, Pepita, "The Avowed and Unavowed Sources of Kant's Theory of Ethics," *Ethics*, (1961–62), 157–68.

° ———, "The Concept of Man as an End-in-Himself," *Kant-Studien*, Band 53 (1962).

° Harrison, Jonathan, "Kant's Examples of the First Formulation of the Categorical Imperative," *Philosophical Quarterly*, 7 (1957), 50–62.

° ———, "The Categorical Imperative," *Philosophical Quarterly*, 8 (1958), 360–64.

° Kemp, J., "Kant's Examples of the Categorical Imperative," *Philosophical Quarterly*, 8 (1958), 63–71.

Hirst, E. W., "The Categorical Imperative and the Golden Rule," *Philosophy*, 9 (1934), 328.

Hoernle, R. F. A., "Kant's Concept of the 'Intrinsic Worth' of Every 'Rational Being'," *Personalist*, 24, 130.

———, "Kant's Theory of Freedom," *Personalist*, 20, 391.

Jensen, O. C., "Kant's Ethical Formalism," *Philosophy*, 9, (1934), 195.

Reich, Klaus, "Kant and Greek Ethics," *Mind*, 48 (1939), 338, 446.

Kolenda, K., "Professor Ebbinghaus' Interpretation of the Categorical Imperative," *Philosophical Quarterly*, 5 (1955), 74–77.

° Matson, W. I., "Kant as Casuist," *Journal of Philosophy*, 51 (1954), 855–860.

Paton, H. J., "The Aim and Structure of Kant's *Grundlegung*," *Philosophical Quarterly*, 8 (1958), 112–130.

Schrader, George, "Autonomy, Heteronomy and Moral Imperatives," *Journal of Philosophy*, 60 (1963), 65–77.

Schroeder, H. H., "Some Common Misinterpretations of the Kantian Ethics," *Philosophical Review*, 49 (1940), 424.

Silber, John R., "The Importance of the Highest Good in Kant's Ethics," *Ethics*, (1962–63), 179–197.

———, "The Context of Kant's Ethical Thought," *Philosophical Quarterly*, 9 (1959), 193–207, 309–318.

° ———, "The Copernican Revolution in Ethics: The Good Reexamined," *Kant-Studien*, Band 51 (1959).

Singer, Marcus, "The Categorical Imperative," *Philosophical Review*, 63 (1954), 577–591.